Dear Reader,

Thank you for choosing *HTML 3.2 QuickStart*—your best resource for learning HTML 3.2.

The material in this book is classroom tested and written by Logical Operations, one of the world's foremost computer training organizations. Every exercise and explanation has been adapted from a Logical Operations course specially designed for people just like you. Since we opened our door in Rochester, New York in 1982, we've taught more than 20,000 people annually how to master dozens of software programs.

Since you can't come to our classrooms, we've created the QuickStart series to bring the instructor to you. QuickStart books feature easy-to-learn, detailed step-by-step instructions and plain-English explanations to make learning complex software easier and faster.

Our research shows two things that are very important to get the most out of learning: practice and fun. You'll get the most out of this book if you have a computer with the software nearby so you can try things out as you learn them. And when you have completed the book, be sure to practice with the software as much as possible. The more you use the software, the more your learning will become permanent.

You'll also learn more if you make your learning experience as enjoyable as possible. Pick a time and place to read this book where you're comfortable and won't be distracted. The QuickStart series is designed to challenge any idea you may have about learning being a chore–with this book and a positive attitude, you'll have fun.

So, find a great spot, crack the cover of this book, relax, and enjoy learning HTML 3.2.

Bill Rosenthal
President

HTML 3.2

QUICKSTART

HTML 3.2

QUICKSTART

**RICHARD SCOTT,
SUE REBER, TIM POULSEN,
AND GAIL SANDLER**

FOR  **Logical Operations®**

Ziff-Davis Press
An imprint of Macmillan Computer Publishing USA
Emeryville, California

Acquisitions Editor	Lysa Lewallen
Copy Editor	Nicole Clausing
Technical Reviewer	Logical Operations
Project Coordinator	Edith Rex
Proofreader	Jeff Barash
Cover Illustration, Design	Megan Gandt
Book Design	Bruce Lundquist
Page Layout	Janet Piercy
Indexer	Valerie Robbins

Ziff-Davis Press imprint books are produced on a Macintosh computer system with the following applications: FrameMaker®, Microsoft® Word, QuarkXPress®, Adobe Illustrator®, Adobe Photoshop®, Adobe Streamline™, MacLink®Plus, Aldus® FreeHand™, Collage Plus™.

Ziff-Davis Press, an imprint of
Macmillan Computer Publishing USA
5903 Christie Avenue
Emeryville, CA 94608

ISBN 1-56276-493-4

Manufactured in the United States of America

10 9 8 7 6 5 4 3 2

CONTENTS AT A GLANCE

TABLE OF CONTENTS

INTRODUCTION

Welcome to HTML 3.2 QuickStart, a hands-on instruction book that will introduce you to the sundry joys of HTML. And congratula7tions on stepping up to HTML; you have much to look forward to.

We at Logical Operations believe this book to be a unique and welcome addition to the teeming ranks of "How To" computer publications. Our instructional approach stems directly from over a decade of successful teaching in a hands-on classroom environment. Throughout the book, we combine theory with practice by presenting new techniques and then applying them in hands-on activities. These activities use specially prepared sample files, which are stored on the enclosed data disk.

Unlike a class, this book allows you to proceed at your own pace. And, we'll be right there to guide you along every step of the way, providing landmarks to help chart your progress and hold to a steady course.

When you're done working your way through this book, you'll have a solid foundation of skills in

- Creating basic HTML documents
- Centering tags for the HTML document, and the HEAD and BODY section
- Recognizing elements contained in the HEAD section—including the window title and links
- Formatting text in the BODY section—entering text, centering, bolding, and italicizing text, and creating headings
- Using tables to display information
- Using links to jump to other Web pages
- Embedding graphics in your Web pages
- Validating your Web pages to make sure the code is correct
- Including JavaScript and Java applets in your Web pages to make them interactive
- Creating frames to display more than one document on a Web page

WHO THIS BOOK IS FOR

We wrote this book for the beginning HTML user. While experience with personal computers and the Internet is certainly helpful, it is not required. You should know how to turn on your computer, monitor, and printer, how to use your keyboard and mouse, and how to connect to your network (if you're on one) and the Internet (if you have access). We'll explain everything beyond that.

HOW TO USE THIS BOOK

You can use this book as a learning guide, a review tool, and a quick reference.

AS A LEARNING GUIDE

Each chapter covers one broad topic or set of related topics. Chapters are arranged in order of increasing proficiency; skills you acquire in one chapter are used and elaborated on in later chapters. For this reason, you should work through the chapters in sequence.

Each chapter is organized into explanatory topics and step-by-step activities. Topics provide the theory you need to master HTML and Web page creation; activities allow you to apply this theory to practical, hands-on examples.

You get to try out each new skill on a specially prepared sample file stored on the enclosed data disk. This saves you typing time and allows you to concentrate on the technique at hand. Through the use of sample files, hands-on activities, illustrations that give you feedback at crucial steps, and supporting background information, this book provides you with the foundation and structure to learn HTML quickly and easily.

AS A REVIEW TOOL

Any method of instruction is only as effective as the time and effort you are willing to invest in it. For this reason, we strongly encourage you to spend some time reviewing the book's more challenging topics and activities.

AS A QUICK REFERENCE

General procedures are presented as a series of bulleted steps; you can find these bullets (•) easily by skimming through the book. Bulleted procedures can serve as a handy reference. At the end of every chapter, you'll find a quick reference table that lists the steps necessary to perform the techniques introduced in that chapter.

WHAT THIS BOOK CONTAINS

This book contains the following 13 chapters and 2 appendices:

Chapter 1:   Getting Started

Chapter 2:   Overview of HTML

Chapter 3:   Formatting Text with HTML

Chapter 4:   Adding Local and Remote Links to Your Web Pages

Chapter 5:   Adding Graphics and Sounds to Your Web Pages

Chapter 6:   Creating Tables in HTML

Chapter 7:   Setting Background and Text Colors for Your Web Pages

Chapter 8:   Web Page Publishing and Design

Chapter 9:   Validating Your HTML Documents

Chapter 10:   Adding Links to Other Internet Services

Chapter 11:   Creating Forms with HTML

Chapter 12:   Creating Dynamic and Interactive Documents

Chapter 13:   Adding Frames to Your Web Pages

Appendix A: Creating Your Work Folder

Appendix B: HTML and Web References

SPECIAL LEARNING FEATURES

The following features of this book will facilitate your learning:

- Carefully sequenced topics that build on the knowledge you've acquired from previous topics

- Frequent hands-on activities that sharpen your HTML skills

- Numerous illustrations that show how your screen should look at key points during these activities

- The data disk, which contains all the files you will need to complete the activities (as explained in the next section)

- Easy-to-spot bulleted procedures that provide the general step-by-step instructions you'll need to perform HTML tasks

- A quick reference at the end of each chapter, listing the mouse/keyboard actions needed to perform the techniques introduced in the chapter

THE DATA DISK

One of the most important learning features of this book is the data disk, the 3½-inch floppy disk that accompanies the book. This disk contains the sample files you'll retrieve and work on throughout the book.

To perform the activities in this book, you will first need to create a work folder on your hard disk, as explained in Chapter 1, "Getting Started" and Appendix A "Creating Your Work Folder." You'll then copy the files from the data disk to your work folder. This folder will also hold all the files that you will be creating, editing, and saving during the course of this book.

WHAT YOU NEED TO USE THIS BOOK

To create and view HTML code, you need a computer with a hard disk and at least one floppy-disk drive, a monitor, a keyboard, and a mouse (or compatible tracking device). You must have a browser such as Netscape Navigator and a text editor such as WordPad installed on your computer.

A SPECIAL NOTE

We created this book on the Windows 95 platform, using WordPad and Netscape Navigator 2.0. If you are working on a different platform, using a different text editor, or using a different browser, your screens might not match ours, and you might not be able to follow all of the steps as they are written in the book.

Chapter 1
Getting Started

The hands-on activities in this book are your key to learning HTML quickly and thoroughly. To perform these activities, you must first

- Familiarize yourself with the book's conventions

- Create a work folder in which you store the practice files from the accompanying data disk

To meet these requirements, you must work diligently through this entire chapter. In Chapter 2, you'll begin learning the nuts and bolts of HTML.

CONVENTIONS USED IN THIS BOOK

The following conventions used in this book will help you learn HTML easily and efficiently.

- Each chapter begins with a short introduction and ends with a Quick Reference section that includes a keystroke guide to the techniques introduced in that chapter.

- Main chapter topics and subtopics explain HTML features.

- Hands-on activities allow you to practice using these features.

- Three "skill builder" sections in the book allow you to practice what you've learned so far.

In the hands-on activities, any keystrokes, menu choices, and anything you are asked to type are all printed in **boldface**. Here's an example from Chapter 2:

1. Double-click on the **home** icon to return to the Jetaway Travel home page.

Activities adhere to a cause-and-effect approach. Each step tells you what to do (cause) and then what will happen (effect). From the example above,

- Cause: Click on the **home** icon.

- Effect: The icon opens Jetaway Travel's home page.

A plus sign (+) is used with the Shift, Ctrl, and Alt keys to indicate a multikey keystroke. For example, "press **Ctrl+V**" means "Press and hold down the Ctrl key, then press the letter V, then release both keys."

To help you distinguish between steps presented for reference purposes (general procedures) and steps you should carry out at your computer as you read (specific procedures), we use the following system:

- A bulleted step, like this, is provided for your information and reference only.

1. A numbered step, like this, indicates one in a series of steps that you should carry out in sequence at your computer. In addition, the first in a series of steps you should carry out at your computer is preceded by the icon shown here.

MOUSING SKILLS

A mouse (or trackball) is a hand-operated device that enables you to communicate with your computer by manipulating—selecting, deselecting, moving, deleting, and so on—objects displayed on your screen. When you slide the mouse (or roll the trackball), the mouse pointer moves across the screen. You use this pointer to "point" to the onscreen object that you want to manipulate. On the mouse are two (or more) buttons. You use these buttons to communicate with your computer in various ways, as shown in Table 1.1.

Table 1.1   Mousing Techniques

Technique	How to Do It
Point	Slide the mouse until the tip of the mouse pointer is over the desired object. "Point to the word *File*" means "slide the mouse until the tip of the mouse pointer is over the word *File*."
Click	Press and release the *left* mouse button. For example, "click on the word *File*" means "point to the word *File*, and then press and release the *left* mouse button."
Right-click	Press and release the *right* mouse button. For example, "right-click on *the navigation icon* to display the shortcut menu."
Double-click	Press and release the *left mouse button* twice in rapid succession. "Double-click on the file name *Jway.htm*" means "point to the file named Jway.htm, and then press and release the *left mouse button* twice."
Drag	Press and hold the *left* mouse button while sliding the mouse. "Drag the scroll box upward" means "point to the *scroll box*, press and hold the *left* mouse button, slide the mouse upward, and then release the mouse button."
Right-drag	Press and hold the *right* mouse button while sliding the mouse.
Scroll	Click on a scroll arrow or a scroll bar, or drag a scroll box to change the screen display.
Check/Uncheck	Click on a check box to check (turn on) or uncheck (turn off) that option.

CREATING YOUR WORK FOLDER

Throughout this book, you will be creating, editing, and saving several data files. To keep these files together, you will create a work folder or directory for them on your hard disk. (*Folders* are containers that hold files and other folders.) Your work folder will also hold the practice files from the enclosed data disk.

Because you can use HTML on many different platforms, we'll give you general instructions here. If you are using Windows 3.1, Windows 95, or Macintosh System 7 or higher, you can refer to Appendix A for help creating your work folder or directory.

To use the data files on the data disk you will need to

- Determine whether your hard disk has enough free space for your new work folder and data files. You will need at least 1 MB (megabyte) of free hard-disk space. If this is not the case, you'll have to delete (or move) enough files from your hard disk to increase its free-byte total to at least 1,000,000. Otherwise, you won't be able to create your work folder and perform the hands-on activities in this book while still maintaining an adequate amount of free hard-disk space. Make sure to back up all important files before deleting them! (For help deleting and backing up, consult your local system guru.)

- Create a new folder or directory (preferably at the root of your hard drive, for example, c:\).

- Name the new folder or directory *HTMLWork*.

- Copy the data files from the data disk in the back of this book to your HTMLWork folder or directory.

Note: The hands-on activities in this book assume that your work folder is on drive C and is named HTMLWork. If you specified a different hard-disk drive or a different folder name, please remember to substitute this drive and/or name whenever we mention drive C or HTMLWork.

SOFTWARE USED IN THIS BOOK

You can create HTML with any text editor or word processor and you can view the results in just about any browser. Instead of trying to guess what setup you have, we tried to make this book as generic as possible. In general, the steps in this book will work with any text editor or word processor and can be viewed with any browser. However, we created the HTML data files using the Windows 95 WordPad program. Whenever we have you view the results of HTML onscreen, we are using Netscape Navigator 2.0. If you are using a different browser (for example, Internet Explorer 3.0 or Mosaic), your screens will look a little different. Or, the steps you need to take may be slightly different.

Don't panic, this is just a minor setback. Depending on how familiar you are with your browser, you'll be able to figure out what you need to do. If there are any major differences between Internet Explorer 3.0 and Netscape Navigator, we'll try to let you know.

BEFORE YOU PROCEED FURTHER

The activities within each remaining chapter proceed sequentially. In many cases, you cannot perform an activity until you've performed one or more of the activities preceding it. For this reason, we recommend that you allot enough time to work through an entire chapter in one continuous session. Feel free to take as many breaks as you need: Stand up, stretch, take a stroll, drink some decaf, share a joke with a friend. Don't try to absorb too much information at any one time. Studies show that people assimilate and retain information most effectively when it is presented in digestible chunks and followed by a liberal amount of hands-on practice.

In the next chapter, we'll take you on a whirlwind tour of HTML. You'll learn what HTML is and how to work with HTML.

Good luck, good learning, and . . . bon voyage!

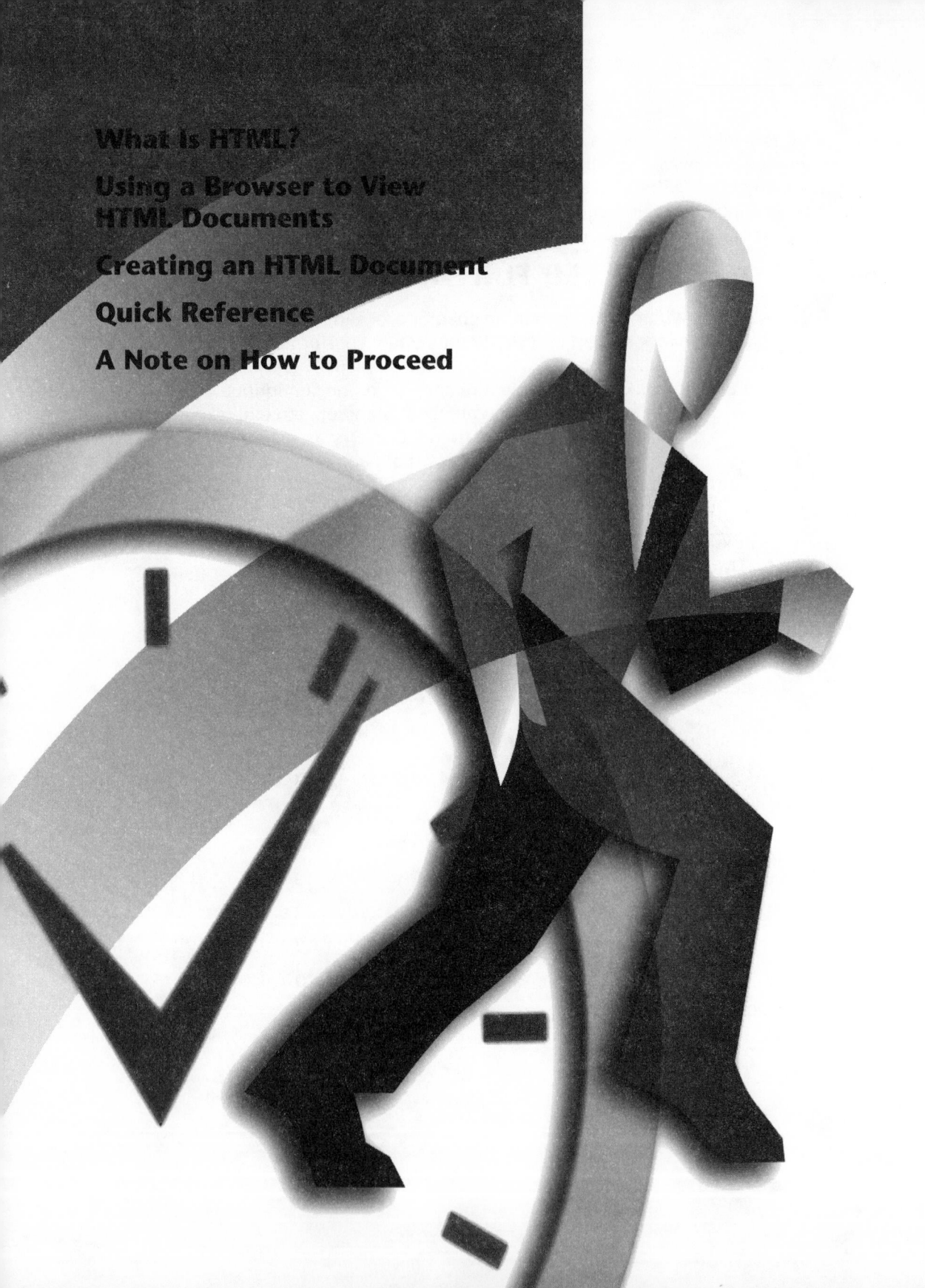

Chapter 2

Overview of HTML

The Internet, a world-wide network of computers, allows you to communicate with people across the world using any computer that supports the TCP/IP networking protocol. The Internet also serves as the pipeline for several popular programs, including the World Wide Web.

The World Wide Web, often called simply the Web, is arguably the most popular service on the Internet. The Web is graphical, easy to access, and increasingly filled with high quality information. Two "behind-the-scenes" technologies power the Web: HTTP, the Hypertext Transfer Protocol, and HTML, the Hypertext Markup Language. You use HTML to create Web pages; computers on the Web transmit the Web page data by using the Hypertext Transfer Protocol; and a Web browser program (such as Netscape Navigator or Microsoft Internet Explorer) receives, interprets, and displays the data. Unless you are a programmer who plans to create custom programs to access the Web, you do not need to be concerned with the Hypertext Transfer Protocol.

When you are done working through this chapter, you will know

- What HTML is
- What a browser is
- How to create a simple HTML document

WHAT IS HTML?

Hypertext Markup Language (HTML) is a simple, yet powerful language that you can use to create Web pages. It is made up of *tags* or codes that you insert into your text to create the elements of your Web pages. These codes act as instructions, telling your browser (in our case, Netscape Navigator 2.0) where to place the elements and how they should look. For example, to designate that a section of text is supposed to be the heading for your Web page, you enter a tag before and after that text telling Netscape that the text is supposed to be the page heading.

There are several standardization levels of HTML.

- Level 0, accepted by the first World Wide Web browsers.
- Level 1, the first update to the HTML standard. It includes level 0 elements and images.
- Level 2, which includes all the elements of level 1, plus tags defining user input fields. Currently, this is the standard supported by all popular browsers.
- Level 3, intended to include many new features, including tables, scientific equations, and better control over page layout and design. HTML 3 was never implemented because vendors and participants couldn't agree on the contents of this proposed standard.
- Level 3.2, the newest standard, includes HTML level 2; many of the more popular features of HTML 3; new tags; and attributes for color, client-side image maps, Java applets, and most Netscape extensions.

USING A BROWSER TO VIEW HTML DOCUMENTS

Creating an HTML document is only half the battle. You also need a browser program to interpret and display that document. In fact, the final look of your Web page is determined not by you, but by the user's browser program. There are many browser programs available today; however, the two most popular are Netscape Navigator and Microsoft Internet Explorer.

Netscape Communications Corporation's Netscape Navigator is the most popular Web browser available. Netscape Navigator is a powerful, yet easy-to-use platform for accessing the Web. Figure 2.1 illustrates the major components of Netscape Navigator version 2.

Figure 2.1
The Netscape Navigator 2.0 program window

Menu bar

Toolbar

Location field

Directory buttons

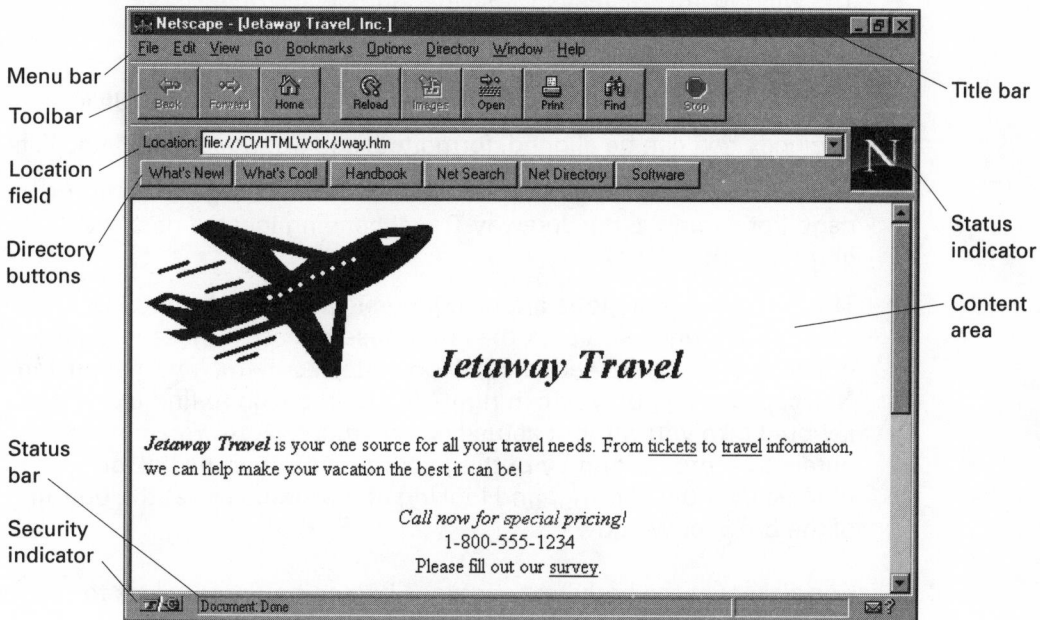

Title bar

Status indicator

Content area

Status bar

Security indicator

Microsoft's Internet Explorer is quickly catching up with Netscape.

Note: We used Netscape Navigator 2.0 and Windows 95 to develop this book. If you are using a different version of Netscape, a different browser, or a different platform, your screens may not match ours. In addition, some steps may be different. Wherever possible, we'll let you know about any major differences; however, use your head and we're sure you'll be able to figure out what you need to do and what you should be seeing.

Let's use a browser to take a look at an HTML document stored in your HTML-Work folder:

1. Start your browser. If you are using Netscape Navigator on Windows 95, you'll probably find Netscape Navigator somewhere in the Programs folder under your Start menu. **Note:** You do not need to be connected to the Internet to start your browser and look at an HTML document stored locally.

2. If you are using Netscape Navigator 2.0, choose **File, Open File**, select your HTMLWork folder and double-click on **Jway.htm**. The file opens in the Netscape Navigator program window (see Figure 2.1). This is the home page for our fictional company, Jetaway Travel, Inc.

3. Note the following major components of the Netscape Navigator program window and the Jway.htm file (refer to Figure 2.1).

   • The window title displays *Netscape—[Jetaway Travel, Inc.]*

   • The plane is an embedded graphic.

   • The text *tickets* and *travel* are links that take you to other pages.

   • The body text can be aligned, formatted, and arranged in bulleted lists.

   • You can create headings or titles for sections of a page or an entire page (for example, the Jetaway Travel heading located near the graphic of the plane).

   • The house and the globe are navigation icons that take you to other pages when you click the left mouse button. If these icons are not visible, you will need to scroll down to see them. If you are using Netscape Navigator, you can right-click on the icon to find out where it would take you without actually going there. **Note:** You can also obtain this information by putting your mouse over the link or graphic (without clicking) and looking at the status bar at the bottom of the browser window.

4. Click on **tickets** in the body text sentence beginning *From tickets to travel...* This is a link to the Tickets page for Jetaway Travel, Inc. (se Figure 2.2). Notice that the window title *reads [Jetaway Travel—Tickets Page]* and that there is a table listing ticket prices on this page.

5. Click on the **Home** icon to return to the Jetaway Travel home page.

VIEWING THE SOURCE CODE FOR A WEB PAGE

When you use HTML to create a Web page, you are simply using markup tags to describe what information you want on the Web page and where and how you want that information displayed relative to the page (for example, as a window title, a page heading, or formatted text). You, the Web page designer, are at the mercy of the user's browser settings when it comes to the final look (the font, size, color, and so on) of that Web page.

HTML files are text files that contain your data (the text and graphics) and the tags that you enter to indicate where and how that data is displayed. You can create these text files with any text editor or word processor. In fact, many

Figure 2.2
The Tickets page for Jetaway Travel, Inc.

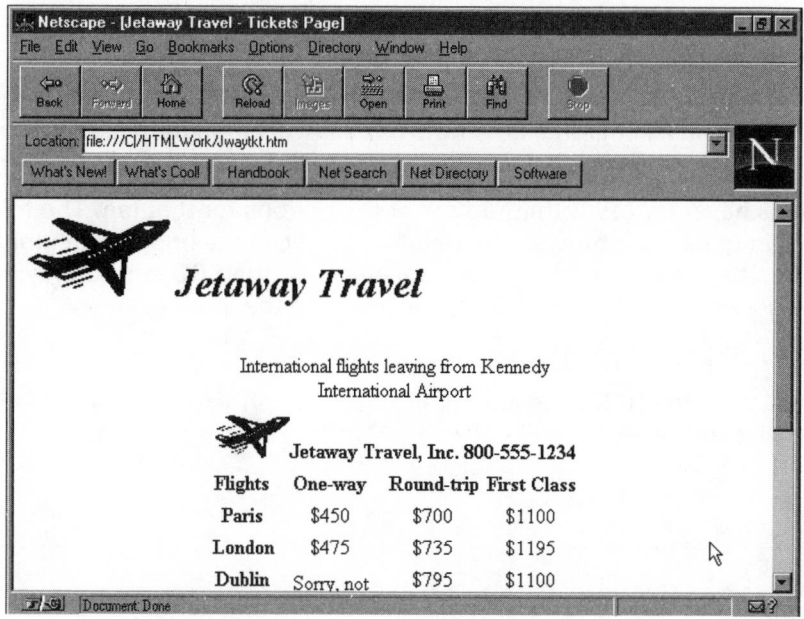

word processors now will walk you through the process of creating an HTML file either from scratch or from an existing document.

You must name HTML files with an .HTM or .HTML extension. If you do not, your browser will not recognize that the files are Web files and will instead load them as if they were plain text files. **Note:** If you are using Windows 95, Windows NT, or the Macintosh, you can use an .HTML extension. Windows 3.1 does not support more than 3-digit extensions.

HTML TAGS

While they may look confusing at first, HTML tags are easy to understand. Tags consist of individual elements inside angle (greater-than and less-than) brackets. There are two types of tags: *container* and *empty* tags.

A *container* tag has an opening and closing tag element. The opening tag begins with the left angle bracket (<) followed immediately by the tag name, any attributes (special instructions regarding the tag) separated by spaces, then the right angle bracket (>). The closing tag is exactly the same except that there is a slash (/) between the left angle bracket and the tag name. Also, closing tags do not contain attributes. Any data to be acted upon is placed between the opening and closing tags. Generally, container tags follow this format:

```
<tag_name>data</tag_name>
```

In the example

```
<TITLE>My First Web Page</TITLE>
```

<TITLE> is the opening tag. *My First Web Page* is the data. And </TITLE> is the closing tag.

An empty tag has only an opening tag element. It is used to indicate one-time instructions such as line breaks or horizontal lines. For example, the tag <BR> inserts a line break. Text following the <BR> tag begins at the left margin.

Some tags have *attributes* that represent the options for that tag. The following empty tag tells the browser to insert a specific inline image (the globe icon you saw in the Jway.htm file). It has one attribute, the SRC attribute, which tells the browser the source of the file containing the image:

```
<IMG SRC= globe.gif >
```

When you view the HTML file containing this code in your browser, this is what you'll see:

Both container and empty tags can have attributes. If a container tag has an attribute, the attribute is listed in the opening tag, not the closing tag.

Now that you're thoroughly confused, let's take a look at the source document for the Jetaway Travel home page.

1. From the Netscape Navigator menu bar, choose **View, Document Source**. The source code for the Jetaway Travel Home page is displayed in a new window (see Figure 2.3). If you're using a browser other than Netscape Navigator, you'll need to find the correct menu command to view the source code.

2. Observe the <HTML> code at the top of the window. This identifies the file as an HTML file.

3. Observe the <TITLE>Jetaway Travel, Inc.</TITLE> code. This is a container tag that tells Netscape Navigator what data (text) to display in the title bar.

4. Double-click on the **Control-menu** box in the upper-left corner of the source code window to close the source code window and return to Netscape Navigator.

Figure 2.3
The source code for the Jetaway Travel home page

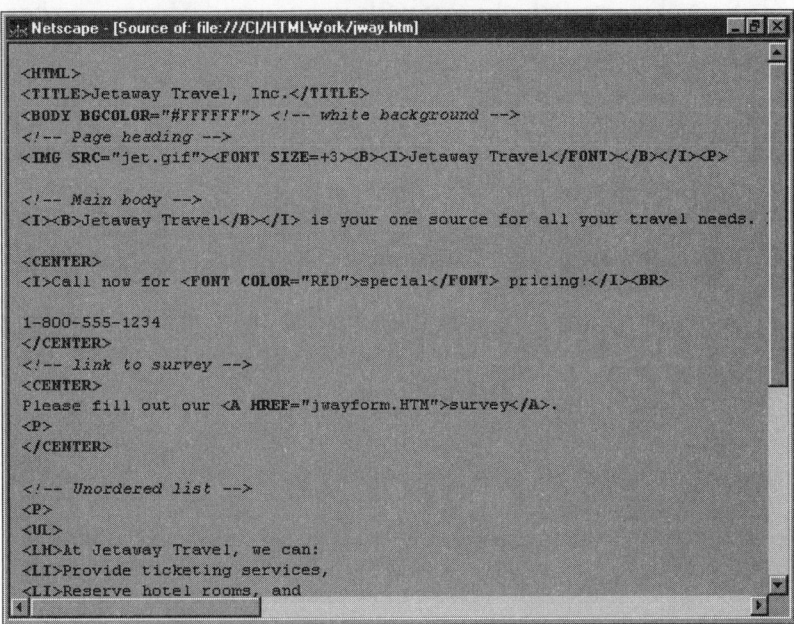

CREATING AN HTML DOCUMENT

As we told you earlier, you can create an HTML document in any text editor program or even in your favorite word processing program (as long as you save your file as a text-only file). Windows WordPad is a suitable, albeit simple, program for creating HTML files.

Using your editor, you enter both the data for your Web page and the tags that will format that text. The HTML specification includes many tags, some of which you will learn about in this book. For a complete list of HTML tags, you can visit one of these Web sites:

U.S. Sandia National Labs HTML Elements page:

```
http://www.sandia.gov/sci_compute/elements.html
```

The World Wide Web Consortium (W3) HTML specifications page:

```
http://www.w3.org/pub/WWW/MarkUp/Wilbur
```

PAGE STRUCTURE

An HTML file begins and ends with the tags <HTML> and </HTML> indicating it is a Web page. It is divided into two parts, a head and a body. The head contains information about the document and the body contains the text of the document. Table 2.1 describes some container tags you can use to define the basic elements of your Web page.

Table 2.1   **Basic Elements of a Web Page**

Opening Tag	Closing Tag	Purpose
<HTML>	</HTML>	Identifies the file as an HTML file. This tag is optional, but recommended.
<HEAD>	</HEAD>	Identifies the portion of the file that contains information about the document. This tag is optional.
<BODY>	</BODY>	Identifies the portion of the file that describes the body elements of the data. This tag is optional, but recommended.
<TITLE>	</TITLE>	Text within the tags appears as the window title.

Let's create a very simple Web page.

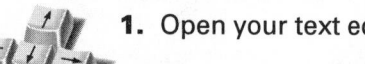

1. Open your text editor.

2. Type **<HTML>** and press **Enter** to indicate that this is going to be an HTML file.

3. Type **<TITLE>My first HTML file</TITLE>** to create a window title. In most cases, this title appears in the browser program's title bar.

4. Using Figure 2.4 as a guide, complete the HTML file (type your name rather than the name displayed in the figure). Press **Enter** at the end of each line. (**Note:** When you view the file, your browser will not show any extra white space. So, it isn't necessary to press Enter at the end of each line; however, it makes your HTML file a little easier to decipher.)

5. Choose **File, Save As** and save the file to your HTMLWork folder as **MYFIRST.HTM. Note:** Save your file as a text only file. If you don't you

Figure 2.4
Creating a basic HTML file

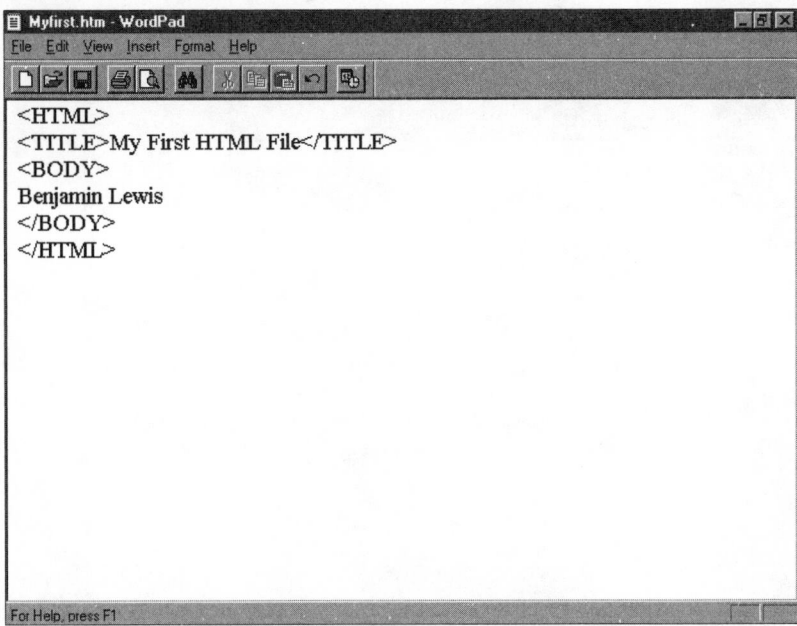

might wind up seeing strange characters on-screen when you try to open the document in your browser.

6. Switch to your browser and open the file **MYFIRST.HTM**. (**Note:** If you are working with Windows 3.1, Windows 95, or Windows NT, you can press **Alt + Tab** to switch among open programs.)

7. Observe the file (see Figure 2.5):

   • The title bar displays the title *My first HTML file.*

   • The body portion of the window displays your first and last name.

MODIFYING WEB FILES

Once you create a Web page, you can always modify it by changing the HTML file. Once you make and save changes to an HTML file, you must "inform" your browser of those changes. With Netscape Navigator, you can reload the document from the disk by choosing *View, Reload,* or by clicking on the *Reload* toolbar button.

Let's modify the HTML file.

Figure 2.5
MYFIRST.HTM in the Netscape Navigator window

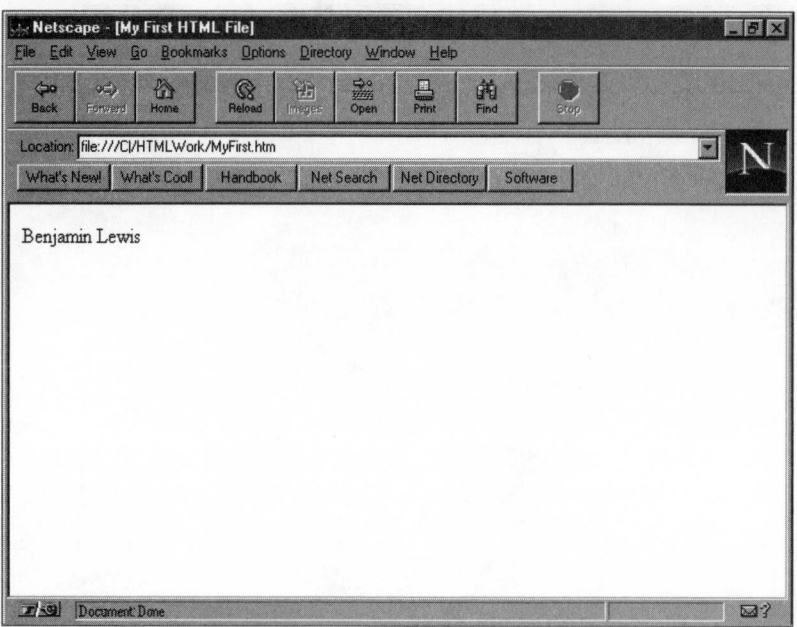

1. Switch to your text editor (remember, if you're using Windows 3.1, Windows 95, or Windows NT, you can press **Alt + Tab** until your text editor is displayed).

2. Add a blank line immediately above the </BODY> tag (press **Enter**).

3. Type **HTML is fun!**

4. Save your changes and switch to your browser. Do you see your changes? Probably not. You must first reload the document before you can see the changes.

5. Choose **View, Reload** (if you are using Netscape Navigator) and observe the changes. Your new message now appears in the body portion of the window. But wait a minute, it's right next to your name. That doesn't look right.

Earlier you learned that your browser ignores any white space in your HTML file. So, how do you tell the browser to start a new line? Remember the <BR> or line break tag we talked about briefly earlier in this chapter? When you add a <BR> tag to your HTML file, it tells the browser to start the text after the

 tag at the left margin of the next line. You'll learn more about the <BR> tag in the next chapter, but for now, let's add a **
** tag to MYFIRST.HTM so everything in the body of the window doesn't appear as a huge run-on block of text.

1. Switch back to your text editor.

2. Place the insertion point at the end of your name and type **
**. This tells the browser that any text after the tag should start at the left margin of the next line.

3. Save the file and return to your browser. Remember, you can't see the changes until you reload the document.

4. Reload the document and notice that the text *HTML is fun!* now appears on the line below your name.

Note: This is the process you follow to enter and test HTML code. You enter the code in your text editor, save changes, switch to your browser, and reload the file to see if your code was interpreted correctly by the browser.

PRACTICE YOUR SKILLS

Let's add some more text to your HTML file.

1. Switch back to your text editor.

2. Enter some text of your choice in the body portion of your file. Feel free to use the line break tag <BR> whenever you want to start a new line.

3. Save your changes and view them in your browser window.

ADDING COMMENTS TO AN HTML FILE

Comments are notations that you record in your HTML files but which do not appear in the browser window. You can use comments to record descriptions of the purpose or functionality of sections of the code in your files.

You might wish to add comments before major sections of your files. For example, before you begin the body text of your file, you could enter a comment such as "Body text begins here." Later, if you need to update the file, your comments help you quickly identify pertinent parts of the file. Table 2.2 describes the opening and closing tags that you can use to enter comments in your HTML files.

Table 2.2 **Creating Comment Tags**

Opening Tag	Closing Tag	Purpose
<!--	-->	Text within the tags does not appear in your browser. Instead, it serves as a place to record comments and reminders.

Let's add some comments to our HTML file.

1. Switch to your text editor.

2. Add a blank line immediately above your <TITLE> line, then enter the following text:

```
<HTML>
<!-- This is a comment -->
<!--
This is another comment -->
This will appear in the Netscape window<BR>  <!-- This will not -->
<TITLE>My First HTML File</TITLE>
<BODY>
Benjamin Lewis
<BR>HTML is fun!
</BODY>
</HTML>
```

3. Save your file, switch to your browser window and view the changes. (You'll need to reload the document.) Your comments do not appear in the Navigator window.

PRACTICE YOUR SKILLS

1. Observe the source code for your Web page (from the browser, choose **View, Document Source**). The comments appear in italics in the source code window (see Figure 2.6).

2. Close the source code window.

WORKING WITH THE HEAD SECTION

As you learned earlier, HTML documents consist of two parts: the head and the body. The head contains information about the document (for example,

Figure 2.6
Viewing the Source Code for MYFIRST.HTM

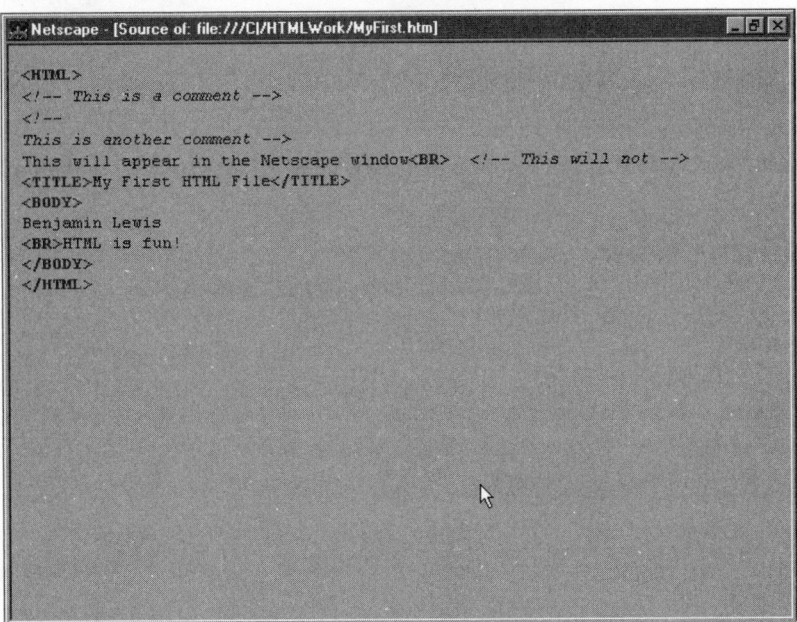

the document title and any relationships between HTML documents and file directories). The body contains the text of the document (all the information that will be displayed by the end user's browser).

In this section, we'll give you some guidelines for creating the head section of your HTML document. **Note:** You'll learn more about the body in the next chapter.

There are several elements you can use in the head section of your HTML document. One must is the title element. The title has nothing to do with the file name (for example, Jway.htm). It simply names your Web page (for example, Jetaway Travel Home page). Your title should be descriptive, but not too long. *My Web Page* or *Page 1* are not good Web page titles unless no one but you is going to visit your Web page. *A play by play description of Carson Lee's second birthday celebration* is also not a good Web page title. It may be descriptive, but it's long. Keep in mind that most browsers will display this title in the title bar or at the top of the Web page.

Generally, when you create a Web page, you'll want to link it to one or more other pages. You can use the <LINK> tag in the head section of your document to define relationships between the current document and other documents or to the author of the document. You'll learn more about links in Chapter 4.

In addition, if you would like your Web page to have simple interactivity and your Web server has a search engine, you might use an <ISINDEX> tag to allow users to search for specific information. The <ISINDEX> tag indicates that there is a searchable index for the document available on the Web server. If your document's server does not have a search engine, users will not be able to perform a search.

Finally, you can use the <META> tag to embed special information about the document (such as sending an http command to the server) in the head section.

QUICK REFERENCE

You learned what HTML is, how to view an HTML document in your browser, and how to create and modify a simple HTML document.

Here's a quick reference guide to the features introduced in this chapter:

Desired Result	How to Do It
Indicate an HTML document	In the text editor, type **<HTML>** at the beginning of the document Type **</HTML>** at the end of the document
Indicate the head section of an HTML document	In the text editor, type **<HEAD>** at the beginning of the section; type **</HEAD>** at the end of the section
Indicate the body section of an HTML document	In the text editor, type **<BODY>** at the beginning of the section; at the end of the section, type **</BODY>**
Add a document title	Within the head section, type **<TITLE>** *Your document title text***</TITLE>**
Save a document as an HTML file	In any text editor or word processor, save the file as a text-only file with the extension .HTM or .HTML
Add a comment to an HTML document	Type **<!--** *Your comment text here***-->**
View the source code for a document in Netscape Navigator	Choose **View, Document Source**
Navigate among open programs in Windows 3.1, Windows 95, or Windows NT	Press **Alt + Tab**

Congratulations, you made it through Chapter 2. You now have a basic understanding of how a Web page is created, shared, and displayed. In the next chapter you'll learn how to create and format the body section of your Web page.

A NOTE ON HOW TO PROCEED

If you wish to stop here, feel free to do so. If you wish to press onward, please proceed directly to the next chapter. Remember to allot enough time to work through an entire chapter in one sitting.

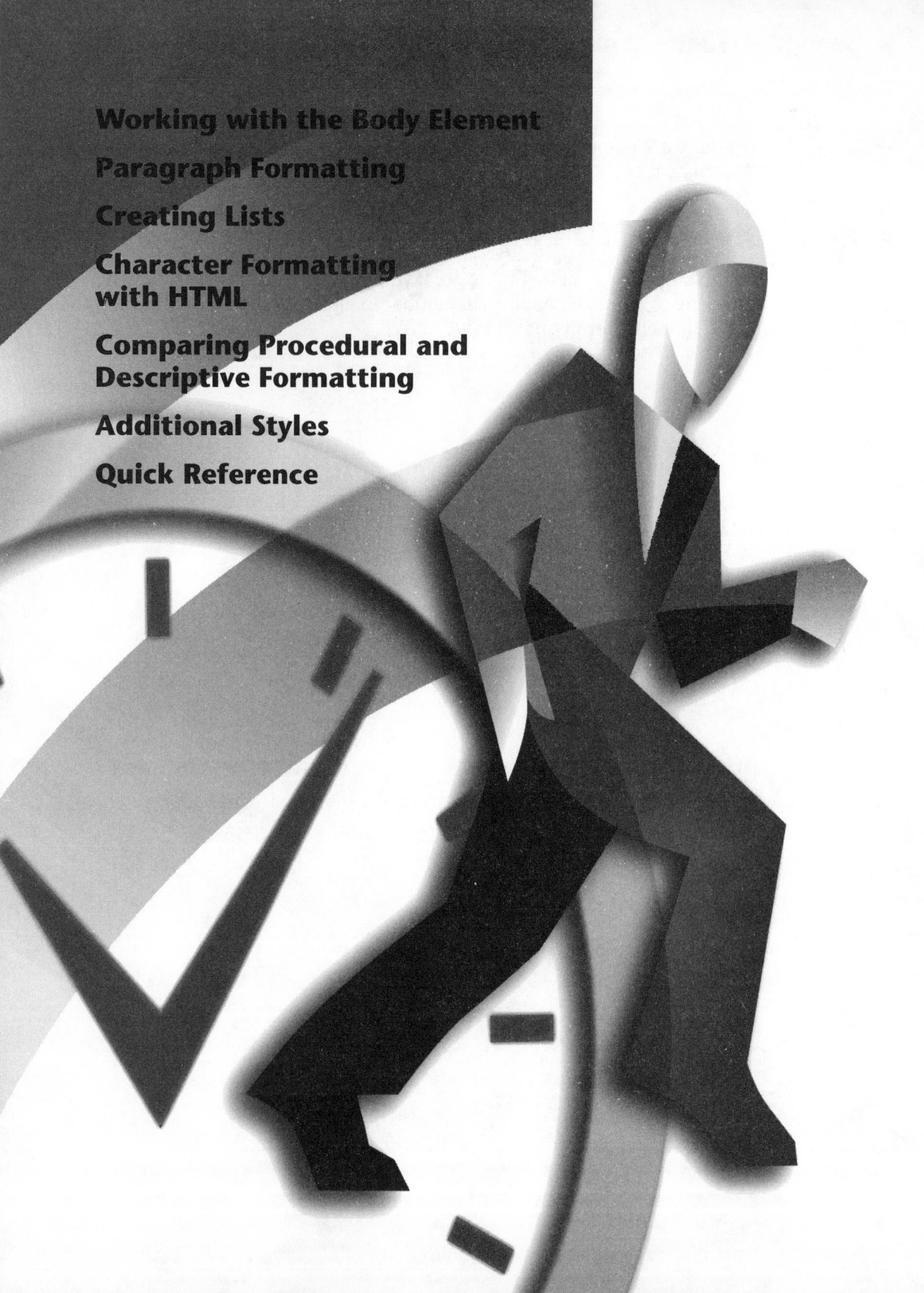

Chapter 3

Formatting Text with HTML

Web pages are what you make them. In Chapter 2, you learned how to create the two basic sections of an HTML document, the head and the body. Now it's time to take a closer look at the content that visitors to your Web page will see in the body. You'll want to use paragraph and character formatting to make the content of your Web page more visually appealing. In this chapter, you'll learn about some HTML tags that will help you do so.

When you're done working through this chapter, you will know

- How to use HTML tags to format paragraphs in Web pages

- How to use HTML tags to format characters in Web pages

- The difference between procedural formatting and descriptive formatting

WORKING WITH THE BODY ELEMENT

Your HTML document is divided into two sections, the head and the body. As you learned in the last chapter, the head section supplies the document title and establishes relationships between HTML documents and file directories.

The body section is the meat of your Web page. It is the largest portion of an HTML document and contains the text and images that make up the content of your Web page.

Before you can begin working with the body of your document, you must lay out the framework. As you learned in Chapter 2, HTML documents must follow a defined pattern of elements if you want Web browsers to interpret them correctly. For example,

- The HTML document should begin and end with the <HTML> and </HTML> tags.

- The head section is contained within the <HEAD> and </HEAD> tags.

- Within the head element you need a document title (indicated by the <TITLE> and </TITLE> tags).

- The body section is contained within the <BODY> and </BODY> tags.

Not all of these tags are required; however, it's a good idea to prevent any section of your document from being misinterpreted as plain text (or gibberish).

So, at the very least before you begin working with the body of your document, you should have a document that looks like this:

```
<HTML>
<HEAD>
<TITLE>This is my window title</TITLE>
</HEAD>

<BODY>


</BODY>
</HTML>
```

Once you get this far, you can simply enter the text that you want to appear in the browser window between the <BODY> and </BODY> tags.

If your text editor and browser are not running, please start them now. Let's start by taking a look at an HTML document:

1. If necessary, switch to your text editor. (Remember, if you're using Windows 95 or Windows 3.1, you can press **Alt+Tab** to cycle between open applications.)

2. Open **XDEFAULT.HTM** from your HTMLWork folder. **Note:** You might not be able to see the .HTM files until you choose **(All Documents *.*)** from the Files of Type list in your text editor's Open dialog box.

PARAGRAPH FORMATTING

While a markup language is extremely useful, there are times when it can be a pain in the neck. You have to mark each section of your document to make sure it appears as you want it to. You might think that if you typed the following paragraphs in your HTML document,

```
<HTML>
<HEAD>
<TITLE>This is my window title</TITLE>
</HEAD>

<BODY>
The optimist fell ten stories.
At each window bar
He shouted to his friends:
"All right so far."
</BODY>
</HTML>
```

that they would appear as you typed them. However, in reality, they would appear like this,

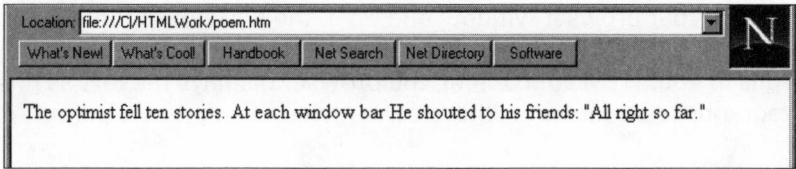

If you don't indicate (with a markup tag) where a new paragraph or line should begin, your text will appear as one giant block no matter how many times you press Enter in the HTML document.

Table 3.1 illustrates the options available for starting new paragraphs.

Note: The <BR> tag is an example of an empty tag. It does not have a corresponding closing tag.

Table 3.1 **Starting New Paragraphs**

Opening Tag	Closing Tag	Purpose
<P>	</P>	Defines a paragraph, inserts a carriage return and a blank line. Additional text you enter will follow the blank line and start at the left margin. The </P> tag is optional.
 		Identifies a line break, inserts a carriage return. Additional text will start at the left margin of the next line.

Let's enter some body text for your Web page and use the <P> tag:

1. Immediately following the line that begins with <BODY> enter the following text

```
<HTML>
<HEAD>
<TITLE>Jetaway Travel, Inc.</TITLE>
</HEAD>
<BODY>
Jetaway Travel is your one source for all your travel needs. From
tickets to travel information, we can help make your vacation the
best it can be!
Call now for special pricing!
1-800-555-1234
</BODY>
</HTML>
```

2. Save the file as the text document **Default.htm**.

3. Switch to your browser window and open the file. Notice that your paragraphs do not appear as you typed them. Even though you typed paragraphs in your HTML document, the browser displays the text as one giant paragraph. You need to tell the browser where to start new paragraphs.

4. Switch to your text editor and place the insertion point to the left of the *J* in the line beginning *Jetaway Travel is*.

5. Type **<P>** to add an opening paragraph tag. Remember, the paragraph tags <P> and </P> define paragraphs in your Web pages.

6. Place the insertion point at the end of the line that ends with "*best it can be!*" Type **</P>** to enter a closing paragraph tag at the end of the line. This tells your browser that all the text between the paragraph tags is one paragraph. Any text after the closing paragraph tag belongs in a new paragraph.

7. Save the file, switch to your browser and reload the document to view your changes. Notice that your browser ends the paragraph where you inserted the tag, inserts a blank line, and *starts "Call for special pricing!"* at the left margin as a new paragraph (see Figure 3.1).

Figure 3.1
Defining paragraphs for Web pages

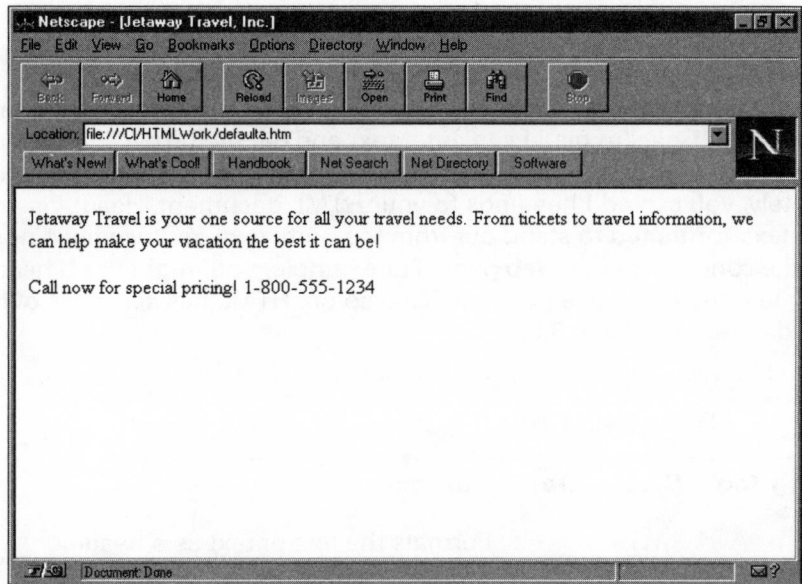

When you add a paragraph tag in your HTML document, your browser knows to separate the paragraphs with a blank line. But, what if you don't want a blank line between paragraphs? What if you just want to start a new line at the left margin without a blank line between? Those HTML wizards thought of everything. Instead of inserting a new paragraph tag, you can insert a line break tag (<BR>). Let's take a look at the difference between a line break and a new paragraph.

1. Switch to your text editor and place the insertion point at the end of the line *"Call for special pricing!"*

2. Type **
** to add a line break tag at the end of the line.

3. Save the file, switch to your browser and reload the document. Notice that the phone number now appears on its own line and there is no blank line between *"Call for special pricing!"* and the phone number. Now that you know about line breaks, you can add some poetry to your Web page.

Note: A word of warning about using line breaks. You don't have any control over the browser or hardware of the person viewing your Web page. Browsers automatically wrap text at the end of a line and that will be at a different place depending on the browser, the size of the user's monitor, and so on. What does this mean to you? Keep in mind that using a line break tag does not necessarily mean all of the text before the line break will appear onscreen as one line.

HEADINGS

At this point, you have an HTML document that probably bores you to tears. You're saying "Gee, I'm glad I can enter text and tell the browser where to start new lines and paragraphs, but how do I make it look more interesting?" Fortunately, you can add headings to your HTML document. Headings are lines of text, formatted to stand out from the body text. You use headings to organize the content of your Web page. For example, you might use a heading to indicate a section title, a page title, and so on. HTML has six levels of headings as described in Table 3.2.

Table 3.2   **HTML Headings**

Opening Tag	Closing Tag	Purpose
<H1>	</H1>	Formats the line of text as a heading level 1 paragraph
<H2>	</H2>	Formats the line of text as a heading level 2 paragraph
<H3>	</H3>	Formats the line of text as a heading level 3 paragraph
<H4>	</H4>	Formats the line of text as a heading level 4 paragraph
<H5>	</H5>	Formats the line of text as a heading level 5 paragraph
<H6>	</H6>	Formats the line of text as a heading level 6 paragraph.

Each of these heading tags includes the functionality of a new paragraph tag (<P>). Headings always appear on their own line and are separated from other text by a blank line before and after. This makes headings stand out more clearly from the body text.

Debugging HTML Code

Wouldn't it be nice to be perfect? Unfortunately, most of us aren't. There will probably be times when we'll mistype some piece of code or forget something and our HTML page will look funny at best. Debugging is the process of discovering and correcting errors in your HTML code. If you enter incorrect HTML code, your Web page will usually show the approximate location of your error. For example, if you forget to include an </H1> tag at the end of your heading line, the remainder of the document will appear in the heading format rather than in the body text format. Table 3.3 describes some common errors and the effects they will have on your Web pages.

Table 3.3   Debugging HTML Code

Common Error	Effect on Your Web Page
Forgetting to close a container tag, for example, not including an </H1> tag after you enter a line with a heading 1 opening tag (<H1>)	The text of your document is formatted incorrectly from that point forward.
Holding the shift key when you should not, resulting in errors such as <H!>, <?H!>	The text is not formatted as you expect, or, if the error is in the closing tag, the effect is the same as forgetting a closing tag.
Not holding the shift key when you should, resulting in errors such as ,H1> or <H2.	Text is not formatted correctly. If the error is in the closing tag, the effect is the same as forgetting a closing tag.
Entering an incorrect tag, such as <G1> instead of <H1>	The text will not be formatted as you expect.

If you run into a formatting problem, check your HTML tags to make sure they are correct.

Let's open an HTML file and look at the six heading levels and then create some headings in our HTML document:

1. In your browser, open the file **HEADINGS.HTM**. This is a sample file that illustrates the heading format levels.

2. Observe the headings. Heading levels one through six are displayed as follows.

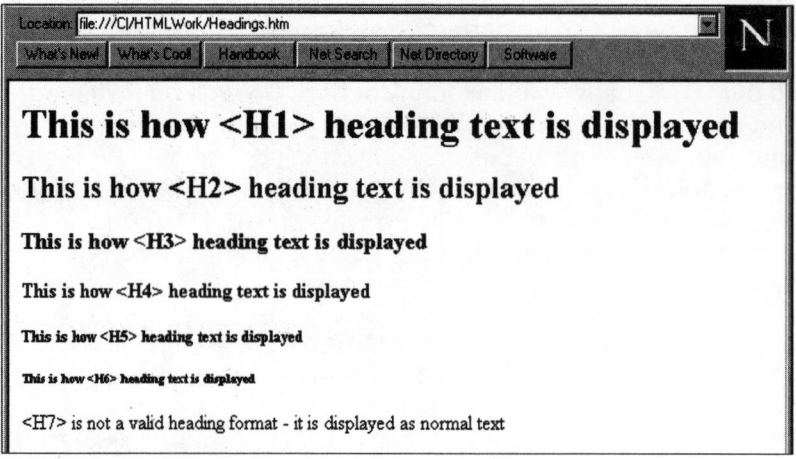

3. Switch to your text editor (the DEFAULT.HTM file should still be open) and place the insertion point at the left edge of the line immediately following the <BODY> tag.

4. Enter the following heading for your page,

```
<BODY>
<!-- Page heading -->
<H1>Jetaway Travel</H1>
```

5. Save the file and switch to your browser window.

6. Open the file **DEFAULT.HTM** and observe the Jetaway Travel heading.

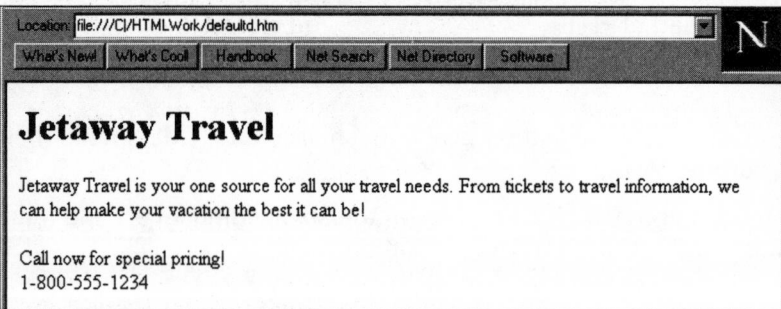

PRACTICE YOUR SKILLS

Let's add some more headings to the HTML document.

1. Switch to your text editor and place the insertion point at the left edge of the line immediately following the <H1> heading line.

2. Add a level 2 heading with the text **Jetaway Travel**.

3. Save the file and view the changes in your browser.

4. Repeat steps 1 through 3 with heading levels <H3> through <H6>. Save and view each heading.

5. Delete each of the lines you entered in this practice, leaving only the <H1> line. Save and view the file.

ALIGNING PAGE ELEMENTS

In addition to setting headings to stand out from body text, you can use the align attribute to align paragraphs and headings and the Center tag to center HTML page elements. Table 3.4 describes how to use the align attribute to align paragraphs.

Table 3.4　　　Using Alignment Attributes

Alignment Value	Purpose
ALIGN=CENTER	Centers the paragraph or heading
ALIGN=RIGHT	Aligns the paragraph or heading along the right margin
ALIGN=LEFT	Aligns the paragraph or heading along the left margin

Using the align attribute looks something like this:

Alignment Value	Purpose
<P ALIGN=CENTER>	Centers the paragraph between the margins.
<H1 ALIGN=CENTER>	This is a centered title</H1> appears in your browser window as follows

Remember that attributes must be listed in the opening tag when you are using a container tag (such as heading 1).

The align attribute isn't just for text. You can also use it to change the alignment for images and horizontal rules. For example, if you want a line that does not extend the entire length of the page and that is centered, you can set the width of the line and center it. The code to do so would look like this:

```
<HR WIDTH=50% ALIGN=CENTER>
```

The Width attribute specifies the length of the line, in this case, 50 percent of the screen, and Align tells the browser to center the line between the margins.

In addition to the align attribute, you can use <CENTER> and </CENTER> to center whatever appears between the tags in relation to the browser window. When you use the Center tags, any text or HTML element you enter between the tags is centered in the browser window. For example, the following code

```
<CENTER>
Come travel the world with us.<BR>
<IMG SRC="globe.gif"><BR>
</CENTER>
```

looks like this in the browser window

Let's align some text:

1. Switch to your text editor and add a new line before the line *"Call now for special pricing!"*

2. Type **<CENTER>** to enter the opening <CENTER> tag.

3. Add a new line after the line containing the phone number and enter the **</CENTER>** closing tag.

4. Save and view the file. The lines between the tags are centered on the Web page.

Please note that you could have used the ALIGN=CENTER attribute to center those two lines of text.

PRACTICE YOUR SKILLS

Let's use the align attribute to right align some text.

1. Switch to your text editor and place the insertion point to the right of the *P* in the <P> tag. Press the **Spacebar** and type **ALIGN=RIGHT**.

2. Save and view the file. The first paragraph should look similar to this

> Jetaway Travel is your one source for all your travel needs. From tickets to travel information, we can help make your vacation the best it can be!

Ugly, isn't it? Let's fix it.

3. Return to the text editor and use the align attribute to left-align the paragraph you right-aligned in step 1.

4. Save and view the file.

CREATING LISTS

What happens if you want to create a list of items on your Web page? You can create numbered and unnumbered lists. These lists are formatted with sequential numbers or bullet characters, respectively. According to the HTML specification, numbered lists are called *ordered lists*, while unnumbered lists are called *unordered lists*.

Within your ordered and unordered lists, you create *list items*, new lines for each item in the list. Use the tags described in Table 3.5 to create lists.

Table 3.5   **Creating Lists**

Opening Tag	Closing Tag	Purpose
<OL>	</OL>	Creates an ordered (numbered) list
<UL>	</UL>	Creates an unordered (unnumbered) list
<LI>		Creates a list item (a new line in either an ordered or unordered list)

CREATING A LIST

A basic list in HTML consists of a list container tag <OL> or <UL> and the list items tag <LI>. The list container tag tells the browser whether or not the items in the list should be numbered. Each item in a list begins with a list item tag.

Let's create an ordered list:

1. Switch to your text editor and immediately following the </CENTER> line, add the following text

```
<!-- Ordered list -->
<P>
<OL>
<LI>Provide ticketing services
<LI>Reserve hotel rooms, and
<LI>Book sightseeing tours.
</OL>
</P>
```

2. Save and view the file. The HTML tag you entered in step 1 creates the ordered (numbered) list shown below.

```
1. Provide ticketing services,
2. Reserve hotel rooms, and
3. Book sightseeing tours.
```

3. Immediately following the <OL> line, enter the text **At Jetaway Travel we can:** (include the colon).

4. Save and view the file. Because you typed the text after the opening tag for the ordered list, yet didn't enter the <LI> tag before the text you typed in step 3, the text appears indented but it isn't preceded by a number. This text serves as a title for your list.

Now you have a numbered list in your Web page. Let's say you decide it really isn't necessary for the list to be numbered. Let's change the container tag to make the list unordered.

1. Switch to your text editor.

2. Select the **<OL>** tag and type **<UL>** to change the opening tag to an unordered list.

3. Select the **</OL>** tag and type **</UL>** to change the closing tag.

4. Change the comment line to reflect that this is now an unordered list.

5. Save and view the file. Your list should resemble the one shown below.

Jetaway Travel

Jetaway Travel is your one source for all your travel needs. From tickets to travel information, we can help make your vacation the best it can be!

Call now for special pricing!
1-800-555-1234

- Provide ticketing services,
- Reserve hotel rooms, and
- Book sightseeing tours.

ADDITIONAL LIST TYPES

To provide greater flexibility in creating different kinds of lists, HTML enables you to customize ordered and unordered lists from their respective list item marker defaults by using the TYPE=*type* attribute.

Ordered Lists

The default list item marker is 1, 2, 3, and so forth. However, you can use the TYPE attribute to designate list items with markers other than 1,2,3. The syntax is

```
<OL TYPE=type>
```

In addition to the default, HTML offers four list types for ordered lists. They are described in Table 3.6.

Line break tags are not necessary in lists. The <LI> tag automatically separates each list item by a line break.

Let's try using list types in ordered lists.

Table 3.6 **List Types for Ordered Lists**

List Type	Description
I	List item marker is set to uppercase Roman numerals
i	List item marker is set to lowercase Roman numerals
A	List item marker is set to uppercase letters
a	List item marker is set to lowercase letters

1. In your text editor, change the <UL> tag to **<OL TYPE=I>**.

2. Change the </UL> tag to **</OL>**.

3. Save the file as **MyLists.htm** and view the file in your browser.

4. In Your text editor, change the TYPE=I to **TYPE=a**.

5. Save and view the file. Your list should resemble the one shown below.

> a. Provide ticketing services,
> b. Reserve hotel rooms, and
> c. Book sightseeing tours.

PRACTICE YOUR SKILLS

1. Try the remaining list types shown in Table 3.6.

2. Save and view the file after each change.

UNORDERED LISTS

Unordered lists in HTML are lists whose list items are not displayed in a specific order. If you do not specify a list type, then the default list item marker is a bullet. You can use the TYPE attribute to specify a different list type. The syntax is

```
<UL TYPE=type>
```

In addition to the default, HTML offers three list types for unordered lists described in Table 3.7.

Table 3.7   **List Types for Unordered Lists**

List Type	Description
Square	In Navigator, the list item marker is a filled-in square
Circle	In Navigator, the list item marker is a hollow square
Disc	In Navigator, the list item marker is the same as the default bullet

Note: In Navigator 2.0 the circle attribute produces a hollow square, and in Navigator 3.0 the circle attribute produces a hollow circle.

Let's try changing the ordered list to an unordered list and use the list types for unordered lists.

1. In your text editor, change the <OL to **<UL**. This will change the list back to an unordered list.

2. Change the type to **CIRCLE**. Remember, if you are using Navigator 2.0, you will see a hollow square rather than a hollow circle.

3. Change the </OL> to **</UL>**.

4. Save and view the file. Even though this list is unordered, there is still an item indicator at the beginning of each list item; in this case, a circle.

PRACTICE YOUR SKILLS

1. Try the remaining list types shown in Table 3.7.

2. Save and view the file after each change.

NESTED LISTS

Nested lists are useful if you want to create an outline. You can't create an outline with just a single ordered or unordered list. By nesting lists, you can create a document that contains primary and secondary list items, each of which uses different list types. You can also use nested lists to create a master list that is comprised of both ordered (see Figure 3.2) and unordered lists.

Figure 3.2
Nested ordered lists

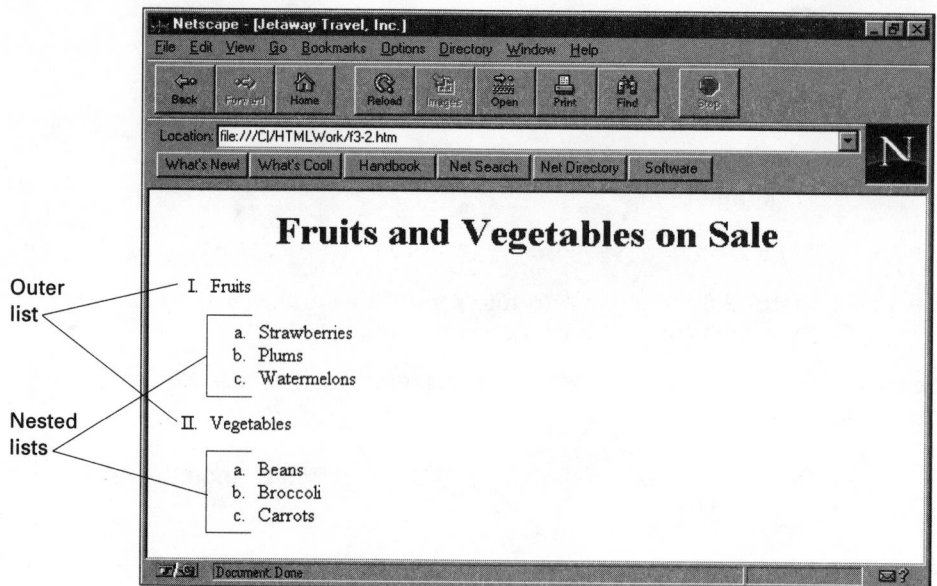

Let's add another list to your document. This one will be a nested list containing both ordered and unordered lists.

1. Switch to your text editor.

2. In the Body section (before the </BODY> tag and below the existing list) add the comment **<!--Nested list types-->**.

3. Add **<OL Type=A>**. This is the beginning of the outer list of the nested lists.

4. Type **<LI>US Destinations**. This is the first list item in the outer list.

5. Type **<UL TYPE=disc>**. This is the opening of the first inner list.

6. Add the following cities as list items: **Boston, Chicago, Dallas**, and **San Francisco**. Remember to use an **LI** (list item) tag in front of each city.

7. Type **</UL>**. This closes the first inner list.

8. Type **<LI> International Destinations**.

9. Type **<UL TYPE=disc>**. This is the opening of the second inner list.

10. Add the following cities as list items: **London, Cologne, Tokyo.**

11. Type **</UL>**. This closes the second inner list.

12. Type **</OL>** to close the ordered (outer) list. Your code should resemble that shown in Figure 3.3

Figure 3.3
Creating nested lists

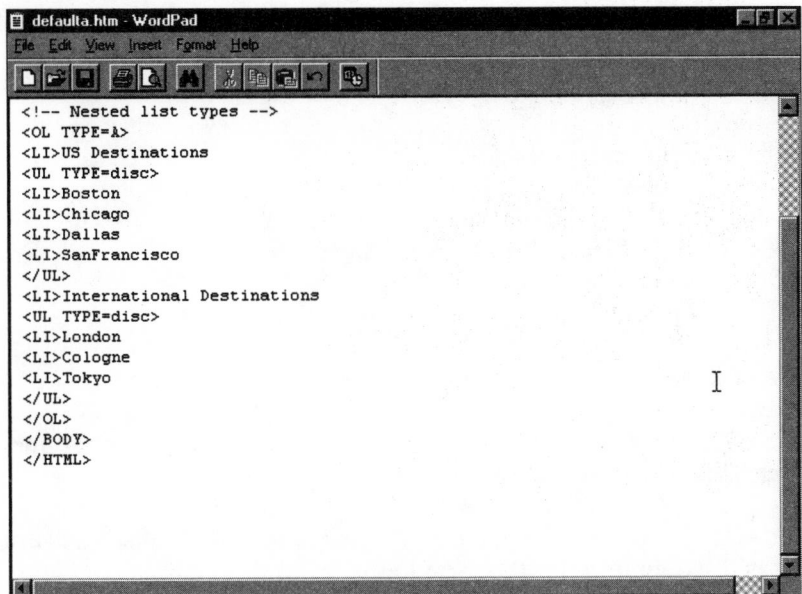

13. Save and view the file.

PRACTICE YOUR SKILLS

1. Change the ordered list to an unordered list with square bullets.

2. Change the unordered lists to ordered lists which number the cities.

DEFINITION LISTS

Definition lists give you the ability to format terms and their definitions through the <DL>, <DT>, and <DD> tags, which stand for definition list, definition term, and definition, respectively. You start a definition list with the <DL> tag, followed by the <DD> tag and the term, followed by the <DT> tag and the definition for the term. You close the list with the </DL> tag.

Definition terms are left-aligned in documents, and separated by a line break from the definition definition. Definition definitions are rendered as indented paragraphs. Multiple definition terms are separated from the previous definition by a line break. If you want more space between a definition and a new term, use the paragraph tag.

Let's create a definition list which lists terms and their definitions.

1. Switch to your text editor.

2. On a new line near the end of the Body section, before the </BODY> tag, type **Glossary of Travel Terms**. Press **Enter**.

3. Type **<!--Definition lists-->**. Press **Enter**.

4. Type **<DL>**. Press **Enter**. This begins the definition list.

5. Type **<DT>Blackout Dates:** (type the colon).Press the **Spacebar** and press **Enter**. This is the term to be defined.

6. Type **<DD>Dates on which special fares are not available**. Press **Enter**. This is the definition for the term in the DT tag.

7. Add the term **<DT>Coach ticket:**. Press the **Spacebar**, press **Enter**, and type the definition **<DD>Unrestricted ticket. Full fare is charged. Changes can be made to the ticket at no extra charge.**

8. On a new line, type **</DL>**. This indicates the end of the definition list.

9. Save and view the file.

Glossary of Travel Terms

Blackout Dates: Dates on which special fares are not available.
Coach ticket: Unrestricted ticket. Full fare is charged. Changes can be made to the ticket at no extra charge.

PRACTICE YOUR SKILLS

1. Add some more terms and definitions of your choice to the file. You can use any word or phrase and its definition.

2. Save and view the file.

CHARACTER FORMATTING WITH HTML

While you can't specify exactly how your Web page will be displayed by a certain browser, you can do a lot to control how body text is displayed by entering character formatting tags within the body text. Table 3.8 describes the some standard HTML character formatting tags you can use in your Web pages.

Table 3.8   Character Formatting Tags

Opening Tag	Closing Tag	Purpose
<B>	</B>	Text within the tags is formatted bold
<STRONG>	</STRONG>	Text within the tags is formatted "strongly" which in most browsers is bold.
<I>	</I>	Text within the tags is formatted in italics.
<EM>	</EM>	Text within the tags is "emphasized" which in most browsers is italic.
<STRIKE>	</STRIKE>	Text within the tags is formatted as strikethrough text. (Strikethrough text looks like this: ~~strikethrough.~~)
<U>	</U>	Text within the tags is underlined.
<BLINK>	</BLINK>	Text within the tags is formatted to blink. Some browsers do not support this tag.

Note: Many Web designers consider the <BLINK> tag to be in poor taste. Because of this, and because not all browsers support the <BLINK> tag, you should limit your use of this tag.

You can enter any of the tags listed in Table 3.8 within your text. Netscape Navigator and most other browsers will recognize these elements as tags even if they appear immediately next to "normal" body text. For example, Navigator will recognize and properly format <B>bolded words</B> even though there are no spaces between the words and the tags.

You can also nest tags; that is, you can apply more than one tag to a block of text by including one set of tags inside another set of tags. Figure 3.4 shows how to nest to produce text that is formatted bold and italic.

Figure 3.4
Tags and nested tags

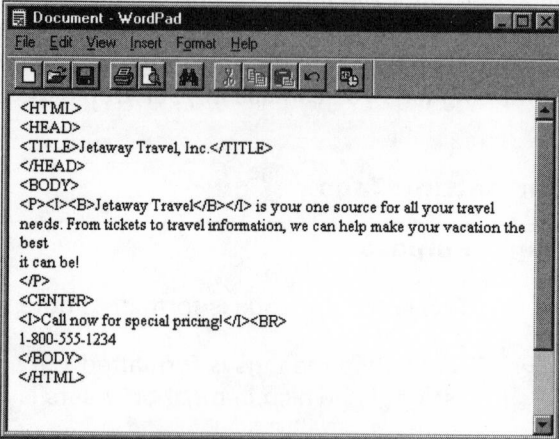

To avoid browser interpretation problems when you nest tags, you should close tags in the reverse order that you open them. For example, if you format text bold and italic by entering the bold tag first then the italic tag, you should close with the italic tag first, then the bold tag. Figure 3.4 demonstrates this convention.

Let's add some variety to the body text of the Jetaway Travel home page:

1. Switch to your text editor and reopen **DEFAULT.HTM**.

2. To the left of the *C* in the line *Call now for special pricing!* type **<I>** to add the opening italic tag.

3. At the end of the line *Call now for special pricing!* (and before the <BR> tag) type**</I>** to add the closing italic tag.

4. Save the file, switch to your browser window and view the file.

> ## Jetaway Travel
>
> Jetaway Travel is your one source for all your travel needs. From tickets to travel information, we can help make your vacation the best it can be!
>
> *Call now for special pricing!*
1-800-555-1234
>
> a. Provide ticketing services,
> b. Reserve hotel rooms, and
> c. Book sightseeing tours.
>
>   A. US Destinations

5. Use your text editor to add **<B>** and **</B>** tags around *Jetaway Travel* in the line that *begins Jetaway Travel is your one source...* to format the company name in bold type.

6. Save and view the file.

> ## Jetaway Travel
>
> **Jetaway Travel** is your one source for all your travel needs. From tickets to travel information, we can help make your vacation the best it can be!
>
> *Call now for special pricing!*
1-800-555-1234

7. Return to your text editor and place the insertion point to the left of the < in the *<B>* tag and type **<I>** to add an opening italic tag. We'll format the company name in bold and italics.

8. Place the insertion point after the > in the *</B>* tag at the end of the line and type **</I>** to add the closing italic tag.

9. Save and view the file.

Jetaway Travel

Jetaway Travel is your one source for all your travel needs. From tickets to travel information, we can help make your vacation the best it can be!

Call now for special pricing!
1-800-555-1234

CHARACTER SIZE

While you cannot specify an exact size that text should appear in a browser window, you can set relative sizing; that is, you can specify that a block of text be a size larger or smaller than normal body text. Table 3.9 describes the tags you can use to set relative sizing.

Table 3.9   Setting Character Size

Opening Tag	Closing Tag	Purpose
<BASEFONT SIZE=#>		Indicates the default font size for the current HTML document. It uses the size attribute to indicate the default text size. Size values can range from 1 to 7. If you don't indicate a size value, Netscape Navigator will use the value 3. This tag is not supported by all browsers.
<FONT SIZE=#>	</FONT>	Sets the size of the text between the opening and closing tags. An absolute or relative size may be specified. Absolute size values range from 1 to 7. Relative sizes are used to specify the size of the text relative to the default font size. For example, <FONT SIZE=+2> increases the size to the text by +2. This tag is not supported by all browsers.

Table 3.9   **Setting Character Size (Continued)**

Opening Tag	Closing Tag	Purpose
<BIG>	</BIG>	Increases the size of the text relative to the surrounding text by an amount determined by the browser.
<SMALL>	</SMALL>	Decreases the size of the text relative to the surrounding text by an amount determined by the browser.

Why would you want to bother increasing or decreasing the text size? Suppose you want to add a copyright notice to your Web page. You might want the text of the copyright notice to be a little smaller than the rest of the body text.

Let's create a copyright notice for the Jetaway Travel Home page.

1. Switch to your text editor and place the insertion point at the end of the file before the </BODY> tag.

2. Type **<!--Copyright footer--><P>** to add a comment letting anyone who views the source code know that this is the copyright notice. You've added the <P> tag at the end of the comment to ensure that the copyright notice always begins on its own line.

3. Press **Enter** and type **Copyright © 1996 by Jetaway Travel, Inc.** to create the text of the copyright notice.

4. Save and view the file. The copyright notice appears at the bottom of your page in normal text.

Call now for special pricing!
1-800-555-1234

At Jetaway Travel, we can:
- Provide ticketing services,
- Reserve hotel rooms, and
- Book sightseeing tours.

Copyright © 1996 by Jetaway Travel, Inc.

Since we want the copyright notice to be a little smaller than the surrounding text, we'll need to add a tag.

5. Return to your text editor and change your copyright notice as follows to set the font size one size smaller than normal text.

```
<!-- Copyright footer><P>
<FONT SIZE=-1>Copyright &copy; 1996 by Jetaway Travel, Inc.</FONT></P>
</BODY>
</HTML>
```

6. Save and view the file. The copyright notice is now formatted in smaller type.

PRACTICE YOUR SKILLS

Let's take a look at some valid text formats.

1. In your browser window, open the file **TEXT.HTM** to view a sample file that illustrates text formats.

2. Observe the Web page as shown in Figure 3.5. These are valid text formats you can use in your documents.

3. View the source code for the Web page (if you are using Netscape Navigator, choose View, Document Source).

```
<HTML>
<TITLE>Valid text formats</TITLE>

<!-- The main body of the document -->
<BODY>

This is how normal BODY text is displayed.<BR>
<B>This is bold text.</B><BR>
<I>This is italic text.</I><BR>
<STRONG>STRONG text is displayed as bold on most systems.</STRONG><BR>
<EM>EM (emphasized) text is displayed as italic on most systems.</EM><BR>
<STRIKE>This is STRIKE (strikethrough) text.</STRIKE><BR>
<U>This is supposed to be U (underlined) text. However, most systems do not su
<FONT SIZE=-2>This is FONT SIZE=-2.</FONT><BR>
<FONT SIZE=-1>This is FONT SIZE=-1.</FONT><BR>
<FONT SIZE=+1>This is FONT SIZE=+1.</FONT><BR>
<FONT SIZE=+2>This is FONT SIZE=+2.</FONT><BR>
<FONT SIZE=+3>This is FONT SIZE=+3.</FONT><BR>
<FONT SIZE=+4>This is FONT SIZE=+4.</FONT>

</BODY>
</HTML>
```

4. Close the source code window.

Figure 3.5
The formatted Web page

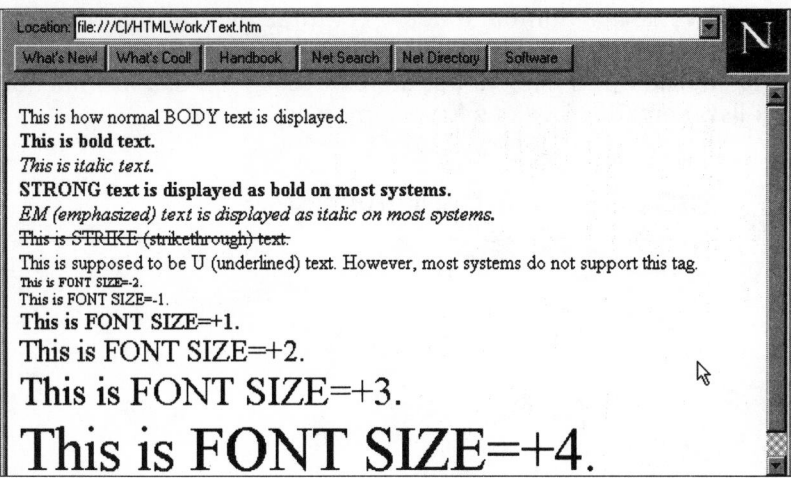

CHARACTER COLORS

In addition to adding emphasis and changing the size of text, you can specify the color for blocks of text. Table 3.10 describes some tags you can use to set text colors. As with the font and basefont tags, these tags are supported by Netscape Navigator 2.0 and Microsoft Internet Explorer 2.0 and higher, but may not be supported by other browsers.

Table 3.10   **Setting Character Colors**

Opening Tag	Closing Tag	Purpose
<FONT COLOR="name"	</FONT>	Sets the font for the text within the tags to the color specified. Some valid color names include: Red, Green, Blue, Black, White, Gray.
<FONT COLOR="#hex_rgb"	</FONT>	Sets the font for the text within the tags to the color specified by the RGB (red, green, and blue) value.

In your <FONT COLOR= > tags, you can enter a color name to indicate the color you want. Or, if you want to be more specific, you can enter an RGB value that describes the red, green, and blue components of the color you want. An RGB value is a number made up of three bytes—one each for a red value, a green value, and a blue value—which gives you a palette of millions of colors to choose from. RGB values are expressed in hexadecimal notation. Table 3.11 lists some RGB values for common colors.

Table 3.11   RGB Values for Common Colors

RGB Value	Color
#FFFFFF	White
#000000	Black
#FF0000	Red
#00FF00	Lime
#0000FF	Blue
#888888	Gray
#008888	Cyan
#880088	Magenta

A few notes of warning about text colors:

- To view the complete range of valid colors, you must configure your computer to display at least 256 colors. If your monitor supports fewer than 256 colors, some valid text colors will not appear properly on your screen.

- Some browsers, such as Netscape Navigator version 1.x and Microsoft's Internet Explorer version 1.x, do not support text colors.

- Defined or valid colors may vary depending upon the browser you are using. Keep this in mind when designing your Web page because the color you intend the text to be may not be what the user sees on his or her screen.

Note: If you are not using a browser that supports color, you will not be able to complete the following exercise.

Let's practice setting character colors. Your Web browser should be open and active.

1. Open **COLORTXT.HTM** in the browser window to view a sample file that illustrates some different text colors.

2. Observe the Web page. The text is formatted in a range of colors. Those color names that are valid are correctly displayed; those that are invalid are formatted in a color other than the one their name suggests.

3. Switch to your text editor and open the file **COLORTXT.HTM** to view the HTML code. Notice the following:

   - Each time you change colors, you must include both the opening and closing FONT tags.

   - The color name appears in quotation marks in the attribute portion of the opening FONT tag.

4. In your text editor, reopen **DEFAULT.HTM** to view the Jetaway Travel home page HTML file. We're going to add some emphasis by changing text color.

5. Place the insertion point to the left of the *s* in *special* in the line *Call now for special pricing!* and type **<FONT COLOR="Red">** to add the opening font color tag.

6. Place the insertion point to the right of the *l* in *special* and type **</FONT>** to add the closing tag.

7. Save and view the file. The word *special* now stands out from the rest of the sentence.

COMPARING PROCEDURAL AND DESCRIPTIVE FORMATTING

Procedural formatting is the type of formatting you do in most word processing programs. For example, with procedural formatting, you might specify that text should be in the Times New Roman font, 12 point, and bold. The text is given only those attributes you specify.

Descriptive formatting, the type used by HTML, leaves the exact formatting to the system that displays the final output; you specify the purpose or the type of text. For example, you might specify that a block of text is a heading. On some systems, headings might be Helvetica, bold, 16 point type; on others they might be Times New Roman, italic, 14 point. On the displaying system, headings will be consistently formatted. However, you cannot guarantee formatting consistency between systems. In other words, what you see on your computer may not be what your next door neighbor sees on his.

Table 3.12 describes some of the advantages and disadvantages of both procedural and descriptive formatting.

Table 3.12   **Comparing Procedural and Descriptive Formatting**

Procedural Formatting	Descriptive Formatting
You can be assured that text will be formatted exactly as you specify.	You do not have to worry whether systems have the proper fonts to display your pages.
As the page designer, you have complete control over the appearance of your pages.	Users can control aspects of the pages they view; for example, they can make the text larger so that it is easier to read.
Typically, the formats you specify on screen are also reproduced on printers if the printer supports the fonts and other formats in your document.	Because you cannot control exact formatting, printed pages might not break appropriately or fill pages properly.

So, which is better? Procedural or descriptive formatting? Each has its place. If you're creating a newsletter to be distributed on paper, you'll definitely want to have complete control over the way that newsletter looks. However, if you decide to distribute that same newsletter electronically, it will be more important for you to get the content across than worry about whether the articles appear in Times New Roman, 10 point type.

The Web uses descriptive formatting because cross-platform compatibility is important to Web users. What good would it do you to create a Web page that could only be viewed by people using Netscape Navigator 3.0 on a Windows 95 system with certain fonts, colors, and so on installed? With descriptive formatting, it doesn't matter if your system is Windows 95, Windows 3.1, or OS/2. It doesn't matter if your browser is Netscape Navigator, Internet Explorer, or Mosaic. You'll still be able to see what's out there on the Web.

Let's take a look at descriptive formatting in action:

1. If necessary, switch to your browser window.

2. Reduce the size of your browser window (if you're using Windows 95 or Windows 3.1, click on the **Restore** button).

3. Resize the window so that it fills about one quarter of your screen (on most systems, you can resize a window by dragging on one of its borders). Notice that the Heading line wraps to a new line when the entire line will no longer fit in the window.

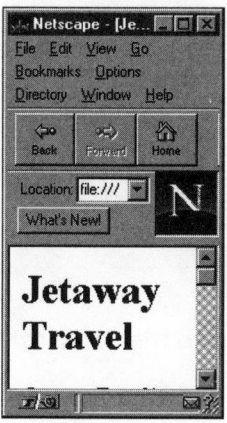

4. Maximize your browser window (click on the Restore button or drag the window border).

BROWSER PREFERENCES

The preferences that you set in your browser can affect how the browser displays Web pages. For example, you can set default sizes and colors, as well as background and link colors. If users of your Web pages have set some of these options, this will affect how your pages appear on their systems.

Let's take a look at how setting browser preferences can affect the display of Web pages:

1. Open the Preferences dialog box for your browser (in Netscape Navigator, choose **Options, General Preferences**).

2. Display the Font preferences, if necessary (in Netscape Navigator, click on the **Fonts** tab).

3. Set the size for the default font to 36 points. If you're using Netscape Navigator, click on **Choose Font** next to the Use The Proportional Font option and make the change in the Choose Base Font dialog box. **Note:** Check the default point size before you change it, so you'll know what to change it back to.

4. Observe the Web page. The text of the Web page is formatted in 36-point type. Nothing wraps where it should.

Jetaway Travel is your one source for all your travel needs. From tickets to travel information, we can help make your vacation the best it can

---

5. Change the size of the proportional font back to the default size (this is probably 12 point).

ADDITIONAL STYLES

The following section describes some additional tags that you might find useful when creating your Web documents.

SUBSCRIPT AND SUPERSCRIPT

By using the and tags, you can physically format characters to display as subscript or superscript. Characters are rendered either below or above the level of regular text. This formatting can be helpful to indicate footnotes or to write mathematical or chemical terminology properly.

QUOTATIONS

You might find it helpful to have quotations stand out from regular text. HTML provides you with two container tags for this purpose. The first is the <BLOCKQUOTE> tag. You can use this logical text formatting tag anywhere inside the body section of a document. Place the <BLOCKQUOTE> tag immediately in front of the quotation; then use the </BLOCKQUOTE> tag at the end of the quotation. Many browsers render a quotation formatted with the <BLOCKQUOTE>

element as an indented paragraph. This typically means the text will be indented on both the left and right. Here is an example of <BLOCKQUOTE>:

```
<BLOCKQUOTE>Put some text here.</BLOCKQUOTE>
```

> This is regular body text. See how it stretches from the left margin to the right margin in the Browser window? This is regular body text. See how it stretches from the left margin to the right margin in the Browser window? This is regular body text. See how it stretches from the left margin to the right margin in the Browser window?
>
> > This is a block quote. Notice that it is indented from the left margin and the right margin. This is a block quote. Notice that it is indented from the left margin and the right margin. This is a block quote. Notice that it is indented from the left margin and the right margin. This is a block quote. Notice that it is indented from the left margin and the right margin.

The second container element you can use to logically format quotations is <CITE>. Many browsers render a quotation formatted with the <CITE> and </CITE> tags in italics.

PROGRAMMING CODE

You might want to show lines of computer code or give instructions on how to accomplish a certain task using a computer in your Web page. You can use the <CODE> container tag for this purpose. Text enclosed in the <CODE> and </CODE> tags is formatted logically. Most browsers display it in a fixed-width font.

ADDRESSES

Use the <ADDRESS container tag in an HTML document to indicate an address. This tag is a logical formatting tag. Most browsers render the text inside the <ADDRESS> and </ADDRESS> tags in italics.

Let's examine a document that contains these additional tags.

1. In your browser, open the file **STYLES.HTM**. This document contains examples of all of the styles listed above.

2. View the Document Source. Notice that each of these additional tags is a container tag with opening and closing tags.

3. Close the Document Source window.

QUICK REFERENCE

Whew, you covered a lot of ground in this chapter! You learned how to format paragraphs and characters, and the difference between procedural and descriptive formatting.

Here's a quick reference guide to the techniques covered in this chapter:

Technique	How to Do It
Cycle among open programs in Windows 3.1 or Windows 95	Press *Alt+Tab*
Indicate the body section of an HTML document	<BODY>, </BODY>
Mark the end of a paragraph	Insert the empty tag *<P>*
Start a new line	Insert the empty tag * *
Create a quote	Surround the quotation with the *<BLOCKQUOTE>* and *</BLOCKQUOTE>* tags or the *<CITE>* and *</CITE>* tags
Center paragraphs or page elements	Surround the paragraph and/or page elements with the *<CENTER>* and *</CENTER>* tags
Left-align paragraphs or lines	Add the *ALIGN=LEFT* attribute to the opening tag for a paragraph, image, or horizontal rule; for example <P ALIGN=LEFT>
Center-align paragraphs or lines	Add the *ALIGN=CENTER* attribute to the opening tag
Right-align paragraphs or lines	Add the *ALIGN=LEFT* attribute to the opening tag
Add a horizontal rule	Use the *<HR>* tag
Change the width of a horizontal rule to a percentage of the screen display	Add the *WIDTH=##%* attribute to the opening tag
Add a comment	Insert the tag *<!--comment text here-->*
Apply bold format to selected text	Surround the text with the *<B>* and *</B>* tags

Technique	How to Do It
Apply strong format to selected text	Surround the text with the *<STRONG>* and *</STRONG>* tags
Italicize selected text	Surround the text with the *<I>* and *</I>* tags
Emphasize selected text	Surround the text with the *<EM>* and *</EM>* tags
Format text as strikethrough	Surround the text with the *<STRIKE>* and *</STRIKE>* tags
Format text as underlined	Surround the text with the *<U>* and *</U>* tags
Format text to blink	Surround the text with the *<BLINK>* and *</BLINK>* tags. This tag may not be supported by all browsers.
Set the default font size for the current HTML document	*<BASEFONT SIZE=#>*; size values can range from 1 to 7
Increase or decrease the font size of selected text relative to the default font size	Surround the selected text with the *<FONT SIZE=#>* and *</FONT>* tags. The value for size can be -7 to +7
Increase the size of selected text relative to the surrounding text	Surround the text with the *<BIG>* and *</BIG>* tags
Decrease the size of selected text relative to the surrounding text	Surround the text with the *<SMALL>* and *</SMALL>* tags
Change the font color for selected text	Surround the text with the *<FONT COLOR="name">* and *</FONT>* tags; the value for color can be a color name or RGB number
Render text above or below the baseline	Surround the text with the *_{* and *}* or *^{* and *}* tags
Indicate programming code in your document	Surround the text with *<CODE>* and *</CODE>* tags
Place an address on your page which will be specially formatted	Surround the address with the *<ADDRESS>* and *</ADDRESS>* tags

Technique	How to Do It
Create an ordered list	Use *<OL>* tag at the beginning of the list and *</OL>* at the end of the list
Create an unordered list	Use the *<UL>* tag at the beginning of the list and *</UL>* at the end of the list
Specify a list item in an ordered or unordered list	Use the *<LI>* empty tag
Change the type of unordered or ordered list	Add the *TYPE* attribute to the <UL> or <OL> tag
Create a definition list	Start the list with the *<DL>* tag; specify the term with the *<DT>* empty tag; specify the definition with the *<DD>* empty tag; close the list with the *</DL>* tag

In the next chapter you'll learn how to create links to other pages.

SKILL BUILDER 1

Periodically throughout this book, we'll provide skill builders to help you put together what you've learned so far. In chapters 2 and 3, you learned how to create and format a basic HTML document. The following skill builder gives you the opportunity to apply these techniques to realistic Web page creation. Chapter references are provided (in parentheses) to inform you where the relevant technique for that step was introduced.

Follow these steps to produce the final document shown in Figures 3.6 and 3.7 from the original document TRAVINFO.HTM.

1. Open **TRAVINFO.HTM** in your text editor.

2. Write the HTML code necessary to set "Jetaway Travel - Travel Information" as the window title. (Chapter 2)

3. Immediately following your window title code, add "**Jetaway Travel**" as an <H1> level heading. (Chapter 3)

4. Immediately following your level 1 heading, add "**Travel Information**" as an <H2> level heading. (Chapter 3)

Figure 3.6
The completed TRAVEL.HTM file

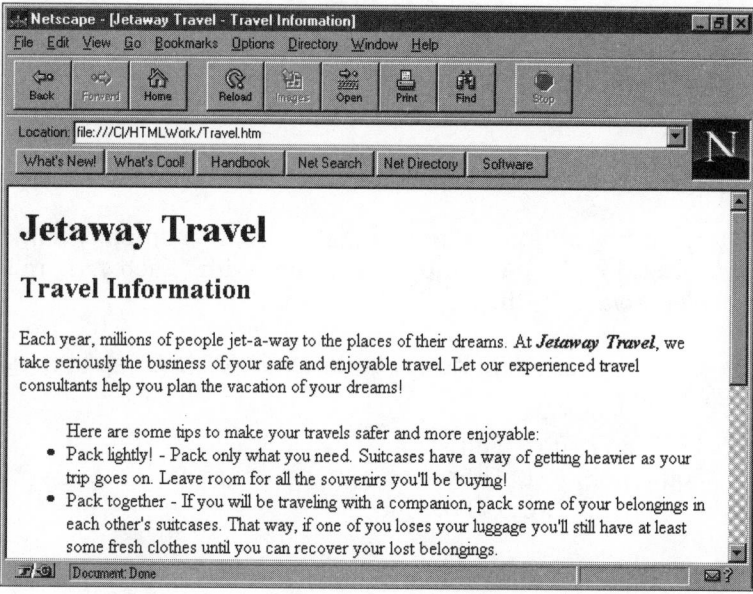

Figure 3.7
The completed TRAVEL.HTM file, continued

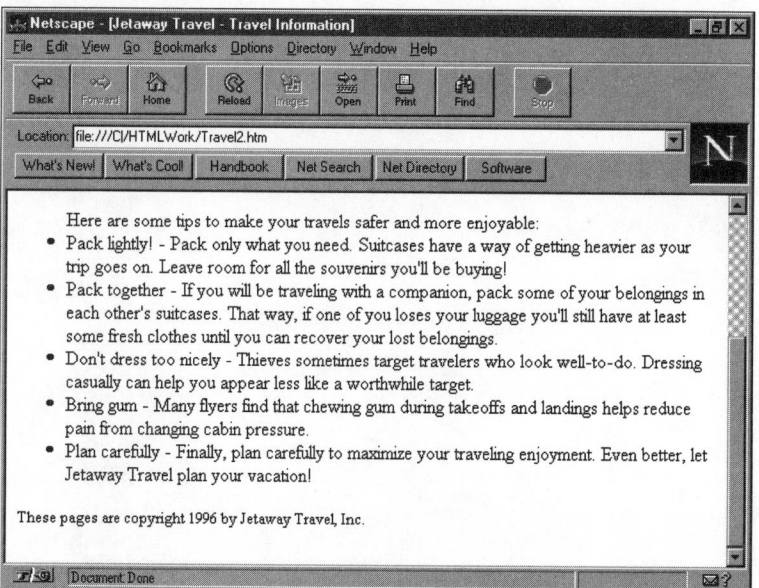

5. Modify the existing HTML code to create an unordered list out of the paragraphs that follow the *<!--This next section is supposed to be an unordered (unnumbered) list-->* comment line. (Chapter 3)

6. Be sure to remove the existing **
** tags from that section of text.

7. Save the file as **TRAVEL.HTM**.

8. View the file in your browser window.

9. Return to your text editor and bold and italicize the company name (*Jetaway Travel*) in the paragraph that begins with "Each year, millions of people jet-a-way..." (Chapter 3)

10. Add the following copyright notice before the </BODY> tag at the end of the file: (Chapter 3)

```
<!--Copyright footer--><P>
<FONT SIZE=-1>These pages are copyright 1996 by
Jetaway Travel, Inc.</FONT></P>
```

11. Save the file and view your changes in the browser.

Adding Local Links to Your Web Pages

Adding Remote Links to Your Web Pages

Guidelines for Linking to Remote Sites

Quick Reference

Chapter 4

Adding Local and Remote Links to Your Web Pages

At the very heart of HTML are its hypertext links, which allow you to jump effortlessly to different documents on your own local computer or on remote computers all over the globe. Without links to connect its millions of HTML pages strewn out over hundreds of thousands of physical locations, the World Wide Web would simply not exist. Links are the "Web" part of the World Wide Web. In this chapter, you'll learn how to create links to local and remote documents.

When you're done working through this chapter, you will know

- How to add local links to your Web pages

- How to add remote links to your Web pages

ADDING LOCAL LINKS TO YOUR WEB PAGES

Links are hotspots; when you click on one, you are connected to the computer and file addressed by the link. Your browser interprets the file's HTML codes and displays the results on your screen. *Et voilà:* You're surfing!

There are two kinds of links: *local* and *remote*. Local links connect to documents on your local computer. When you click on a link that opens an HTML file from your computer's HTMLWork directory, you are using a local link. Remote links connect to documents on remote computers. When you click on a link to go to Yahoo!, you are using a remote link. Over the next few sections we'll discuss local links; later in the chapter we'll take on remote links.

Here are the opening and closing HTML tags you use to add a local link to your Web page:

Opening Tag	**Closing Tag**
<A HREF=*"filename"*>	</A>

And here's the syntax you use to create the local link:

```
<A HREF="filename">local link</A>
```

When you insert this statement in your HTML page, it creates a link to a file named *filename* that resides in the current directory of your computer. The text between the opening and closing tags (*local link*) is highlighted, usually by being formatted as blue underlined characters. The highlighting indicates that users should click on the text to jump to the link; that is, to display the contents of the file *filename*.

RELATIVE ADDRESSING

The <A HREF> syntax presented above uses *relative addressing*. With relative addressing, you specify the file to open and its location *relative to* the current directory—the directory in which the HTML file containing the link resides.

Here are three examples of relative addressing:

```
<A HREF="default1.htm">Link1</A>
```

Link1 links to default1.htm, a file stored on the local computer in the same directory as the HTML file that contains the link.

```
<A HREF="../default2.htm">Link2</A>
```

Link2 links to default2.htm, a file stored on the local computer in the parent of the current directory.

```
<A HREF="Webfiles/default3.htm">Link3</A>
```

Link3 links to default3.htm, a file stored on the local computer in the Webfiles subdirectory, which is a child of the current directory.

Let's begin this chapter's hands-on activities by creating a link to a local file:

1. In WordPad, open **travel.htm**, the Travel Information page.

2. Directly before the copyright footer comment line, insert:

```
<!-- Link to home page -->
<A HREF="default.htm">Back to the Jetaway Travel home
page</A>
```

This creates a link to the local file, default.htm. The <A HREF> tag uses relative addressing; it tells your browser to look for default.htm in the same directory as the file containing the link *travel.htm*. The directory, in this case, is HTMLWork.

3. Save the file, and then open it in Netscape. It should match that shown in Figure 4.1.

4. Click on the link **Back to the Jetaway Travel home page** to jump to the home page. Cool?

ABSOLUTE ADDRESSING

Along with relative addressing, HTML supports *absolute addressing*. With absolute addressing, you must specify the file's exact (absolute) location; its complete *path*. Here's the syntax you use to specify an absolute-address link to a local file:

```
<A HREF="file:///c:/path/filename">local link</A>
```

The file:/// identifier tells the browser that the linked file resides on your local computer.

Important Note: Make sure to use the forward slash "/" to separate directory names in an <A HREF> tag, not the back slash "\" typical of PCs. Why? Because both Netscape and HTML emerged from the UNIX computing environment, which uses the forward slash "/" to specify file paths.

Figure 4.1
Creating a link to a local file

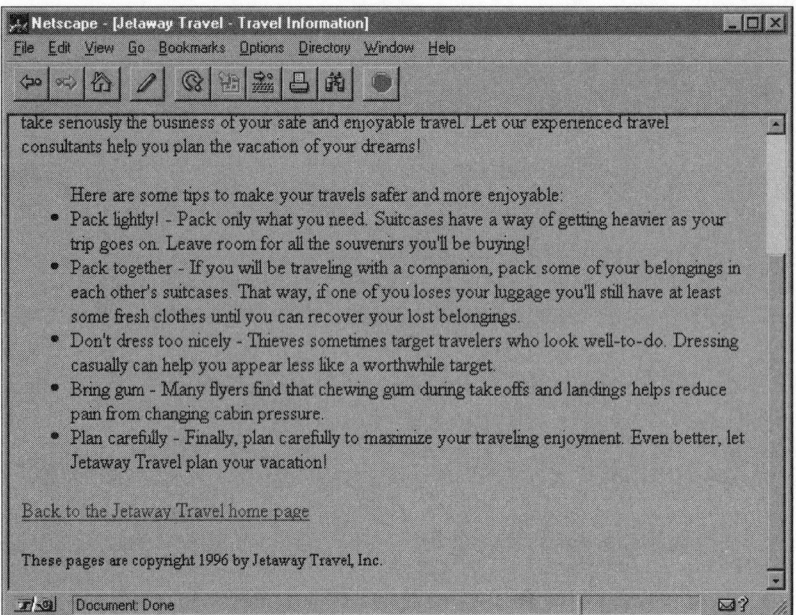

Let's create an absolute-address link to a local file:

1. In WordPad, open **default.htm**.

2. Change the phrase **From tickets to travel information** to **From tickets to <A HREF="file:///c:/HTMLWork/travel.htm">travel</A> information**.

3. Save the file, then open it in Netscape. It should match that shown in Figure 4.2.

4. Click on your new travel link to go to the Travel Information page, which is the local file c:\HTMLWork\travel.htm.

5. Click on **Back** to return to the Jetaway Travel home page.

Let's verify the absolute nature of an absolute address by moving travel.htm to a different directory and then retrying the travel link. First we'll clear Netscape's memory cache, so that it doesn't "cheat" by loading travel.htm from memory instead of from disk.

Figure 4.2
Creating an absolute-address link to a local file

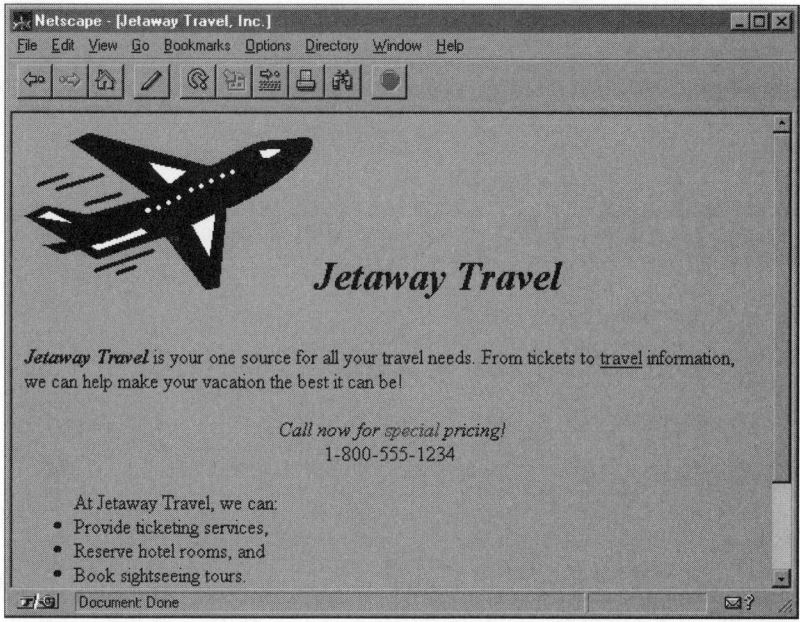

1. Choose **Options, Network Preferences** and click on the **Cache** tab to open the Cache page of the Preferences dialog box.

2. Click on the **Clear Memory Cache Now** button and click on **OK** to clear your Netscape memory cache. Click on **OK** to close the Preferences dialog box.

3. Use **Explorer** (or **File Manager**) to move the travel.htm file from c:\HTML-Work to your c:\ root directory.

4. In Netscape, click on the **travel** link on the Jetaway Travel home page. An error message appears informing you that the file to which the link is trying to connect cannot be found. Why not? Because you just moved it (travel.htm) to a new directory!

5. Click on **OK** to close the error message dialog box.

PRACTICE YOUR SKILLS

1. Move **travel.htm** back to your c:\HTMLWork directory.

2. In Netscape, verify that the travel link once again goes to travel.htm.

ADDING REMOTE LINKS TO YOUR WEB PAGES

Remote links connect to files that are not on your own local computer. You create remote links to Web sites by using the <A HREF> tag as follows:

Opening Tag	**Closing Tag**
<A HREF="http://*URL*">	</A>

Here's the syntax you use to create the remote link:

```
<A HREF="http://URL">remote link</A>
```

When you insert this statement in your HTML page, it creates a link to a World Wide Web page that is addressed by *URL*. The text between the opening and closing tags (*remote link*) is highlighted; you click on it to activate the link. The URL (Uniform Resource Locator) is the address of the remote computer and, optionally, a file on that system. For example, to open the default.htm file stored on a computer at the address "www.company.com" you would use the URL http://www.company.com/default.htm.

Let's add a remote link to our home page:

1. In WordPad, open **default.htm**.

2. After the line beginning with </UL>, insert

```
<!-- Link to Yahoo! -->
<A HREF="http://www.yahoo.com">The Yahoo! Web site</A>
```

3. Save the file, then open it in Netscape. It should match that shown in Figure 4.3. Up to now you could do everything in the book without being connected to the Internet. For this step and some others to come where you are linking to remote sites, you will need to be connected to the Internet.

4. Click on your link **The Yahoo! Web site** to go to the Yahoo! home page.

5. Click on the **Back** button to return to the Jetaway Travel home page.

Figure 4.3
Creating a link to a remote site

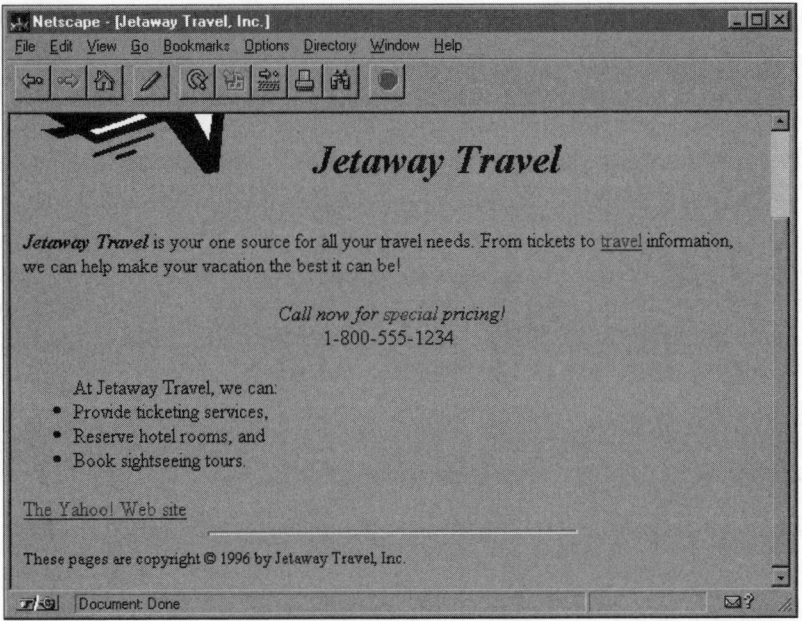

PRACTICE YOUR SKILLS

1. Use WordPad to add a new link after your link to Yahoo!. Use the URL of your favorite site for the link.

2. Save the file, then *reload* it in Netscape (press **Ctrl+R**). The link to Yahoo! and the new link to your favorite site most likely appear on the same line.

3. Use WordPad to skip a line between the graphics (**Hint:** <P>).

4. Save the file, then reload it in Netscape.

5. Verify that your new link works.

6. Return to the Jetaway Travel home page.

GUIDELINES FOR LINKING TO REMOTE SITES

In general, it's a good idea to include links to remote sites on your Web pages. Providing links to useful sites—even to your competitors' sites—may well bring cyberadventurers back to your site regularly as a starting point for their Web excursions.

Beware, however, of including *too many* links. Long lists of links can be ever so dreary and do not generally add great value to a site. Moreover, Yahoo! and other cataloging Web sites probably contain far longer site lists than you could ever create and maintain.

Finally, for every link you provide away from your site, you increase the chances that users will take you up on it and leave—never, perhaps, to return. As long as users stay at your Web site, you can continue delivering your "message" to them.

Here are several common sites to which Web designers create links:

URL of Site	Description of Site
http://www.yahoo.com	The Yahoo! directory, a very popular index of Web sites
http://search.yahoo.com	The Yahoo! search site
http://altavista.digital.com	The AltaVista search site
http://home.netscape.com	The home page for Netscape Navigator
http://www.netscape.com	The home page for Netscape Communications Co.
http://www.microsoft.com	The home page for Microsoft Corp.
http://www.w3.org	The home page for the Worldwide Web Consortium (W3), the organization that defines standards for the Web
http://www.zdnet.com	The home page for ZD Net, a service from the Ziff-Davis Publishing Company, and one of the most popular sites on the Web

Here are some questions that will help get you thinking about what kinds of remote links you might want to include on your Web pages:

- How might it help your Web site to provide links to remote sites?

  Answer: Providing useful links makes your site a good Web jumping-off point and encourages surfers to return.

- How might it hurt your site to provide links to remote sites?

  Answer: Every link that exits on your site increases the chance that users will leave, perhaps never to return.

- Should you set a limit on the number of remote links you provide?

  Answer: Probably. Long link lists are tiresome and may detract from the appeal of your site. Moreover, Yahoo! (and others) contain far more comprehensive link lists than you could ever create/maintain.

- Why should you always get permission from site owners before including a link to their sites in your Web pages?

  Answer: Web page visitors may (falsely) assume that the presence of a link implies an association or endorsement with the linked site.

- To what types of remote sites should you link: utilities, sites supporting or related to yours, edutainment, general interest, other?

  Answer: This one's up to you.

QUICK REFERENCE

In this chapter, you entered the world of hypertext by learning how to add local and remote links to your Web pages.

Here's a quick reference for the techniques you learned in this chapter:

Desired Result	How to Do It
Create relative-address local link	syntax: <A HREF=*"filename"*>*local link*</A>
Create absolute-address local link	syntax: <A HREF="file:///*c:/path/filename*"> *local link*</A>
Create remote link	syntax: <A HREF="http://*URL*">*remote link*</A>

In the next chapter, we'll show you how to add graphics, sounds, and other multimedia goodies to your Web pages.

Chapter 5

Adding Graphics and Sounds to Your Web Pages

Text is okay...it looks authoritative and communicates rather nicely. But come on, admit it: Pictures, animations, movies, sound effects, music, patterns, colors, flashing lights, explosions—that's what you really want on your Web site! In this chapter, we'll introduce you to the world of online multimedia by showing you how to add graphics, sounds, animations, and movies to your Web pages. We'll also show you how to spice up your pages with horizontal rules and special characters.

When you're done working through this chapter, you will know

- How to add graphics to your Web pages

- How to add sounds to your Web pages

- How to add animations and movies to your Web pages

- How to add horizontal rules to your Web pages

- How to add special characters to your Web pages

ADDING GRAPHICS TO YOUR WEB PAGES

Most Web browsers can display several common types of graphic files. Netscape 2.0, for example, can display *GIF* (Graphics Interchange Format), *JPEG* (Joint Photographic Experts Group), and *X-bitmap* (X Windows bitmap) files. Since 90 percent of the graphics on the Web are in one of these formats— mainly GIF and JPEG—you should have no trouble viewing graphics or making them available for your Web page visitors to view.

You can display a graphic in two ways:

- By itself on a page (see Figure 5.1)

- Embedded in a page (see Figure 5.2)

DISPLAYING A GRAPHIC BY ITSELF ON A PAGE

To display a graphic by itself on a page, simply

- Create a link to the graphic file in your Web page.

When a user clicks on this link, the graphic will appear by itself on an otherwise blank page—assuming, of course, that the graphic file type is supported by the user's browser.

You use the same HTML tags to create a link to a graphic file as to any other file:

Opening Tag   **Closing Tag**

<A HREF=*"path/filename"*>   </A>

Here's the syntax you use to create the link:

```
<A HREF="path/filename">link</A>
```

This statement creates a link to a file named *filename* located in the directory specified by *path/*. The text between the opening and closing tags (*link*) is highlighted to identify the link.

Figure 5.1
A graphic by itself on a page

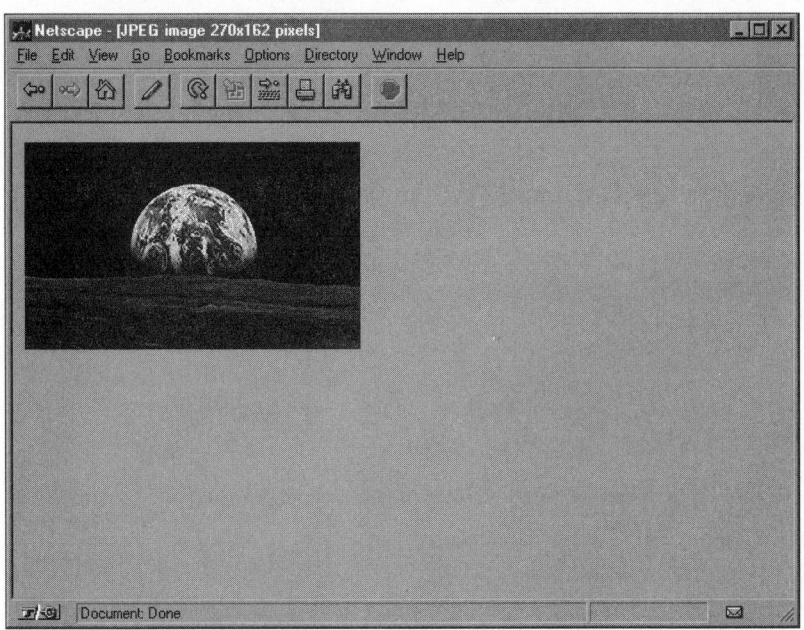

Figure 5.2
A graphic embedded in a page

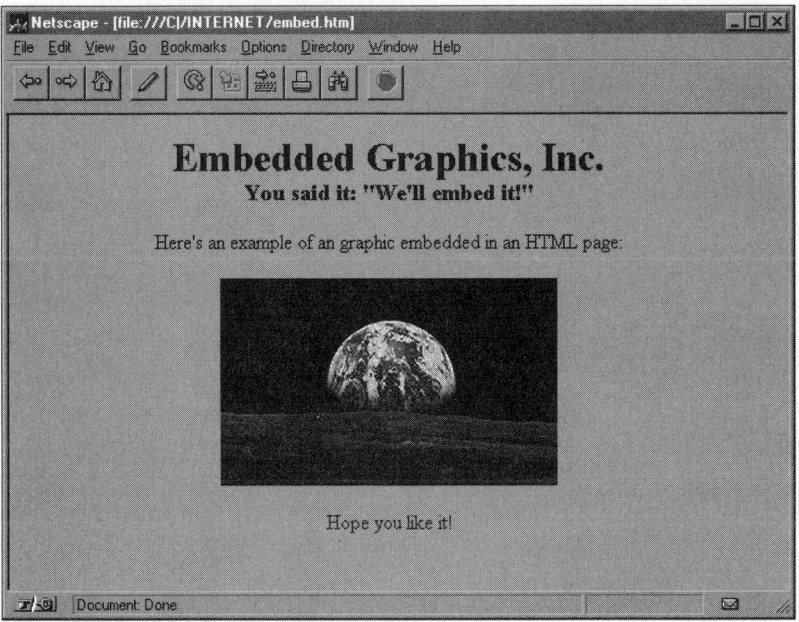

Let's use this technique to display a graphic by itself on a page:

1. In your text editor, open **default.htm** from your HTMLWork directory.

2. Directly below the line <BODY> at the top of the file, insert

   ```
   <!-- A link to the company logo -->
   ```

   Click **<A HREF="jet.gif">here</A>** to view the company's logo.
   This creates a link to the GIF file jet.gif.

3. Save and view the default.htm Web page. (That is: Save the file in your text editor, switch to your browser, and open **default.htm**.)

4. Click on your new link (here) to display the company logo graphic **jet.gif** by itself on a page, as shown in Figure 5.3.

Figure 5.3
Clicking on a link to display jet.gif alone on a page

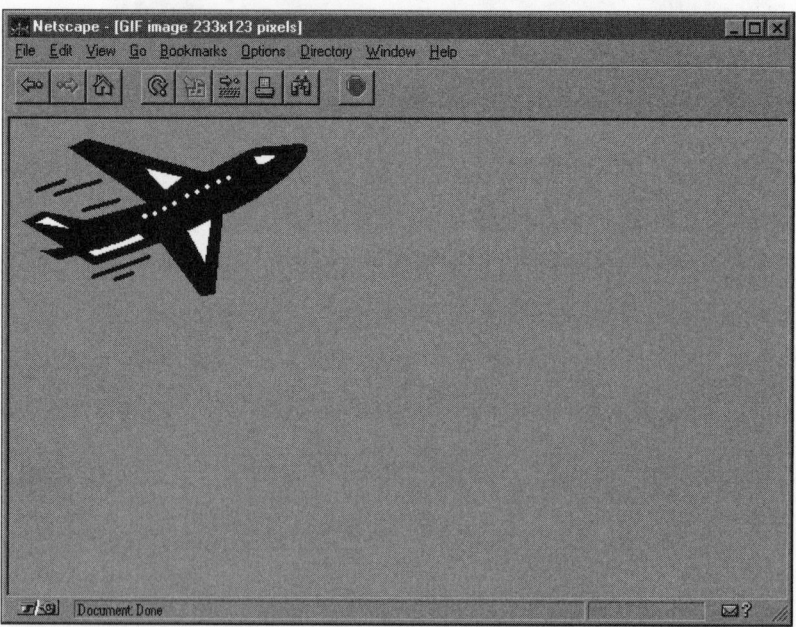

5. Click on **Back** to return to the Jetaway Travel home page.

6. In Your text editor, directly below the company-logo lines you just added, insert

   ```
   <!-- A link to a JPEG file -->
   ```

Click **<A HREF="earth.jpg">here</A>** for a JPEG file.

This creates a link to the JPEG file earth.jpg.

7. Save and view the default.htm file.

8. Click on your new link to display the JPEG file by itself on a page. As mentioned above, Netscape supports both JPEG and GIF files.

9. Click on **Back** to return to the Jetaway Travel home page.

DISPLAYING A GRAPHIC EMBEDDED IN A PAGE

You can display a graphic in a nonempty Web page by *embedding* the graphic file. Here's the HTML tag you use to embed a graphic:

```
<IMG SRC="filename">
```

This inserts the graphic (*filename*) in your page right at the spot you indicate. You can use relative or absolute addressing with this tag. If you use absolute addressing, you must include the "file:///" identifier and use the "/" slashes to separate directories. For example,

```
<IMG SRC="file:///c:/website/graphics/logo.gif">
```

loads an absolutely addressed graphic (*logo.gif*).

Let's embed a graphic in our default.htm page:

1. In your text editor, remove the two links you created in the previous task by deleting the lines

```
<!-- A link to the company logo -->
```

Click **<A HREF="jet.gif">here</A>** to view the company's logo.

```
<!-- A link to a JPEG file -->
```

Click **<A HREF="earth.jpg">here</A>** for a JPEG file.

2. At the beginning of the <H1> header line, insert

```
<IMG SRC="jet.gif">
```

to embed the company logo **jet.gif** in the page. The line should now read

```
<IMG SRC="jet.gif"><H1>Jetaway Travel</H1>
```

3. Save and view the file. It should match that shown in Figure 5.4.

Note that the graphic and header do not appear on the same line, yet they are on the same line in the default.htm file. Why? Because browsers always dis-

Figure 5.4
Embedding jet.gif in a page

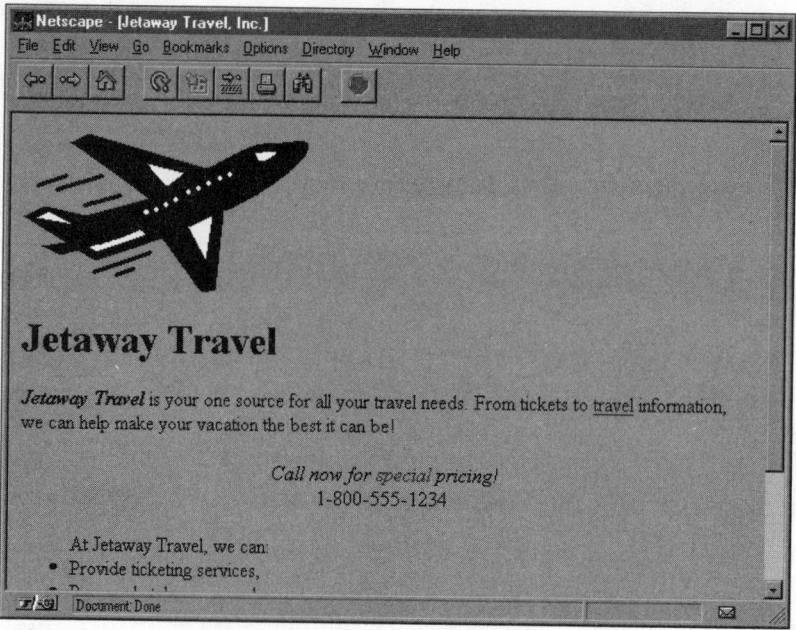

play HTML headers (text enclosed in <HN>...</HN> tags) on lines by themselves. What a shame! But here's a "trick" that enables you to get around this HTML shortcoming:

1. In your text editor add a **<P>** tag before the <IMG SRC="jet.gif"> tag.

2. Change the **<H1>** opening tag for the page header to

   ```
   <FONT SIZE=+3><B><I>
   ```

3. Change the **</H1>** closing tag at the end of the page header to

   ```
   </I></B></FONT></P>
   ```

4. Save and view the file. The graphic and the header now share the same line, as shown in Figure 5.5. <FONT>...</FONT> tags allow you to create header-like text entries that are not displayed on lines by themselves.

ALTERNATIVES FOR NON-GRAPHIC BROWSERS

Some users have non-graphic browsers and will not be able to see or use the graphics you have included in your Web page. Other users turn off graphics to

Figure 5.5
Using <FONT>...</FONT> to make a "header" share a line

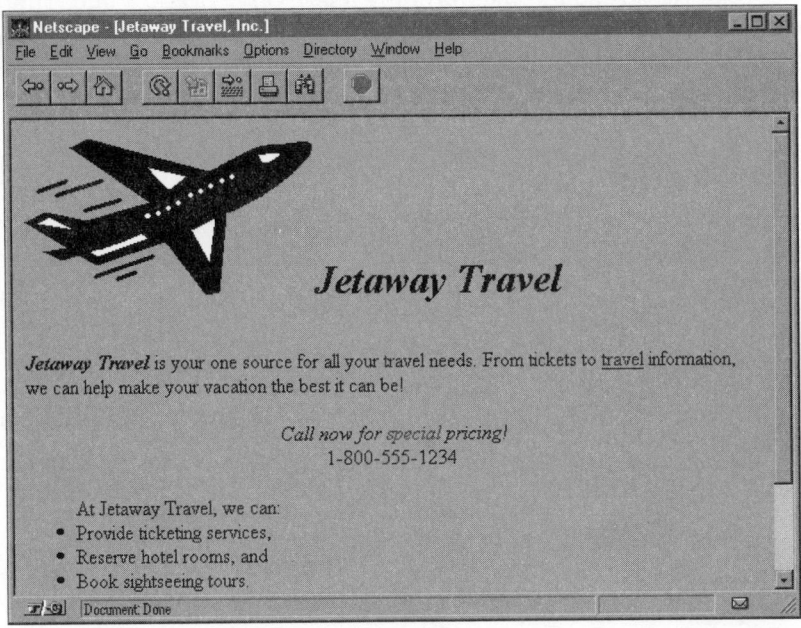

speed up file transfers. You can choose from several alternatives to provide support for non-graphic users:

- Provide a separate page for non-graphic users that is linked from the graphical page.

- Put in regular hypertext links for those who cannot see the graphics used to jump to other pages. Many pages separate these two areas by using the *HR* (horizontal rule) tag.

- Use the *ALT* attribute of the IMG statement. This attribute displays the text defined by the ALT attribute. If users have turned off the graphics, the text is displayed. When they turn the graphics back on, the graphic is displayed. Users will not see both the text and graphics at the same time.

CONTROLLING SIZE AND ALIGNMENT OF GRAPHICS

The IMG tag offers several other attributes to control the size and alignment of graphics.

HEIGHT AND WIDTH

HEIGHT and WIDTH attributes for screen resolutions are expressed in pixels. The lowest standard resolution commonly used today is 600 x 400. Therefore, a 600 x 400 pixel graphic can be resized to whatever size is most appropriate to the page. If you create a 1024 x 768 graphic, users with lower resolutions will need to do a lot of scrolling to view the entire image.

ALIGNING GRAPHICS

The alignment of the graphic is expressed in relation to the text. TOP, MIDDLE, ABSBOTTOM, ABSMIDDLE, TEXTTOP, and BASELINE are all valid values for the Align attribute.

SPACING

You can specify how much space to place around an image. HSPACE is an <IMG> attribute used to add horizontal spacing. The VSPACE attribute adds vertical spacing. The value of these attributes is expressed in pixels. For example, adding the attributes HSPACE=20 VSPACE=30 to an IMG statement will place 20 pixels of horizontal white space and 30 pixels of vertical white space around the image.

OTHER ALIGNMENT METHODS

You can also space text and graphics by placing a transparent GIF file made of a clear square between the graphic and the text (or the margin and the text). Use the alignment, spacing, and sizing attributes of the IMG statement to define the size of the clear square. You can find a description of "The Single-Pixel GIF Trick" at

        http://www.dsiegel.com/tips/wonk5/single.html.

When you debug your document, you can use a square containing a color so that you can see where the clear square is placed. Replace the colored square with the clear square when you are done debugging.

Let's examine a Web page that uses different image and text alignments.

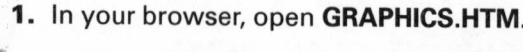

1. In your browser, open **GRAPHICS.HTM**.

2. Observe the alignment of the text and graphics. The text explains each alignment.

3. View the document source. (If you are using Netscape, choose **View, Document Source**.)

4. Examine each IMG statement. The ALIGN attribute in each statement uses a different value to specify the relationship of the graphic to the text.

5. Close the document source window.

Now, let's try changing the relationship of the graphic you added to the DE-FAULT.HTM file.

1. In your text editor, open **DEFAULT.HTM**.

2. Change the <IMG SRC="jet.gif"> tag **to <IMG SRC="jet.gif" HEIGHT=25 WIDTH=25>**. This will change the size of the image on the page.

3. Save the file as **DEFAULT2.HTM** and view the file in your browser.

4. Switch to your text editor and add **ALIGN=ABSBOTTOM** to the IMG tag. The top of the graphic will be aligned with the top of the letters in the text. The tag should now read

```
<IMG SRC="jet.gif" WIDTH=25 HEIGHT=25 ALIGN=ABSBOTTOM>
```

5. Save and view the file.

6. In the DEFAULT2.HTM file in your text editor, add the attribute **HSPACE=20** to the IMG tag. This will add 20 pixels of horizontal white space between the graphic and the text.

7. Save and view the file. It should look like Figure 5.6.

USING GRAPHICS AS BULLETS

You can add an image statement to the <DD> element of a definition list. By default, a definition list does not place any numbers or pre-defined bullet shapes before the list items. However, you can place a graphic at the beginning of the line, and the graphic will act as a bullet, as in Figure 5.7.

Let's see how this works.

1. Switch to your text editor (**DEFAULT2.HTM** should be open).

2. Beginning on a new line in the main body, enter

```
<DL>
<DD><IMG SRC="jet.gif" HEIGHT=20 WIDTH=20 ALIGN=CENTER>
Tickets </DD>
<DD><IMG SRC="jet.gif" HEIGHT=20 WIDTH=20 ALIGN=CENTER>
```

Figure 5.6
Aligning an image with text

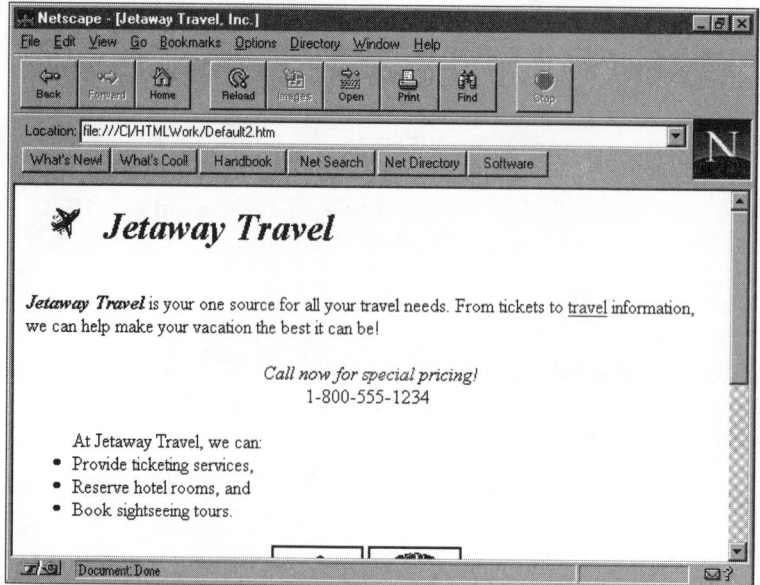

Figure 5.7
Graphics as bullets

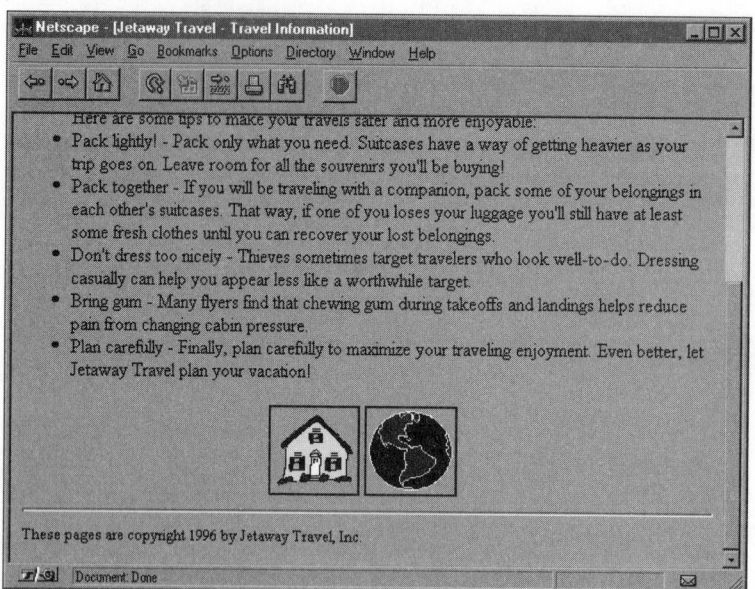

```
Traveler s Checks </DD>
<DD><IMG SRC="jet.gif" HEIGHT=20 WIDTH=20 ALIGN=CENTER>
Reservations </DD>
<DD><IMG SRC="jet.gif" HEIGHT=20 WIDTH=20 ALIGN=CENTER>
Trip Planning </DD>
<DD><IMG SRC="jet.gif" HEIGHT=20 WIDTH=20 ALIGN=CENTER>
Full Travel Services </DD>
</DL>
```

3. Save and view the file.

Figure 5.8
The data definition list with graphics as bullets

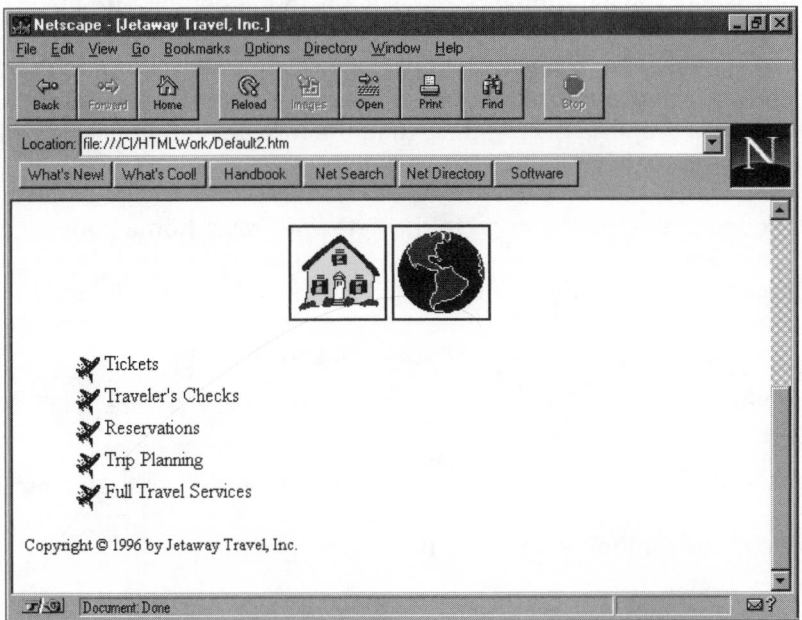

CREATING A LINK FROM AN EMBEDDED GRAPHIC

HTML enables you to create a link from an embedded graphic. To do this,

- Nest an **<IMG SRC>** tag within an **<A HREF>...</A>** tag.

For example, this line creates a link to the Yahoo! Web site from a graphic called yahoolnk.gif.

```
<A HREF="http://www.yahoo.com"><IMG
SRC="yahoolnk.gif"></A>
```

Note: Embedded graphics that are links are displayed, by default, with a blue border in Netscape.

Let's create a link from an embedded graphic:

1. In your text editor open **travel.htm**.

2. Change the comment for the link to the home page to

   ```
   <!-- Navigation bar -->
   ```

3. Change the current link to the home page to

   ```
   <CENTER>
   <A HREF="default.htm"><IMG SRC="home.gif"></A>
   ```

This embeds a graphic (home.gif) that is a link to the default.htm file.

4. Save and view the **travel.htm** Web page. The link to the home page is represented by a graphic of a house. You can tell it's a link—and not just an embedded graphic—by pointing to it; the mouse pointer changes to a hand, which is what it does for all links.

5. Click on the **home** icon to go to the Jetaway Travel home page.

6. Click on the **Back** button to return to the Travel Information page.

7. In your text editor change the current link to Yahoo! to

   ```
   <A HREF="http://www.yahoo.com"><IMG SRC="globe.gif"></A>
   </CENTER>
   ```

   This embeds a globe graphic that is a link to the Yahoo! Web site.

8. Save and view the file to verify this.

9. Click on the **globe** icon to go to the Yahoo! page.

10. Click on the **Back** button to return to the Travel Information page.

PRACTICE YOUR SKILLS

1. Use your text editor to copy the **navigation bar** you just created to the Jetaway Travel home page file default.htm. Replace the navigation bar links that are already in that file. **Note:** You'll copy all of the text from the <!-- Navigation Bar --> to </CENTER>. Use the **Edit, Copy** command, then open **Default.htm**, select the existing links, and use the **Edit, Paste** command.

2. Save your modified **default.htm**, then view it in your browser.

3. Use the text editor to add the graphic **jet2.gif** to the header of travel.htm (just as you did with default.htm). Replace the <H1> and </H1> tags from the header with tags to set the font size to **+3**, **bold**, and **italic**. Make sure to include **<P>** and **</P>** tags around your header.

4. Save **travel.htm**, then view it in your browser.

CREATING AND USING IMAGEMAPS

An imagemap is a picture used to go to different URLs. Different areas or regions of the picture are defined to link users to different URLs.

When you click on one of these defined regions, your browser sends the coordinates to the Web server which in turn looks up the coordinates and figures out what you clicked on. The corresponding URL is then accessed and displayed for you.

There are two categories of imagemaps: server-side and client-side. Server-side imagemaps can be used by most browsers. Client-side imagemaps were introduced with Netscape Navigator 2.0, so only the most recent browsers can support client-side imagemaps.

ADVANTAGES AND DISADVANTAGES OF USING IMAGEMAPS

Many users find imagemaps easier to use than text hyperlinks. However, not everyone either wants to use them or *can* use them.

Some advantages of using imagemaps include:

- They are easy to use when the graphic relates directly to the URL users will move to. For example, clicking on a map is easier than picking a city from a list.

- Because so many Web pages include graphics, users are beginning to expect to see them.

- An imagemap can be used to get users to the part of your site you most want them to go to.

You should always try to achieve some consistency between the pages on your site. By using imagemaps on each page, you can work towards this goal.

Some disadvantages of using imagemaps include:

- The imagemap graphics can be quite large and take a long time to download. If you think that people would not be willing to wait for a graphic to download, you should consider either using a smaller imagemap or using a different method for the link.

- Not all Web servers can correctly process imagemaps.

- To test your imagemaps, you need to be able to place them on a Web server. This might not be possible, or it might be a bothersome extra step.

- Not all users can view graphics.

TERMINOLOGY

Before you can understand server-side imagemaps, you need to be aware of the following terminology:

- An *imagemap graphic* is the picture users see on your Web page. These files must be GIF files.

- An *imagemap definition file*, or a .MAP file, lists the coordinates and URLs for each region defined in the imagemap.

- The clickable area of a graphic is defined in the definition file as a *region*. A region can be one of four different types: rectangle, circle, polygon, or point. You express the coordinates for the region as the distance, in pixels, from the upper-left corner of the imagemap graphic.

- An *imagemap program* is a CGI program which interprets the mouse clicks and returns the corresponding URL.

If your Web server does not directly support imagemaps, you will need to add a program which adds this support. Server-side imagemaps require a Web server that runs imagemap software.

CERN AND NCSA FORMATS

The format of your imagemap .MAP file must correspond to the server software that your Web server runs. This software can be of two different types, CERN or NCSA.

CERN, the Conseil European pour la Recherche Nucleaire, developed the concept of the Web, as well as the format for imagemaps. The CERN format defines a region type, region coordinates in parentheses and separated by commas, and the related URL.

NCSA, the National Center for Supercomputing Applications, defined another format for imagemaps. This format includes region shape, URL, and coordinates separated by commas.

Examples of the code for each are shown in Table 5.1.

Table 5.1   **Examples of CERN and NCSA Code**

Type	Example
CERN	RECT (25,3)(60,48) http://www.yahoo.com
NCSA	RECT http://www.yahoo.com 25,3,60,48

CLIENT-SIDE IMAGEMAPS

Client-side imagemaps are a Netscape extension to the HTML specification. They do not require any special server programs. The information normally contained in a .MAP file is included inside your current HTML document. Not all browsers support client-side imagemaps, so you may want to provide both server-side and client-side imagemaps in your page. Users will take advantage of client-side imagemaps if their browser supports these imagemaps; if not, they will use the server-side imagemaps.

You can add a client-side imagemap to your Web page by adding some code to your IMG statement, and by defining the imagemap definition and area. You need two ingredients to create a client-side imagemap: a graphics file and a map definition.

You can create the map definition within your HTML file by using the MAP and AREA tags. This definition specifies the different sections of the graphic file in coordinates and associates each section with an HREF. After you define the map, you can use the IMG tag to display the graphics in the browser. You can reference the map by using the USEMAP attribute of the IMG tag.

Table 5.2 describes the different tags and attributes needed to create a client-side imagemap.

Table 5.2   **Client-Side Imagemap Tags and Descriptions**

Tag	Description
<IMG ...USEMAP=>	Defines the image file to use. The USEMAP attribute references a map that is defined with the MAP tag. The value of USEMAP is "*#map_name*", where map_name is defined within the MAP element.
<MAP>	Identifies an imagemap definition; that is, a section of your HTML document that contains AREA tags which define the regions of the image. The NAME attribute of the opening MAP tag defines the map.

Table 5.2   **Client-Side Imagemap Tags and Descriptions (Cont.)**

Tag	Description
<AREA>	Defines the clickable areas of the image and the URL or HTML files that they point to. The area is defined in pixels. This tag has the following attributes: SHAPE, COORDS, and HREF. The SHAPE value can be RECT, POLY, CIRCLE, or DEFAULT. The COORDS attribute specifies a list of coordinates that correspond to the region being defined. The HREF specifies the URL to be loaded when the region is clicked on.

Each region shape needs its coordinates defined in a specific order. Table 5.3 lists the order in which the numbers will be listed.

Table 5.3   **Image Map Shape and Coordinates**

Shape	Coordinates
RECT	upper left x, upper left y, lower right x, lower right y
POLY	x1, y1, x2, y2, ... xn, yn
CIRCLE	center x, center y, radius

Let's examine an HTML document which contains a client-side imagemap.

1. In your browser, open the file **POLYGON.HTM**.

2. Move the cursor around within the blue box. The area has been defined as a polygon. Only the area within the polygon is clickable.

3. View the document source. Examine the line beginning with <AREA SHAPE="POLYGON". You will need to scroll right to see the entire list of coordinates. Each of the vertices of the region is represented by the COORDS parameters (Xn, Yn, Xn, Yn...). An HREF follows the coordinates to indicate the action to be performed when the user clicks inside the polygon.

4. Examine the IMG statement. The USEMAP attribute indicates the map name that is defined by the MAP tag in this document.

5. Close the document source window.

INCORPORATING IMAGEMAPS IN A WEB PAGE

When using server-side imagemaps you need to put two elements in your HTML code. An anchor element references the imagemap definition file. When you use server-side imagemaps, the IMG tag must include the ISMAP attribute. An example of the code to use a server-side imagemap is:

```
A HREF= mapname.map ><IMG SRC= graphic.gif  ISMAP></A>
```

The client-side imagemap IMG statement uses the USEMAP attribute. The value of USEMAP is the name defined in the MAP element. If the name can be found within the current document it is written USEMAP="#name" or if found in another location it is written USEMAP="path#name".

Let's add a client-side imagemap to a document. This is a tri-colored flag where each color connects the user to a different URL.

1. In your text editor, open **FLAG.HTM**.

2. In the body section, enter the following code:

```
<IMG SRC="flag.gif" USEMAP="#colors">
<MAP NAME="colors">
<AREA SHAPE="RECT" COORDS="4,3,89,138"
HREF="http://www.yahoo.com >
<AREA SHAPE="RECT" COORDS="89,3,175,138"
HREF="http://www.w3.org">
<AREA SHAPE= RECT  COORDS=175,3,258,138"
HREF="http://www.search.com">
</MAP>
```

The first two numbers of each of the COORDS parameters define the upper left coordinates of the rectangle, and the second two numbers define the lower right coordinates of the rectangle.

3. Save and view the file.

4. Verify that each region accesses the appropriate HREF by pointing to or clicking on them. Pointing to the region will display the defined URL in the status bar of most browsers.

**Figure 5.9
The FLAG.HTM page**

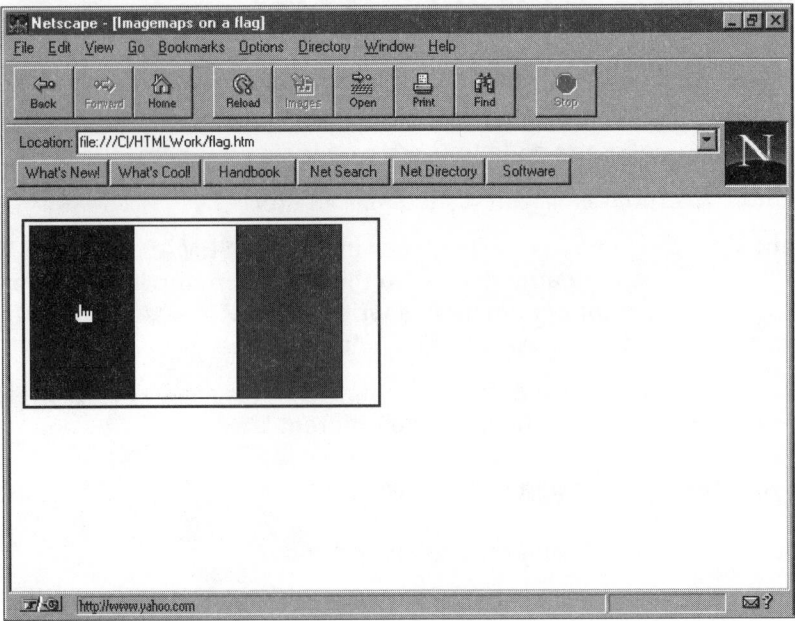

ADDING SOUNDS, ANIMATION, AND MOVIES TO YOUR WEB PAGES

Most browsers, including Netscape, do not directly support multimedia files, such as animation or sounds. To view or play these files, you need to obtain and install *helper applications*. Some helper applications, such as Future-Splash animation viewers require software only; others, such as sound players, require software and hardware (sound cards).

You must configure your browser to automatically launch helper applications when multimedia Web files are accessed. To configure a helper application in Netscape 2.0:

- Choose *Options, General Preferences*.

- Click on the *Helper applications* tab.

- In the File Type list box, select the type of file for which you want to configure a helper application.

- Select *Launch The Application*.

- Type the application's path and filename in the text box. (If necessary, use the Browse button to locate the path\filename.)

- Click on *OK*.

Table 5.4 lists several common multimedia file types that you'll encounter on the Web.

Table 5.4   **Multimedia File Types on the Web**

File Type	Medium	Description
.WAV	Sound	Developed for Microsoft Windows family of operating systems; helper applications are available for Microsoft Windows, Apple Macintosh, and Unix computers
.AU	Sound	Developed for Sun Microsystems and NeXT Corporation workstations; helper applications are available for Microsoft Windows, Apple Macintosh, and Unix computers
.AIFF	Sound	Developed for Macintosh computers and Silicon Graphics workstations; helper applications are available for Microsoft Windows, Apple Macintosh, and Unix computers
.AVI	Animation/ movie	Standard Microsoft AVI movie format; helper applications are available for Apple Macintosh, Microsoft Windows, and Unix computers
.MOV	Animation/ movie	QuickTime movie; helper applications are available for Apple Macintosh, Microsoft Windows, and Unix computers
.MPG	Animation/ movie	MPEG (Motion Picture Expert Group), a standard animation/movie file format; helper applications are available for Microsoft Windows, Apple Macintosh, and Unix computers

To create a link to a multimedia file, you proceed just as you would to create a link to any other file. Here's the syntax

```
<A HREF="path/filename">link text</A>
```

For example, the line

```
<A HREF="sounds/boom.wav">Click here for a Boom!</A>
```

creates a link (*Click here for a Boom!*) to the sound file boom.wav, which resides in the subdirectory *sounds*.

Here are some "minds-on" questions for you to mull over:

1. What hardware and/or software do you need to play Web sounds on a Windows 95 computer?

    Answer: You need a sound board and drivers to play Web sounds on a Windows 95 computer.

2. What HTML code would you use to create a link to a sound file named *hello.wav*?

    Answer:

```
<A HREF="hello.wav">Click here to play hello.wav.</A>
```

ADDING HORIZONTAL RULES AND SPECIAL CHARACTERS TO YOUR WEB PAGES

You can use the <HR> tag to add a *horizontal rule* (a separator line) to your Web pages. The <HR> tag is an empty tag, meaning that it has no closing tag; that is, there is no </HR>.

Let's add a horizontal rule to one of our sample pages:

1. In your text editor, open **travel.htm**.

2. Change the **<P>** in the copyright footer comment line to **<HR>**. This will insert a horizontal rule rather than a blank line before the copyright message.

3. Save and view the file.

PRACTICE YOUR SKILLS

1. In default.htm, replace the blank line before the copyright message with a horizontal rule.

2. Save and view the file.

<HR> TAG ATTRIBUTES

You can use four attributes with <HR> tags to customize your horizontal rules:

<HR> Attribute	What It Does	Default Value
WIDTH	Sets the width of the rule in pixels or as a percentage of the total width of the browser window	The total width of the browser window
SIZE	Sets the size (height) of the rule in pixels	Two pixels high
ALIGN	Sets the horizontal alignment of the rule	Center (other options are left and right)
NOSHADE	Draws the rule as a solid color	Shaded

For example, the unadorned tag

```
<HR>
```

sets the horizontal rule width to the total width of the browser window, the size (height) to two pixels, and the alignment to center. The adorned tag

```
<HR WIDTH=50% SIZE=10 ALIGN=left>
```

sets the rule width to 50 percent of the total width of the browser window, the size (height) to ten pixels, and the alignment to left.

Let's insert a centered horizontal rule that is 50 percent as wide as the browser window:

1. In default.htm, change the **<HR>** tag you entered in the previous task to **<HR WIDTH=50%>**. This sets the horizontal rule to half the width of the browser window and center-aligns it.

2. Save and view the file. See?

PRACTICE YOUR SKILLS

1. In travel.htm, set the horizontal rule to a width of 50 percent of the browser window and left-align it.

2. Save and view the file.

SPECIAL CHARACTERS

Special characters are

- Characters for which the keyboard does not provide a key, such as the copyright and registered-trademark symbols (© and ®).

- Characters that are reserved keywords in HTML, such as less-than (<) and greater-than (>).

You can insert special characters in your Web pages by entering their HTML character codes. Here are a few commonly used special characters and their codes. Note that all the special-character codes begin with *&* and end with *;.*

Character Name	Character	HTML Code
Copyright	©	&copy;
Trademark	™	&trade;
Registered trademark	®	&reg;
Greater than	>	&gt;
Less than	<	&lt;
Double quote	"	&quot;
Ampersand	&	&amp;

Note: For a complete list of special characters that you can include in your HTML files, check out either of these Web pages:

```
http://stiwww.epfl.ch/html_symbols.html

http://dellsp2.vc.cvut.cz/ascii/cc/icsc/software/ntcpconv/
entities.html
```

Let's add the copyright symbol to the copyright message on our default.htm and travel.htm Web pages:

1. In travel.htm, insert **&copy**; between *copyright* and *1996* in the copyright statement line.

2. Save and view the file.

DEFINING AND USING ICON ENTITIES

Icon entities are a set of small icons known and stored within the browser. Icon entities were part of the HTML 3.0 proposal, but they have been abandoned for now. Netscape 1.1 included a set of icons stored internally, which many browsers now support. They are displayed by using the IMG tag <IMG SRC="*internal-name*">. A browser which cannot interpret these will display an unknown-image icon. You can find a list of the Netscape Navigator 1.1 internal icons at

```
http://www.sandia.gov/sci_compute/icons.html.
```

The Netscape 1.1 internal icon entities include icons for gopher objects, icon objects, and news postings. Because these icons are defined within the browser, the browser does not need to go to the network to retrieve the image. They are displayed by using the internal icon name in the IMG statement. For example, if you wanted to indicate that a binary file was available for downloading, you could include the command <IMG SRC="internal-gopher-binary">. For a movie file, you might use <IMG SRC="internal-gopher-movie">.

QUICK REFERENCE

In this chapter, you learned how to embellish your Web pages by adding graphics, sounds, animations and movies, horizontal rules, and special characters to them.

Here's a quick reference for the techniques you learned in this chapter:

Desired Result	How to Do It
Display graphic by itself on page	Create link to graphic file in page
Embed graphic file	syntax: <IMG SRC="*path\filename*">
Specify the size of a graphic	Use the IMG attributes *HEIGHT*=n or *WIDTH*=n or both attributes

Desired Result	How to Do It
Specify the alignment of a graphic with text	Use the *ALIGN* attribute of the IMG tag
Add horizontal or vertical spacing around a graphic	Use the *HSPACE* or *VSPACE* attributes of the IMG tag or both attributes
Tell users without graphic capabilities what they are missing	Use the *ALT* attribute of the IMG statement to provide alternate text when graphics are turned off or users are using a non-graphics browser
Use graphics as bullets	Use a *definition list* and place an *IMG* statment at the beginning of each data definition
Create link from embedded graphic	Nest <IMG SRC> tag within <A HREF>...</A> tag
Configure helper application in Netscape 2.0	Choose *Options, General Preferences*; click on *Helper applications* tab; select type of file; select *Launch Application*; specify application's path and filename; click on *OK*
Create link to multimedia file	syntax: <A HREF=*"path/filename">link text*</A>
Insert horizontal rule in page	tag: <HR> attributes: WIDTH, SIZE, ALIGN, NOSHADE
Create a client-side imagemap	Add the *USEMAP* attribute to the IMG statement. Define the MAP name and AREA shape, coordinates, and URL
Define a client-side imagemap	Use the *<MAP NAME="name">* and *</MAP>* tags
Define the clickable area of a client-side imagemap	Use *<AREA SHAPE="shape" COORDS="X1,Y1,X2,Y2" HREF="url">*
Insert special characters in page	Insert HTML character codes

In the next chapter, we'll show you how to add tables to your Web pages.

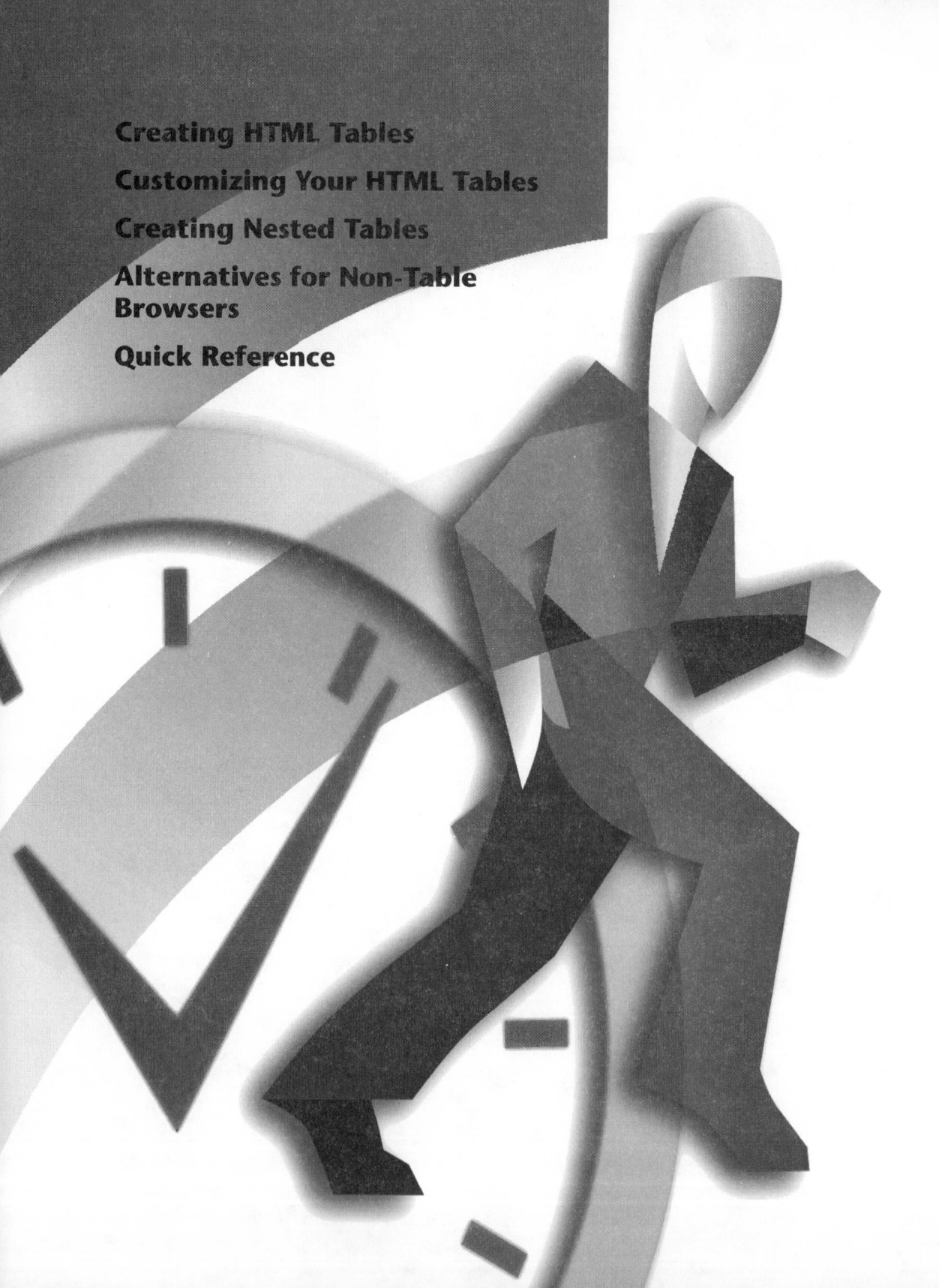

Creating HTML Tables

Customizing Your HTML Tables

Creating Nested Tables

Alternatives for Non-Table Browsers

Quick Reference

Chapter 6

Creating Tables in HTML

In Chapter 3, you learned the basics of character and paragraph formatting in HTML. In this chapter, we'll broaden your formatting horizons by teaching you how to add *tables* to your HTML documents.

When you're done working through this chapter, you will know

- How to create basic HTML tables
- How to customize your HTML tables
- How to nest tables to assist in page layout

CREATING HTML TABLES

You use the following HTML tags to create tables on your Web pages:

Opening Tag	Closing Tag	Purpose
<TABLE>	</TABLE>	Encloses all of the data that defines an HTML table.
<TR>	</TR>	Encloses the data that defines a single table row.
<TD>	</TD>	Encloses the data that defines a single table cell.
<TH>	</TH>	Encloses the data that defines a single table header (column or row). Most browsers format table headers in bold.

Let's begin by viewing a table and the HTML code used to create it:

1. In your browser, open the file **jwaytkt.htm** from your HTMLWork directory.

2. Observe the HTML table, as shown in Figure 6.1. It has four columns, seven rows, column and row headers, and a caption. Some cells span multiple rows or columns. The first row of the table contains a graphic.

Figure 6.1
The table from jwaytkt.htm

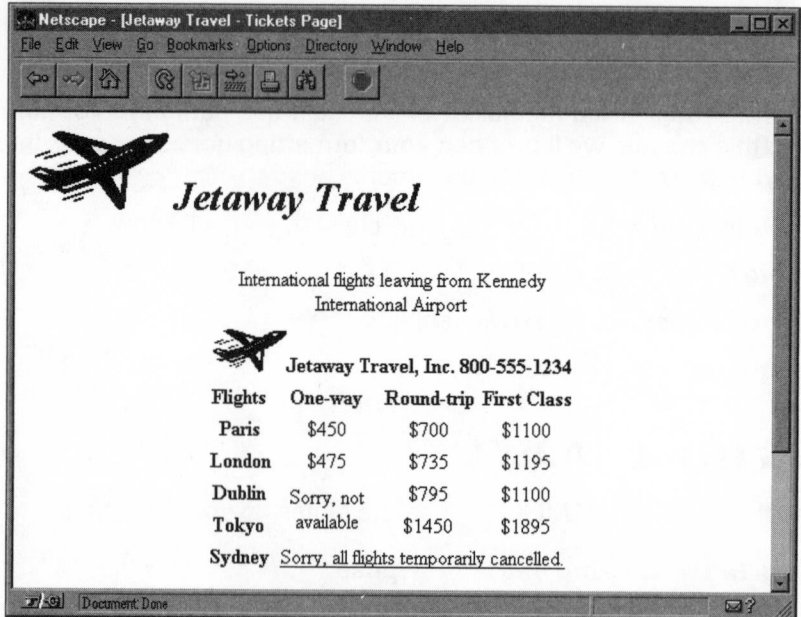

3. View the page's **HTML source code**. (If you are using Netscape, choose **View, Document Source** to view the page's HTML source code).

4. Observe the HTML code enclosed within the opening <TABLE> and closing </TABLE> tags. This block of code defines the entire table.

5. Observe the <TR>...</TR> tags. These blocks define the table rows. Note that the code enclosed within each pair of <TR>...</TR> tags is indented. These indents are not required—nor are any indents in HTML code. We use them, and recommend that you do also, to visually clarify the code logic. In this case, indenting makes each table row easy to spot. Without any indents, paragraph returns, or comments, HTML source code can be very difficult to read—particularly for someone encountering the code for the first time.

6. Observe the <TH>...</TH> tags. These define the column and row headers (hence the H in the tag).

7. Observe the <TD>...</TD> tags. These define the data that appear in the table cells.

8. Close the Source window.

CREATING A TABLE

When creating a table, you enclose all of its HTML code within the <TABLE>...</TABLE> tags. Then, you define table rows and, within each row, you define cells of data.

The following code creates the simple two-row, two-column table shown in Figure 6.2.

```
<TABLE>
<TR> <!-- Row #1 -->
    <TD>Cell #1</TD> <TD>Cell #2</TD>
</TR>
<TR> <!-- Row #2 -->
    <TD>Cell #1</TD> <TD>Cell #2</TD>
</TR>
</TABLE>
```

Note: You do not actually define columns when you create a table; you define individual cells. Therefore, you can easily create a table with one row that has four columns (four individual cells) and another row that contains only three columns (three cells).

Let's create a simple two-column, one-row table:

1. In your text editor, open **tickets.htm**, a partially completed HTML document.

2. Directly below the line that begins

```
<!-- INSERT TABLE HERE -->
```

Figure 6.2
A simple two-row, two-column table

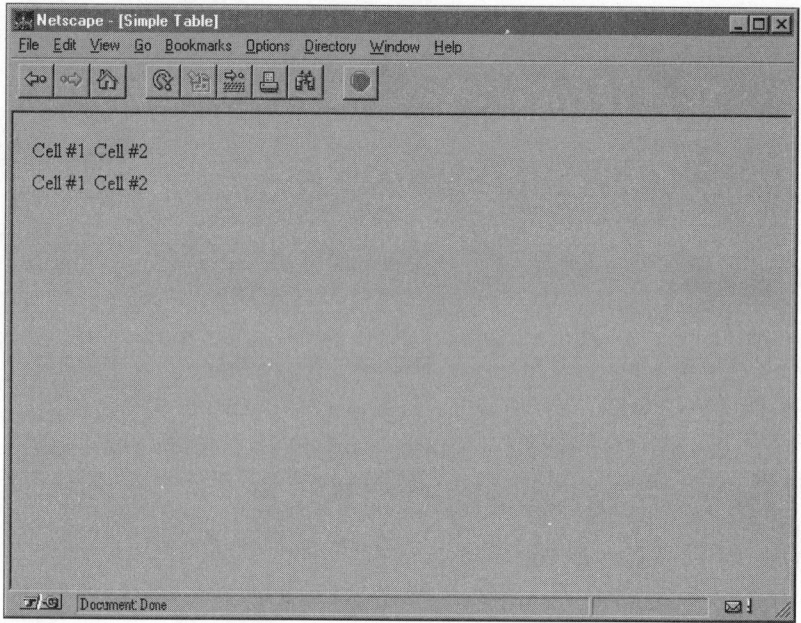

insert the following HTML code

```
<TABLE>
<TR> <!-- Row #1 -->
    <TD>column #1</TD> <TD>column #2</TD>
</TR>
</TABLE>
```

With these five short lines, you've fully defined a one-row, two-column table!

3. Save the file.

4. In your browser, open **tickets.htm** to view your table-creation handiwork. It should match that shown in Figure 6.3. (Not impressed? Just wait!)

TABLE CODING GUIDELINES

HTML tables can be quite complex—multirow columns, multicolumn rows, headers, captions, individual cell alignment and formatting, and so on. Here are some guidelines to help you keep your table code as clear as possible:

• Use comments to identify each row.

Figure 6.3
Creating a one-row, two-column table

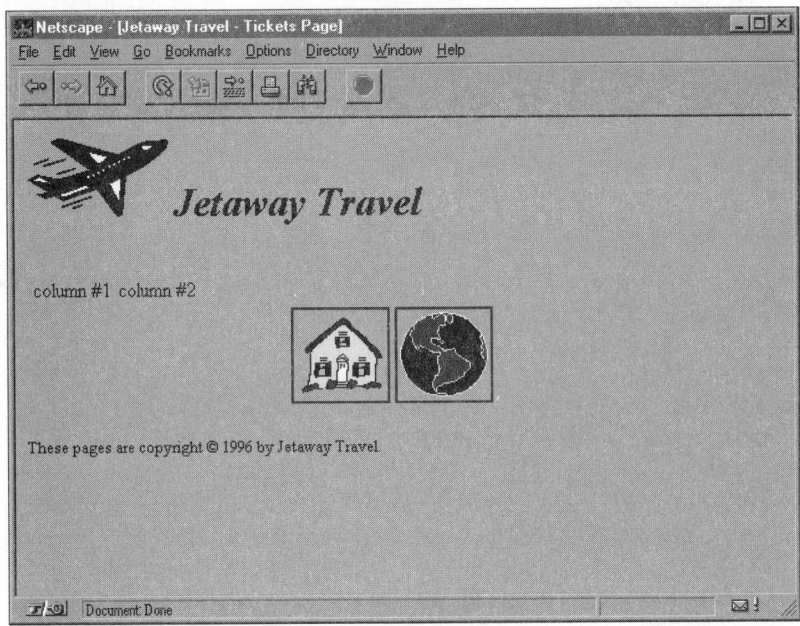

- Place each row's opening <TR> and closing </TR> on a separate line.

- Indent each row's data between its <TR>...</TR> tags.

- Insert a space (or two) between each cell.

The paragraph returns that you insert in an HTML document do not show up in the Web page, nor do the spaces between table cells. So, you can insert as many returns and spaces as you want to clarify your table code *without* affecting how the table will actually look on the page.

Let's create a new table:

1. In your text editor, delete all of the HTML code between the <TABLE> and </TABLE> tags. This erases the entire table, so that you create a new one from scratch.

2. Between the <TABLE> and </TABLE> tags, insert

```
<TR> <!-- Row #1 -->
    <TD>Flights</TD> <TD>One-way</TD> <TD>Round-trip</TD>
</TR>
<TR> <!-- Row #2-->
    <TD>Paris</TD> <TD>$450</TD> <TD>$700</TD>
</TR>
<TR> <!-- Row #3 -->
    <TD>London</TD> <TD>$475</TD> <TD>$735</TD>
</TR>
```

As you'll see in a moment, this code block creates a three-row, three-column table.

3. Observe the spacing and formatting of your new table code. Note that it uses all of our table-coding guidelines—comments, indentation, and vertical/horizontal spacing—to make the code logic visually clear.

4. Save the file, then reload/view it in your browser (by pressing **Ctrl+R**). Your table should match that shown in Figure 6.4.

Figure 6.4
Creating a three-row, three-column table

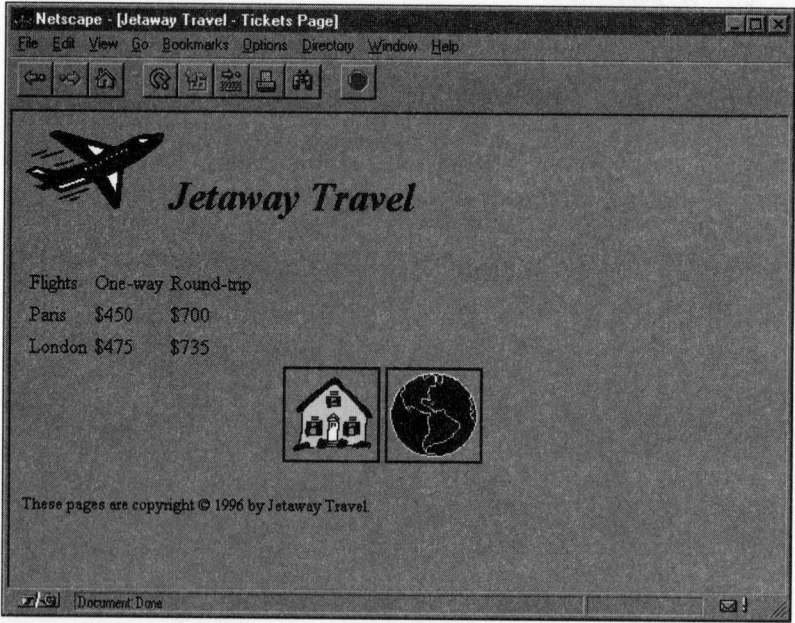

5. If your table does not match the one in Figure 6.4, you probably made a typo entering your table code. To fix things up,

- Use your text editor to edit *tickets.htm* so that the exact code specified in step 2 appears between your <TABLE> and </TABLE> tags.

- Resave the file.

- In your browser, reload/view the file.

PRACTICE YOUR SKILLS

Add to your table the fourth column shown in Figure 6.5. (**Hint:** After editing the file in your text editor, resave it, then reload/view it in your browser by pressing **Ctrl+R**.)

Figure 6.5
Adding a fourth column to the table

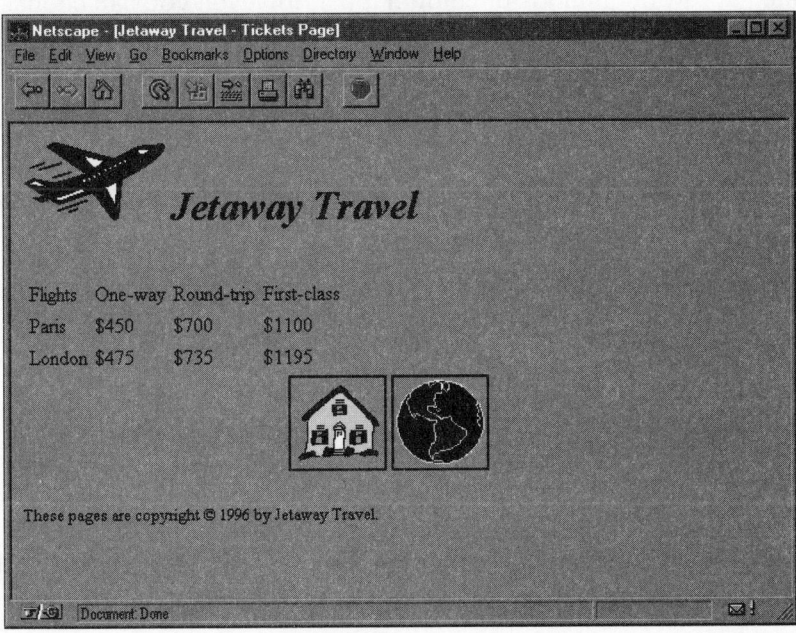

CUSTOMIZING YOUR HTML TABLES

Now that you know how to create basic HTML tables, let's move on to the fun part: customization! Over the next several sections, we'll show you

- How to format cells as table headers
- How to add borders and captions to your tables
- How to format cells to span multiple columns and rows
- How to align cell contents
- How to set cell width and height
- How to place links in cells
- How to place graphics in cells

FORMATTING CELLS AS TABLE HEADERS

Table headers are cells that display bold, centered text. Normally, header cells are located at row beginnings or column tops. However, you can choose to format any cell in your table as a header.

To format a cell as a table header, simply

- Enclose the cell's data in *<TH>...</TH>* tags.

Let's format our table's entire first row and first column as table headers:

1. In your text editor, change all of row one's <TD>...</TD> tags to **<TH>...</TH>**, as follows. (**Note:** You should have added the *<TH>First-class</TH>* entry to your row-one table code in the preceding Practice Your Skills activity.)

```
<TR> <!-- Row #1 -->
    <TH>Flights</TH> <TH>One-way</TH>
    <TH>Round-trip</TH> <TH>First-class</TH>
</TR>
```

2. Change the Paris and London cells' <TD>...</TD> tags to **<TH>...</TH>**. (Do not change the other cells' tags in rows two and three.)

3. Save the file, then reload/view it in your browser. As shown in Figure 6.6, all the cells of the first table row and column are now table headers displaying bold, centered text.

Figure 6.6
Formatting cells as table headers

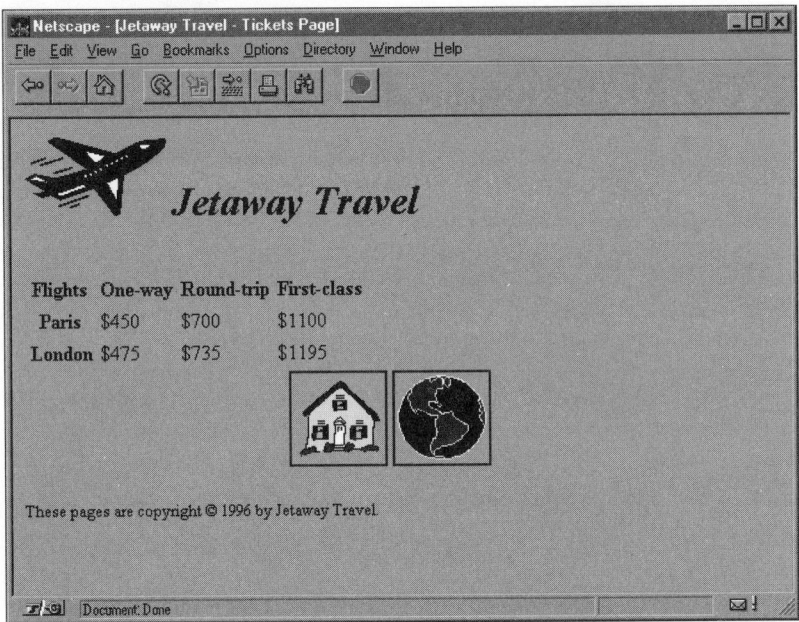

ADDING BORDERS AND CAPTIONS TO TABLES

You can add cell borders to your table to make its rows and columns visually crisp and well-defined. Beware, however, for borders can make a table look "noisy" and perhaps even confusing to some users. We recommend that you use borders only when you are sure that they make the table data *clearer* to read.

You can add a caption (title) to your table. You can specify that the caption appear above or below the table. The caption is automatically centered width-wise across the table. No caption line can be wider than the table; so, if you specify a long caption, it may well wrap into multiple lines.

You use the following tags to add borders and captions to your tables:

Opening Tag	Closing Tag	Purpose
<TABLE BORDER>	</TABLE>	Including the BORDER attribute in a <TABLE> tag adds a border to the table.
<CAPTION ALIGN= alignment>	</CAPTION>	Defines the caption for a table. The ALIGN attribute specifies whether the caption appears above (ALIGN=TOP) or below (ALIGN=BOTTOM) the table. If you do not include ALIGN, the caption appears by default above the table.

Let's add a border and a caption to our tickets.htm table:

1. In your text editor, change the <TABLE> tag to **<TABLE BORDER>**. That's all there is to it!

2. Save the file, then reload/view it in your browser. Your table now has a border around every cell, as shown in Figure 6.7.

**Figure 6.7
Adding cell borders to the table**

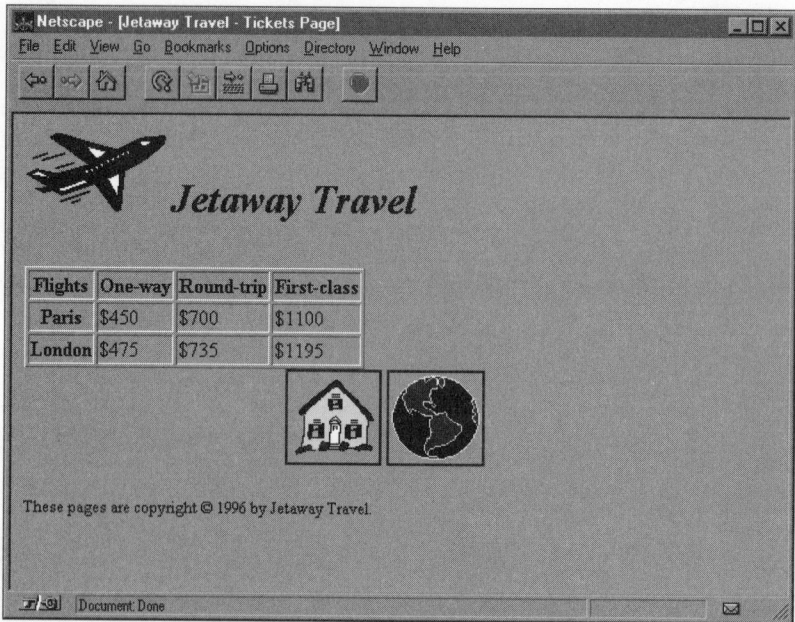

3. In your text editor, directly below the <TABLE BORDER> line, insert

   ```
   <CAPTION>International flights leaving from Kennedy
   International Airport</CAPTION>
   ```

   This adds a caption to the table. Because we did not include the ALIGN attribute in the <CAPTION> tag, the caption will appear in its default location, above the table.

4. Save the file, then reload/view it in your browser. The caption is displayed above the table, as shown in Figure 6.8. Note that, since no caption line can ever be longer than its table, our caption automatically wrapped to two lines. (This wrap has, of course, nothing to do with where the caption text might have wrapped in your editor!)

Figure 6.8
Adding a caption to the table

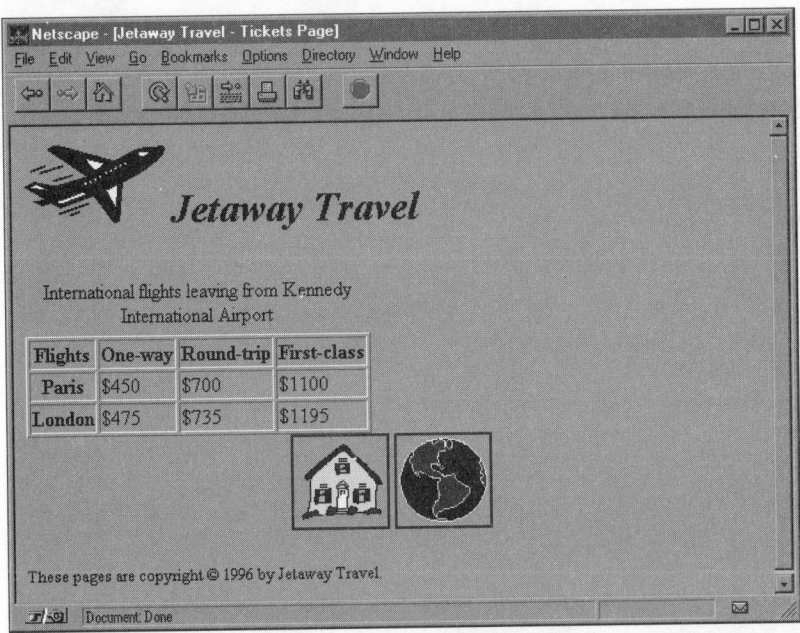

5. In your text editor, change the <CAPTION> tag to **<CAPTION ALIGN= BOTTOM>** to display the caption below the table.

6. Save the file, then reload/view it in your browser. Observe the new caption location.

PRACTICE YOUR SKILLS

1. Reset the caption to display above the table. Verify the change (by saving the modified file, then reloading/viewing it in your browser).

2. Remove the **border** from the table. Verify the change.

3. Add to the table the **three new rows** shown in Figure 6.9. Note that the city-name cells are formatted as table headers. (**Hint:** Don't forget to add comments to identify your rows!) Verify it.

4. Your table should now match ours shown in Figure 6.9. Yes?

Figure 6.9
Modifying the table

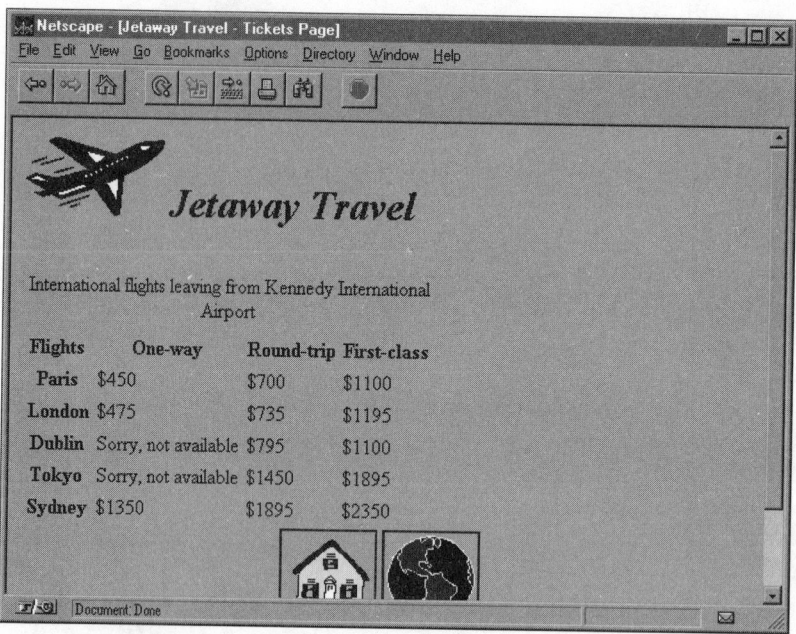

FORMATTING CELLS TO SPAN MULTIPLE COLUMNS AND ROWS

You can format cells to *span*—that is, to extend across—multiple columns and rows. To do this, you include the ROWSPAN or COLSPAN attributes in the <TD> or <TH> tags, as follows:

Opening Tag	Closing Tag	Purpose
<TD ROWSPAN=#>	</TD>	Creates a cell that spans # rows
<TD COLSPAN=#>	</TD>	Creates a cell that spans # columns
<TH ROWSPAN=#>	</TH>	Creates a cell header that spans # rows
<TH COLSPAN=#>	</TH>	Creates a cell header that spans # columns

Let's format one of our table cells to span two rows:

1. In your text editor, edit the row for Dublin flights as follows:

    ```
    <TR> <!-- Row #4 -->
        <TH>Dublin</TH> <TD ROWSPAN=2>Sorry, not available</TD>
        <TD>$795</TD> <TD>$1100</TD>
    </TR>
    ```

    This formats the column-two cell *Sorry, not available* to span two rows.

2. In the Tokyo row—not in Dublin!—delete the column-two cell **Sorry, not available**. (Make sure to delete the cell's opening/closing **<TD>...</TD>** tags also.) Why did we have you delete this cell? Because it is no longer needed; Dublin's column-two cell (also *Sorry, not available*) now spans two rows, Dublin's and Tokyo's. If you had not deleted Tokyo's column-two cell, the Tokyo row would have had an extra cell: its own four plus the spanned column-two cell from Dublin.

3. Save the file, then reload/view it in your browser. Note that the second Dublin cell now spans two rows, as shown in Figure 6.10.

Now let's format a cell to span three columns:

1. In your text editor, change the row for Sydney flights to match the following:

    ```
    <TR> <!-- Row #6 -->
        <TH>Sydney</TH>
        <TD COLSPAN=3>Sorry, all flights temporarily
    canceled.</TD>
    </TR>
    ```

Figure 6.10
Formatting a cell to span two rows

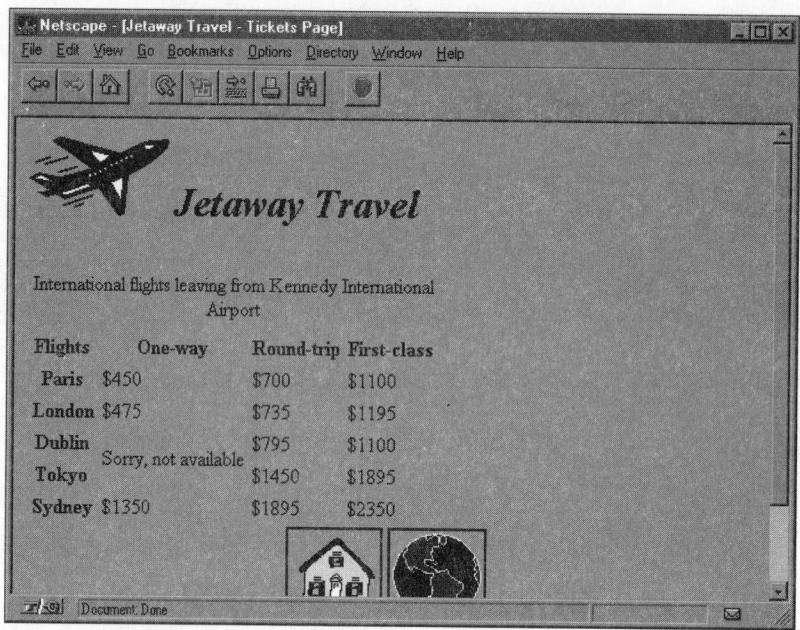

2. Save the file, then reload/view it in your browser. Sydney's second cell now spans three columns, as shown in Figure 6.11.

PRACTICE YOUR SKILLS

1. Add the following new *first* row to your table. Format the row as a table header and span it across all four table columns. (**Hint:** Make sure to edit your row comments to reflect the new numbering.)

```
Jetaway Travel, Inc. 800-555-1234
```

2. Center the entire table on the page. (**Hint:** Nest everything from <TABLE> to </TABLE> within a pair of <CENTER>...</CENTER> tags.)

3. Your table should now match that shown in Figure 6.12.

Figure 6.11
Formatting a cell to span three columns

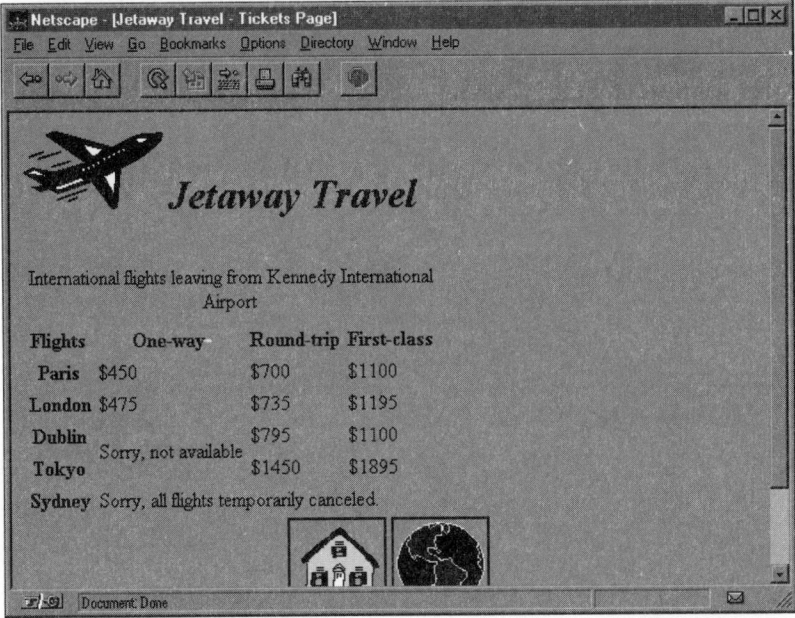

ALIGNING CELL CONTENTS

You can align the contents of your table cells, either individually or for entire rows. You can specify that cell data be centered, left-aligned, or right-aligned with respect to the left and right borders of the cell. You can also specify that cell data be top-, middle-, or bottom-aligned with respect to the top and bottom borders of the cell. To do all of this, you include the ALIGN or VALIGN attributes in the <TD>, <TH>, or <TR> tags, as follows:

Opening Tag	Closing Tag	Purpose
<TD ALIGN= alignment>	</TD>	To align a cell's contents horizontally with respect to its left/right borders. Options include LEFT, RIGHT, and CENTER.
<TD VALIGN= alignment>	</TD>	To align a cell's contents vertically with respect to its top/bottom borders. Options include TOP, BOTTOM, and MIDDLE.
<TH ALIGN= alignment>	</TH>	Same as <TD ALIGN>, but applies to table header cells.

Figure 6.12
Spanning a new first row and centering the table on the page

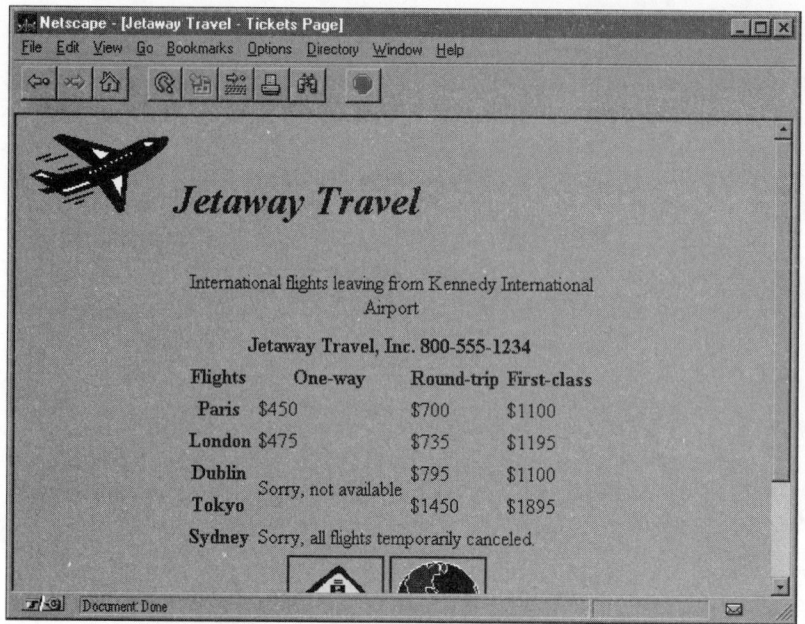

Opening Tag	Closing Tag	Purpose
<TH VALIGN= alignment>	</TH>	Same as <TD VALIGN>, but applies to table header cells.
<TR ALIGN= alignment>	</TR>	To horizontally align the contents of all the cells in a row. Options include LEFT, RIGHT, and CENTER.
<TR VALIGN= alignment>	</TR>	To vertically align the contents of all the cells in a row. Options include TOP, BOTTOM, and MIDDLE.

Let's align:

1. In your text editor, change each <TR> to **<TR ALIGN=CENTER>** to center-align the contents of all the cells in each table row; that is, to center-align the contents of the entire table. (This action is somewhat redundant, since header cells are, by default, center-aligned.)

2. Save the file, then reload/view it in your browser. Your table should match the one in Figure 6.13.

Figure 6.13
Aligning cell contents

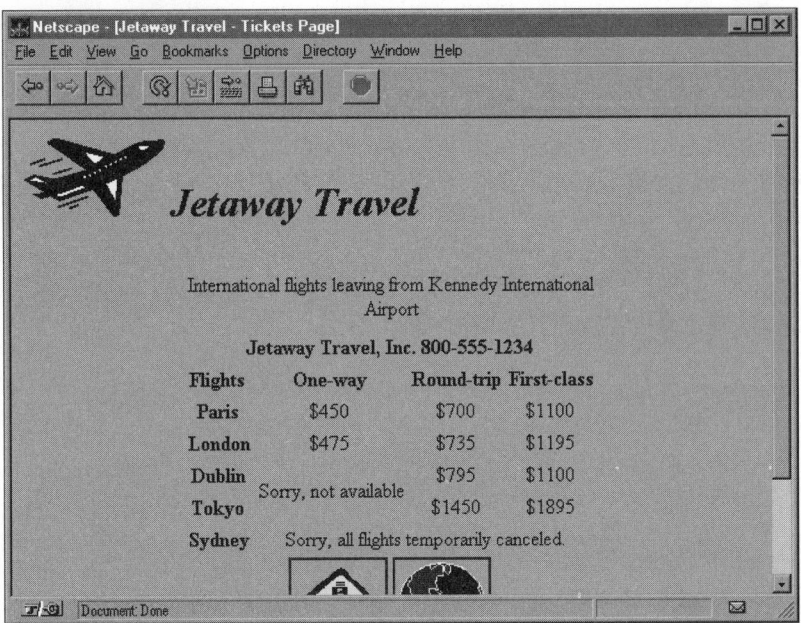

SETTING CELL WIDTH AND HEIGHT

You can specify the width and height of your table cells. You must specify these attributes individually for each cell. However, when you set the width for the widest cell in a column, you effectively set the width for the entire column; likewise for height and rows.

To specify cell width and/or height, you include the WIDTH and/or HEIGHT attributes in the <TD> and <TH> tags, as follows:

Opening Tag	Closing Tag	Purpose
<TD WIDTH=# HEIGHT=#>	</TD>	Sets the width and height of a cell to # pixels
<TH WIDTH=# HEIGHT=#>	</TH>	Sets the width and height of a table header cell to # pixels

Let's reduce the width of Dublin's *Sorry, not available* cell:

1. In your text editor, in the Dublin row, insert **WIDTH=80** in the <TD> tag of the *Sorry, not available* cell to reduce its width to 80 pixels. (This is the same cell that we formatted to span two rows.)

2. Save the file, then reload/view it in your browser.

3. Observe the results, as shown in Figure 6.14. The cell's column width is reduced, causing *Sorry, not* to appear on one line and *available* on the next.

Figure 6.14
Narrowing Dublin's *Sorry, not available* cell

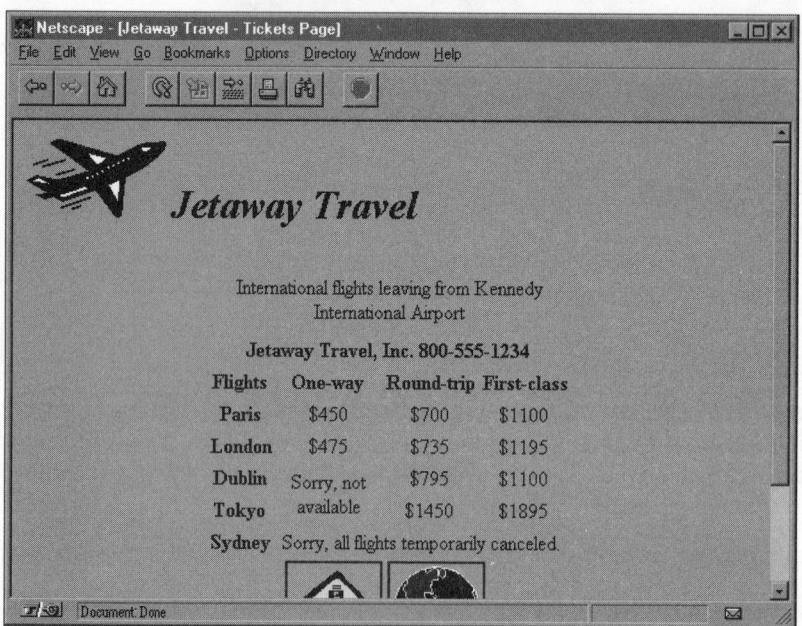

PLACING LINKS IN CELLS

You can place links in your table cells by nesting the tags that define the links (<A HREF>...</A>) within the tags that define the cells (<TD>...</TD> or <TH>...</TH>). For example, the following HTML code creates a link to Yahoo! in the cell of a one-row, one-column table:

```
<TABLE> <!-- One row, one column table -->
<TR ALIGN=CENTER> <!-- Row #1 -->
   <TD><A HREF="http://www.yahoo.com">Yahoo!</A></TD>
</TR>
</TABLE>
```

Note how the link's <A HREF>...</A> tags are nested snugly within the cell's <TD>...</TD> tags.

Let's place a link in one of our table cells:

1. In your browser, open the file **cancel.htm** from your HTMLWork directory. This file contains information on flight cancellations to Sydney.

2. Click on the **Back** button to return to the Tickets page.

3. In your text editor, still in the file tickets.htm, modify the row for Sydney flights as follows to create a link to the cancel.htm file:

```
<TR ALIGN=CENTER> <!-- Row #7 -->
    <TH>Sydney</TH>
    <TD COLSPAN=3><A HREF="cancel.htm">Sorry, all flights
temporarily canceled!</A></TD>
</TR>
```

4. Save the file, then reload/view it in your browser. It should match that shown in Figure 6.15.

Figure 6.15
Placing a link in a table cell

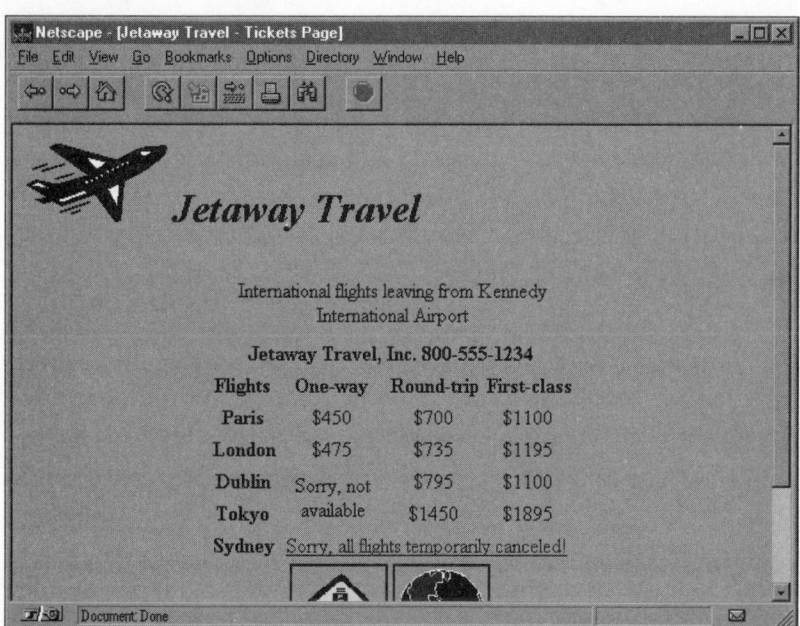

5. Click on your new **Sorry, all flights temporarily canceled!** link to jump to the Sydney flight cancellation page.

6. Click on the **Back** button to return to the Tickets page.

PLACING GRAPHICS IN CELLS

You can place a graphic in a table cell by nesting the graphic tag <IMG SRC> within the cell tags (<TD>...</TD> or <TH>...</TH>). For example, the following HTML code places the graphic jet3.gif in the cell of a one-row, one-column table:

```
<TABLE> <!-- One row, one column table -->
<TR ALIGN=CENTER> <!-- Row #1 -->
    <TD><IMG SRC="jet3.gif"></TD>
</TR>
</TABLE>
```

Let's add the Jetaway Travel corporate logo to our table:

1. In your text editor, modify the HTML code for row one—the Jetaway Travel, Inc. row—as follows:

```
<TR ALIGN=CENTER> <!-- Row #1 -->
    <TH COLSPAN=4><IMG SRC="jet3.gif">Jetaway Travel, Inc.
800-555-1234</TH>
</TR>
```

2. Save the file, then reload/view it in your browser.

3. Observe the results, as shown in Figure 6.16. The corporate logo (jet3.gif) appears in the first row, whose single cell spans across all four columns of the table.

CREATING NESTED TABLES

Nested tables are a Netscape enhancement to the HTML specification, which are also supported by Microsoft Internet Explorer. If a user's browser does not support nested tables, all the information in the tables might be lost to the viewer or, at the very least, not displayed in tabular format.

Nested tables can be useful in organizing the information on your page. They can also be used to create special effects such as a double-lined border.

Some advantages of using nested tables include the ability to place two tables side-by-side. In order to do this, you create an outer table and place the two tables inside that table, each acting as a cell in the outer table. Nesting also allows you to create tables that help with page layout. A disadvantage of using

Figure 6.16
Placing a graphic in a table cell

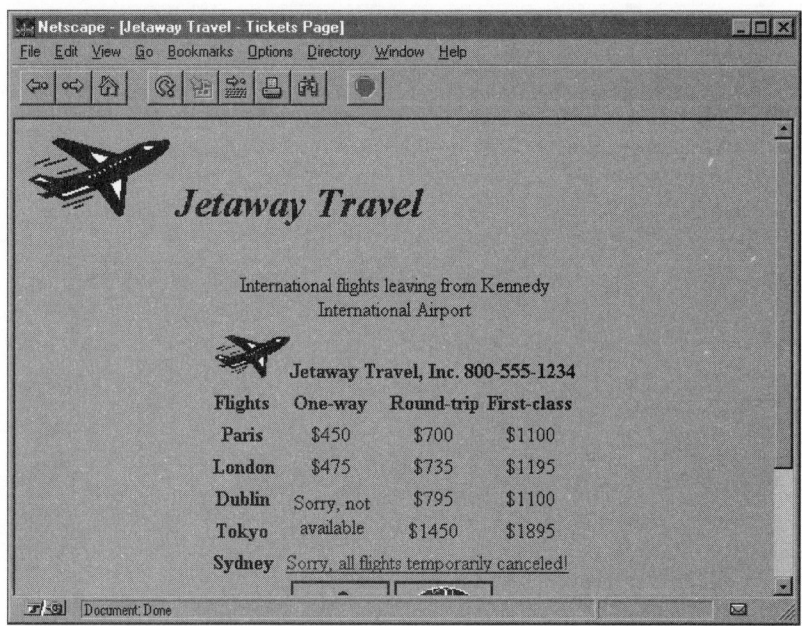

nested tables is that any users who access your page with a browser that does not support nested tables may not be able to view your data.

Figure 6.17 shows an example of code for two tables nested within another table. In the following exercise, we'll take a look at this code and try to figure out where the outer table and the two nested tables are. Let's examine the code for a nested table.

1. In Figure 6.17, locate the first <TABLE> tag (immediately after the <BODY> tag) and the last </TABLE> tag (it appears at the bottom of the figure just before the copyright footer comment). Draw a **box** around the outer table. (Yes, we really are telling you to write in the book!) The box will go from the first <TABLE> tag on line six to the line before the <!-- Copyright footer --> comment where the </TABLE> tag closes this outer table.

2. Draw a **box** around the first table contained within the outer table. This box will go from the second <TABLE> tag (this code appears as the first <TABLE BORDER> tag on or near the tenth line of the HTML code) to the first </TABLE> tag (on or near line 15 of the HTML code).

Figure 6.17
An example of code for a nested table

```
<HTML>¶
<HEAD>¶
<TITLE>Nested tables</TITLE>¶
</HEAD>¶
<BODY>¶
<TABLE BORDER>¶
<TR><TH ALIGN=RIGHT VALIGN=TOP>Jetaway Travel</TH>¶
<TD ROWSPAN=3><IMG HEIGHT=250 WIDTH=100 SRC="food.gif"></TD></TR>¶
<TR><TD VALIGN=TOP>¶
<TABLE BORDER>¶
<TR><TH COLSPAN=2>Accommodations</TH></TR>¶
<TR><TD>Economy</TD><TD><TT>$ 60- 80/night</TT></TD></TR>¶
<TR><TD>Moderate</TD><TD><TT>$ 80-120/night</TT></TD></TR>¶
<TR><TD>Deluxe</TD><TD><TT>$120-180/night</TT></TD></TR>¶
</TABLE>¶
</TD>¶
<TD VALIGN=TOP>¶
<TABLE BORDER>¶
<TR><TH COLSPAN=2>Tours</TH></TR>¶
<TR><TD>Shopping</TD><TD>6 hours</TD></TR>¶
<TR><TD>Art Galleries</TD><TD>4 hours</TD></TR>¶
<TR><TD>Concerts</TD><TD>3 hours</TD></TR>¶
<TR><TD>Local History</TD><TD>6 hours</TD></TR>¶
<TR><TD>Local Attractions</TD><TD>8 hours</TD></TR>¶
</TABLE>¶
</TD>¶
</TR>¶
<TR><TD ALIGN=RIGHT VALIGN=BOTTOM>Vacation Plans</TD>¶
<TD VALIGN=BOTTOM>for all budgets</TD></TR>¶
</TABLE>¶
</BODY>¶
</HTML>¶
```

3. Draw a **box** around the second table contained within the outer table. This box will go from the third <TABLE> tag (also a <TABLE BORDER> on or near line 18 of the HTML code) to the second </TABLE> tag (on or near line 25 of the HTML code).

Drawing boxes around each of the tables gives you a better idea of what information is included in each of the tables. Now, let's take a look at how the code for these nested tables actually appears when you open the document in your browser (**Note:** If your browser doesn't support nested tables, you may not see anything):

1. In your browser, open and view **NESTED.HTM** (see Figure 6.18). This is the table created by the code in Figure 6.17.

2. Switch to your text editor and open **NESTED.HTM**.

3. Add a **border** to the outer table. (Remember, just change the first <TABLE> tag to **<TABLE BORDER>**.)

4. Save and view the file. Now you should really be able to see the tables clearly in your browser.

Figure 6.18
Viewing nested tables in Netscape

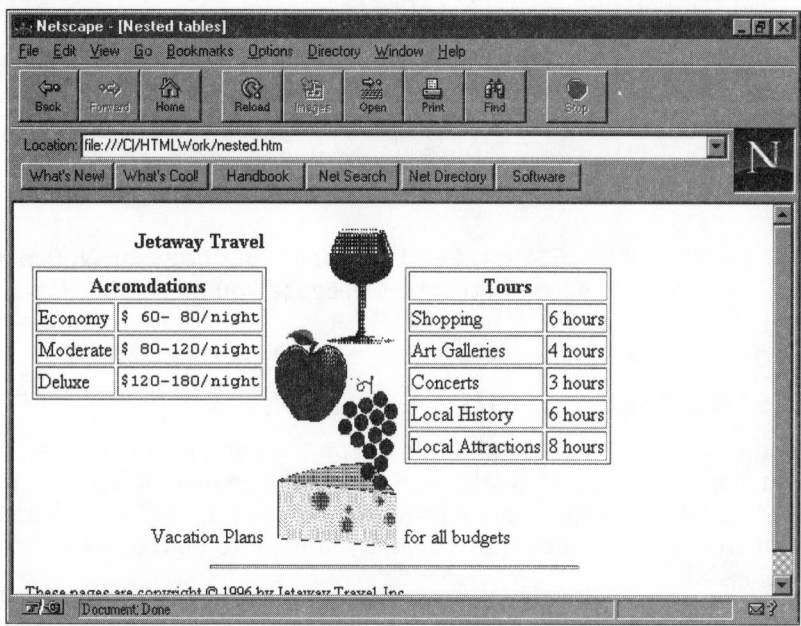

When you create nested tables, make sure to work from the outside in (or vice versa) when creating the code. If the tables are not opened and closed in the proper order, they will not be displayed properly. Some browsers will attempt to interpret what you meant, but others will just be so confused that they give up.

Let's create those nested tables you saw in Figure 6.18.

1. In your browser, open **MTNEST.HTM**. This file contains only the outer table. You will be adding two nested tables inside of this table.

2. Switch to your text editor and open **MTNEST.HTM**.

3. After the Insert Accommodations comment line, enter the following code:

```
<TABLE BORDER>
<TR><TH COLSPAN=2>Accommodations</TH></TR>
<TR><TD>Economy</TD><TD>$60 - $80/night</TD></TR>
<TR><TD>Moderate</TD><TD>$80 - $120/night</TD></TR>
<TR><TD>Deluxe</TD><TD>$120 - $180/night</TD></TR>
</TABLE>
```

4. After the *Insert Tour* comment line, enter the following code:

```
<TABLE BORDER>
<TR><TH COLSPAN=2>Tours</TH></TR>
<TR><TD>Shopping</TD><TD>6 hours</TD></TR>
<TR><TD>Art Galleries</TD><TD>4 hours</TD></TR>
<TR><TD>Concerts</TD><TD>3 hours</TD></TR>
<TR><TD>Local History</TD><TD>6 hours</TD></TR>
<TR><TD>Local Attractions</TD><TD>8 hours</TD></TR>
</TABLE>
```

5. Save the file as **MYNEST.HTM** and view it in your browser. Notice how you can easily see each of the tables because you placed borders around each of the inner tables.

USING TABLES FOR PAGE LAYOUT

Tables can be used to help you align things on the page as you saw earlier when you placed graphics in a table cell. You can also use tables to align fields in forms. Nested tables can also be used to facilitate page layout. By not using borders on the table, you can make the page appear to be regular text or text with graphics.

Let's examine a page that uses tables for page layout.

1. In your browser, open **PGLAYOUT.HTM** (see Figure 6.19). The graphics appear to be in the middle of the text. You will be adding more text via nested tables to this page shortly.

2. View the **document source**. The graphics and the text are all contained in a table. In the next exercise, we'll add some nested tables to this page.

3. Go ahead and close the source window.

Now that you have seen a completed page that used tables to help with page layout, let's make one.

1. In your text editor, open **PGLAYOUT.HTM**. The outer table is already in the document and you will add more tables to the document.

Figure 6.19
Viewing Pglayout.htm in Netscape

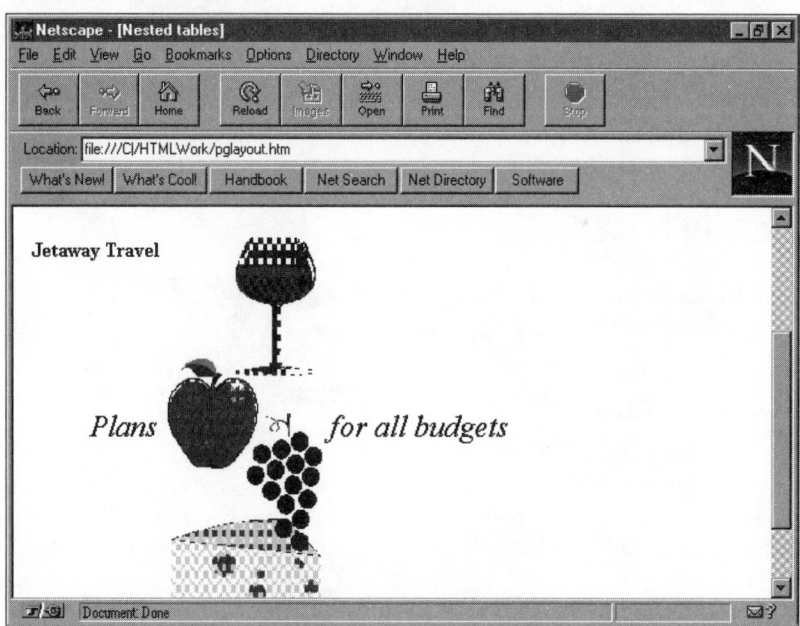

2. After the comment line for the first nested table, enter the following code:

```
<TABLE>
<TR><TH COLSPAN=2>Meal Plans</TH></TR>
<TR><TD>Breakfast, Lunch and Dinner: $100/day</TD></TR>
<TR><TD>Breakfast and Dinner: $80/day</TD></TR>
<TR><TD>Dinner only: $60/day</TD></TR>
</TABLE>
```

3. After the comment line for the second nested table, enter the following code:

```
<TABLE>
<TR><TH COLSPAN=2>Meal Choices</TH></TR>
<TR><TD>For breakfast, you can choose a Continental
breakfast or from a selection of fine Cafes near your
hotel. You will be given passes which will cover the cost
of breakfast at these selected Cafes.</TD></TR>
<TR><TD>Lunch varies depending on the tour package you
have chosen. In most cases, it will be either a boxed
lunch or a pass to selected restaurants featuring
regional cuisine.</TD></TR>
<TR><TD>Dinner will be a multi-course feast. You can
```

```
choose from standard American fare or a regional
cuisine.</TD></TR>
<TR><TD>All meals are available as Vegetarian and
Kosher.</TD></TR>
</TABLE>
```

4. Save and view the file (see Figure 6.20).

Figure 6.20
Using tables for page layout

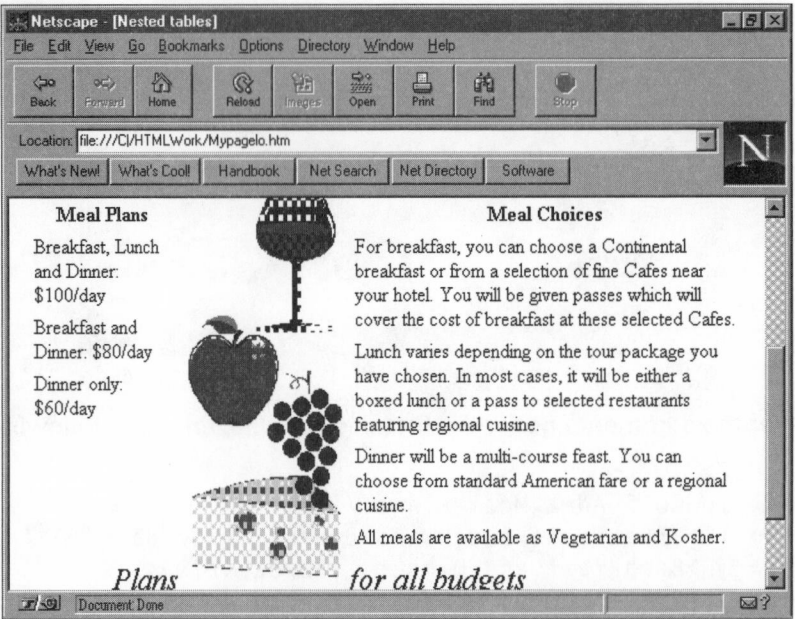

ALTERNATIVES FOR NON-TABLE BROWSERS

Not all browsers support tables, although most of the popular graphical browsers are capable of displaying them. Since not all users will be able to view your tables, it is a good idea to provide another page that contains a text-only page linked from the page containing the table. Some browsers that cannot display nested tables might also need an alternate page.

One way to make sure that the information is displayed in the way that you want it to be seen is to use preformatted text. By using the PRE tags, the spacing you enter into your HTML document will be the spacing used to display the text on screen.

Let's take a look at a document with and without the PRE tags.

1. In your browser, open **PREFRMT.HTM**. It is a plain text file and is not laid out in any order, so it looks very messy.

2. Switch to your text editor and open **PREFRMT.HTM**.

3. On a new line after the <BODY> line, enter **<PRE>**. This is the opening tag and any text after it will be displayed using the spacing found in this source document.

4. On a new line just before the copyright line, enter **</PRE>**. This is the closing tag to define where the end of the preformatted text is.

5. Save and view the file. With the addition of the PRE tags, the text appears exactly as it is spaced in the PREFRMT.HTM file.

Now that we have two documents with the same information, let's link from one to the other. This way, if someone cannot see the table information in the first document, they can use the link to move to the preformatted text page which they will be able to view.

1. In your text editor, open **MYNEST.HTM**. This is the page you created earlier with nested tables in it.

2. On a new line above the first <TABLE> tag, enter the following code:

```
If your browser does not support tables or nested tables,
<A HREF="prefrmt.htm">a text version of this page is
available.</A>
```

3. Save and view the file **MYNEST.HTM**.

4. Click on the **link** to view the preformatted text page.

5. Use the **Back** button to return to the nested tables page.

QUICK REFERENCE

In this chapter, you learned how to create and customize HTML tables.

Here's a quick reference for the techniques you learned in this chapter:

Desired Result	How to Do It
Create HTML table	*<TABLE>...</TABLE>* encloses data for entire table; *<TR>...</TR>* encloses data for table row; *<TD>...</TD>* encloses data for table cell; *<TH>...</TH>* encloses data for table header
Make table code clear	Comment each row; place each row's <TR> and </TR> tags on separate lines; indent each row's data between *<TR>...</TR>* tags; insert *space(s)* between cells
Format cell as table header	Enclose cell's data in *<TH>...</TH>* tags
Add border to table	<TABLE BORDER>...</TABLE>
Add caption to table	*<CAPTION ALIGN=alignment>...</CAPTION>*—alignment can be *TOP* or *BOTTOM*
Format cell to span multiple rows/columns	*<TD ROWSPAN=#>...</TD>* cell spans # rows; *<TD COLSPAN=#>...</TD>* cell spans # columns; *<TH ROWSPAN=#>...</TH>* cell header spans # rows; *<TH COLSPAN=#>...</TH>* cell header spans # columns
Align cell contents	*<TD ALIGN=alignment>...</TD>* aligns cell's contents horizontally (*LEFT, RIGHT,* or *CENTER*); *<TD VALIGN=alignment>...</TD>* aligns cell's contents vertically (*TOP, BOTTOM,* or *MIDDLE*); *<TH ALIGN=alignment>...</TH>* same as <TD ALIGN>, but for table header cells; *<TH VALIGN=alignment>...</TH>* same as <TD VALIGN>, but for table header cells; *<TR ALIGN=alignment>...</TR>* aligns horizontally contents of all cells in row (*LEFT, RIGHT,* or *CENTER*); *<TR VALIGN=alignment>...</TR>* aligns vertically contents of all cells in row (*TOP, BOTTOM,* or *MIDDLE*)
Set cell width/height	*<TD WIDTH=# HEIGHT=#>...</TD>* sets width/height of cell to # pixels; *<TH WIDTH=# HEIGHT=#>...</TH>* sets width/height of table header cell to # pixels
Place link in cell	Nest link tags (<A HREF>...</A>) within cell tags (<TD>...</TD> or <TH>...</TH>)

Desired Result	How to Do It
Place graphic in cell	Nest graphic tag *<IMG SRC>* within cell tags (<TD>...</TD> or <TH>...</TH>)
Provide an alternative page for non-table browsers	Use preformatted text which displays the spacing in the source document. The opening tag is *<PRE>* and closing is *</PRE>*.

In the next chapter, we'll show you how to change your Web pages' backgrounds and text colors.

SKILL BUILDER 2

In this practice activity, you will add remote-site links to your Travel Information Web page.

1. Open your text editor and open the file **TRAVEL.HTM**.

2. Add a link to preview Travel Inc.'s Web site at the end of the file (after the link to the home page) as follows: (Chapter 4)

```
<P><!--Link to Vacation.com-->
<A HREF ="http://www.vacations.com">The Yahoo! Web
site</A></P>
```

3. Save the file.

4. View the file in your browser.

5. Use your **link**, then return to the **TRAVEL.HTM** Web page.

6. In your text editor, add the link to the **Logical Operations** Web site:

```
<P><!--Link to Logical Operations-->
<A HREF ="http://www.logicalops.com">The Logical
Operations Web site</A></P>
```

7. Save and view the file.

8. Use your link, then return to the **TRAVEL.HTM** Web page.

9. Delete the link to the **Logical Operations** Web site.

10. Save and view the file.

Chapter 7

Setting Backgrounds and Text Colors for Your Web Pages

Okay, so you know how to format your Web pages and adorn them with links, graphics, sounds, animations, movies, and customized tables. But what about colors and those ultra-cool backgrounds you've seen out there on so many sites? Funny you should ask ....

When you're done working through this chapter, you will know

- How to set background colors for your pages
- How to set background graphics for your pages
- How to set text colors for your pages

SETTING BACKGROUND COLORS

The default Web page background color for most browsers is light gray. You can easily change a page's background color by using the BGCOLOR attribute with the <BODY> tag, as follows:

Opening Tag	Closing Tag	Purpose
<BODY BGCOLOR= "#*rrggbb*">	</BODY>	Sets the page's background color to the color that corresponds to the six-digit hexadecimal RGB value *rrggbb*
<BODY BGCOLOR= "*colorname*">	</BODY>	Sets the page's background color to the color that corresponds to *colorname*

As you can see, there are two approaches to setting colors in HTML:

- The RGB method, in which you specify a six-digit hexadecimal RGB value, such as *FFFFFF*
- The colorname method, in which you specify a text color name, such as *black*

The RGB method is more tedious to use, since you need to know—or, more likely, look up—the six-digit hexadecimal (yuck!) number that corresponds to your desired color. However, RGB offers much greater control over the exact color.

The colorname method is easier to use, since most of the color names are easy to remember. However, it offers less control over color, particularly if you are *not* running Netscape: Netscape supports 140 color names; Internet Explorer supports just 16!

We'll present both approaches and let you decide which you prefer.

USING RGB VALUES TO SET COLOR

An *RGB value* is a string of three two-digit numbers: *rrggbb*. The first number (*rr*) specifies the amount of red in the color, the second (*gg*) specifies the amount of green, and the third (*bb*) the amount of blue. These three numbers are expressed in hexadecimal notation; each number has two digits, from 00 (0) to FF (255). This gives you a palette of more than 16 million colors to choose from: 256 times 256 times 256!

Here are the RGB values for some common colors:

RGB Value	Color
FFFFFF	white
000000	black
FF0000	red
00FF00	green
0000FF	blue
888888	gray
008888	cyan
880088	magenta

Note: When specifying BGCOLOR, make sure to precede the RGB value (rrggbb) with a pound sign (#). BGCOLOR="#FFFFFF" is correct; BGCOLOR="FFFFFF" isn't.

Let's use the RGB approach to set the background color of our Jetaway Travel home page to white:

1. In your text editor, open **default.htm** from your HTMLWork directory.

2. Change the <BODY> tag to:
   `<BODY BGCOLOR="#FFFFFF"> <!-- white background -->`
   Don't forget the # before the *FFFFFF* or you'll be in trouble!

3. Save the file, then view it in Netscape. Your background color should now be white, instead of the default gray, as shown in Figure 7.1.

4. In your text editor, change the RGB value (FFFFFF) of your BGCOLOR attribute to one of the other RGB values listed above.

5. Save the file, then reload/view it in Netscape. Is the page as readable with your background color as it was with a white background?

Figure 7.1
Setting a white background

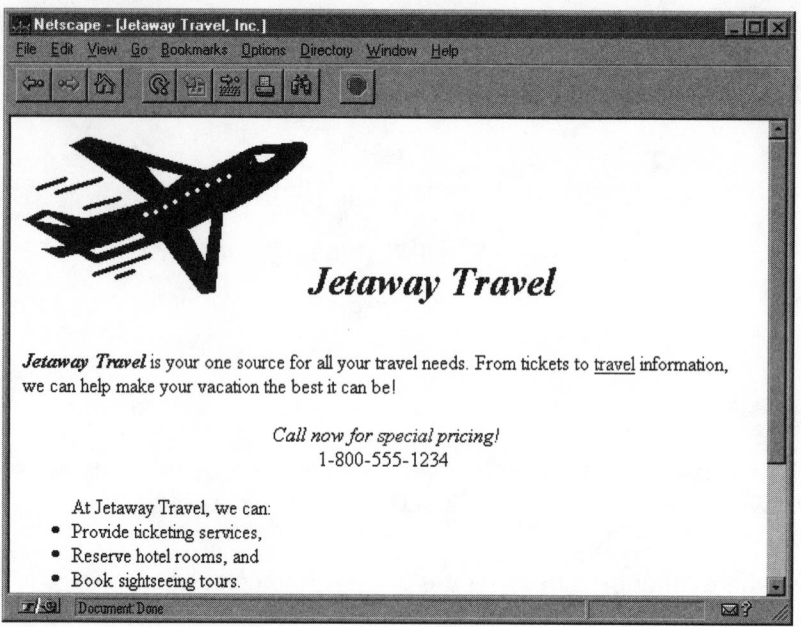

PRACTICE YOUR SKILLS

1. Repeat the previous two steps for some (or all!) of the remaining colors in the RGB list.

2. Adventurers: Devise your very own six-digit RGB values and see what background colors they produce. Remember, each RGB number (*rr*, *gg*, and *bb*) comprises two hexadecimal digits, and each digit can have a value from 0 to F (0 to 15 in conventional decimal notation).

3. When you're done adventuring, set your background color to its default, light gray. (**Hint:** Simply remove the BGCOLOR attribute.)

USING COLOR NAMES TO SET COLORS

A *color name* is a text string that defines a color. Table 7.1 lists the 16 color names supported by both Netscape and Internet Explorer:

Table 7.1   **Color Names (for Netscape and Internet Explorer)**

black	lime
olive	fuchsia
teal	white
red	green
blue	purple
maroon	silver
navy	yellow
gray	aqua

And Table 7.2 gives a sampling of the other 124 color names supported only by Netscape. Note that there are no spaces in the names:

Table 7.2   **Color Names (for Netscape Only)**

gold	hotpink
antiquewhite	cornflowerblue
bisque	khaki
ghostwhite	chartreuse
mistyrose	papayawhip
seashell	thistle
powderblue	wheat
midnightblue	plum

Note: When specifying BGCOLOR with color names, do not precede the color name with a pound sign (#). BGCOLOR="white" is correct; BG-COLOR="#white" isn't.

Let's use the color name approach to set our background color to white:

1. In your text editor, change default.htm's <BODY> tag to:

```
<BODY BGCOLOR="white"> <!-- white background -->
```

2. Save the file, then view it in Netscape. Your background color should now be white, instead of the default gray.

3. In your text editor, change the color name in your BGCOLOR attribute to one of the other color names listed above. (Choose from the second list only if you are using Netscape!)

4. Save the file, then reload/view it in Netscape. How's the page legibility?

PRACTICE YOUR SKILLS

1. Repeat the previous two steps for some (or all!) of the remaining color names in the list(s).

2. View the sample backgrounds color page at

```
http://www.infi.net/wwwimages/colorindex.html
```

This page lists color names *and* the corresponding RGB values for a generous selection of colors. It also provides a color sampler that can help you determine which background/foreground color combinations work well (and which are nauseating).

3. When you're done sampling, change your Jetaway Travel home page background back to **white**, and reload/view the page.

SETTING BACKGROUND GRAPHICS

Bored with solid colors? Well, you can get as unsolid as you want by setting a graphic as your Web page background. If the graphic is not large enough to fill the entire browser window, the browser will automatically *tile* it; that is, display as many copies of the graphic as are necessary to fill the entire window.

To set a background graphic for your Web page, you use the BACKGROUND attribute with the <BODY> tag, as follows:

Opening Tag	Closing Tag	Purpose
<BODY BACKGROUND= "*filename*">	</BODY>	Fills the page background with the graphic stored in *"filename"*

Netscape Communications Corp. maintains a site with free sample backgrounds that you can download and use in your Web pages:

```
http://home.netscape.com/assist/net_sites/bg/
backgrounds.html
```

Let's set a background graphic for our Jetaway Travel home page:

1. In your text editor, change the <BODY> tag to

   `<BODY BACKGROUND="bluerock.gif"> <!-- sets a background graphic -->`

2. Save the file, then view it in Netscape.

3. Observe the text. Is it legible against this background? Not very! The background is dark and grainy, and the text is black, which makes the page very difficult to read.

PRACTICE YOUR SKILLS

1. Change your page background graphic to each of the following, and observe the results. (**Note:** All of these GIF files are stored in your HTML-Work directory.) Which text/background combinations promote legibility?

   - embossed.gif
   - redrock.gif
   - metal.gif
   - bluebar.gif
   - disks.gif

2. Journey to the Netscape site,

   ```
   http://home.netscape.com/assist/net_sites/bg/
   backgrounds.html
   ```

and try out a few of their background graphics on your Jetaway page.

When you're done, set your Jetaway page background back to **bluerock.gif**. (You'll fix the legibility problem in a moment.)

SETTING TEXT COLORS

Along with background color, you can also specify text color. You can set the color for a page's body text and for its link text (the text a user clicks on to jump to another page). You can set different text colors for *unvisited* links, *visited* links, and *active* links. An active link is one that the user is clicking on (while the mouse button is down).

The default color for body text is black, for unvisited links is blue, for visited links is purple, and for active links is red. To change these colors, you use the TEXT, LINK, VLINK, and ALINK attributes with the <BODY> tag, as follows:

Opening Tag	Closing Tag	Purpose
<BODY TEXT="#*rrggbb*"> or <BODY TEXT="*colorname*">	</BODY>	Sets the color of body text to that specified by the RGB value rrggbb or by *colorname*
<BODY LINK="#*rrggbb*"> or <BODY LINK="*colorname*">	</BODY>	Sets the color of unvisited links to that specified by the RGB value *rrggbb* or by *colorname*
<BODY VLINK="#*rrggbb*"> or <BODY VLINK="*colorname*">	</BODY>	Sets the color of visited links to that specified by the RGB value *rrggbb* or by *colorname*
<BODY ALINK="#*rrggbb*"> or <BODY ALINK="*colorname*">	</BODY>	Sets the color of active links to that specified by the RGB value *rrggbb* or by *colorname*

Note: You use the same RGB values or color names to create text colors as you do to create background colors. Netscape Communications Corp. maintains a site with information on how to set background, text, and link colors in your Web pages: http://home.netscape.com/assist/net_sites/bg

Let's set text colors to make your Web page easier to read:

1. In your text editor, change the <BODY> tag to:

```
<!-- white text on graphic -->
<BODY BACKGROUND="bluerock.gif" TEXT="white">
```

(Note that we've moved the comment line above the <BODY> tag.) This sets your home page's text color to white.

2. Save the file, then view it in Netscape.

3. Observe the results. Is the white text easier to read against this background than the default black text? (Yes!)

4. In your text editor, change the <BODY> tag to:

```
<!-- colored text and links on graphic -->
<BODY BACKGROUND="bluerock.gif" TEXT="white"
    LINK="red" VLINK="green" ALINK= blue >
```

(Note that we've split the <BODY> tag into two lines.) This sets white text, red unvisited links (LINK), green visited links (VLINK), and blue active links (ALINK) against the background graphic.

5. Save the file, then reload/view it in Netscape.

6. Observe the page legibility. Are the text and links clearly readable?

7. Observe the links. Those you have not yet visited are red; those you have visited are green; those you click on are blue. Verify this by clicking on an as-yet unvisited (red) link; it turns blue for an instant while it is "active"— that is, before the linked page appears. Then return to the Jetaway Travel home page; the link you just visited is now green.

PRACTICE YOUR SKILLS

1. Change the text and link colors to their **default values**.

2. Remove the background graphic.

3. Set the background color to **white**.

4. Save the file, then reload/view it in Netscape.

QUICK REFERENCE

In this chapter, you learned how to set Web page backgrounds and text colors.

Here's a quick reference for the techniques you learned in this chapter:

Desired Result	How to Do It
Set background color	*<BODY BGCOLOR="#rrggbb">...</BODY>* where *rrggbb* is hexadecimal RGB value; *<BODY BGCOLOR="colorname">...</BODY>* where *colorname* is the color name (see lists in chapter)
Specify RGB color	*rrggbb* where *rr* is red component, *gg* is green, *bb* is blue; each component is hexadecimal number from 00 to FF
Set background graphic	*<BODY BACKGROUND="filename">...</BODY>* where graphic is stored in *filename*
Set body text color	*<BODY TEXT="#rrggbb">...</BODY>*, or *<BODY TEXT="colorname">...</BODY>*
Set unvisited link color	*<BODY LINK="#rrggbb">...</BODY>*, or *<BODY LINK="#colorname">...</BODY>*
Set visited link color	*<BODY VLINK="#rrggbb">...</BODY>*, or *<BODY VLINK="#colornameb">...</BODY>*
Set active link color	*<BODY ALINK="#rrggbb">...</BODY>* or *<BODY ALINK="#colornameb">...</BODY>*

In the next chapter, we'll help you get started designing your own Web pages.

SKILL BUILDER 3

In this activity, you will add a link from the Jetaway Travel home page to your new Tickets page. Figures 7.2, 7.3, and 7.4 show a map of the Jetaway Travel Web site as it should appear at the completion of Skill Builder 3.

Figure 7.2
The Jetaway Travel home page

1. Open your **text editor**, if necessary, and open the **DEFAULT.HTM** file.

2. Add a **link** to the TICKETS.HTM page: Create a link so that the word "tickets" in the sentence "From tickets to travel information, we can make your vacation the best it can be!" is the highlighted link word.

3. Save and view the Jetaway Travel home page with your browser.

4. Test your links.

Figure 7.3
The Jetaway Travel tickets page

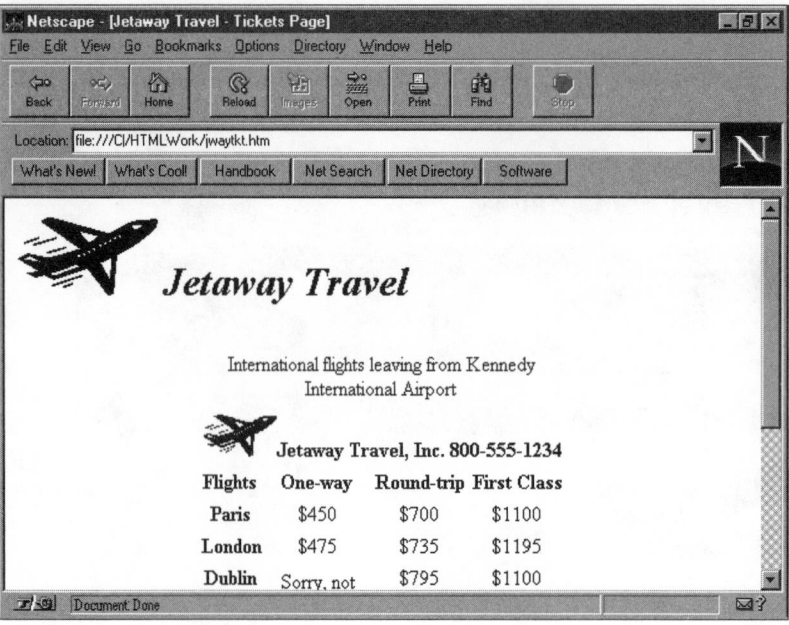

Figure 7.4
The Jetaway Travel Special Notice page

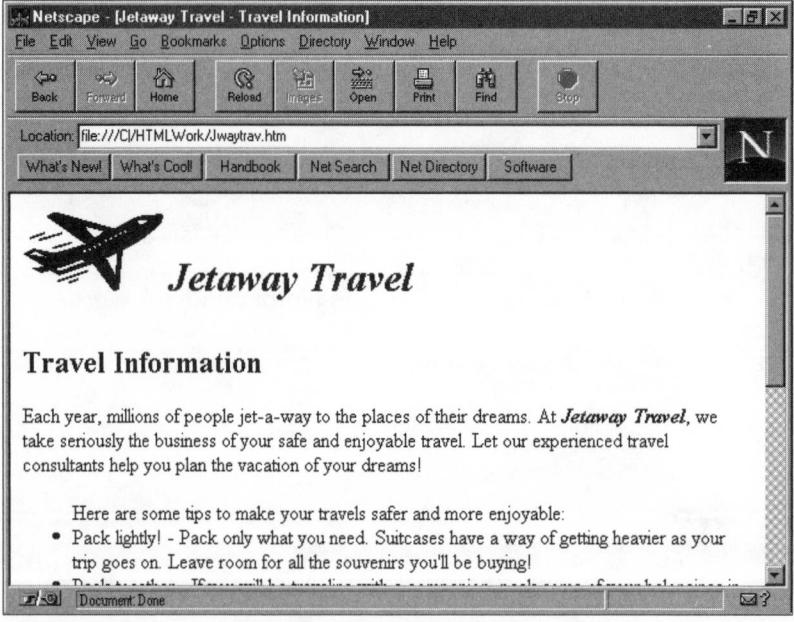

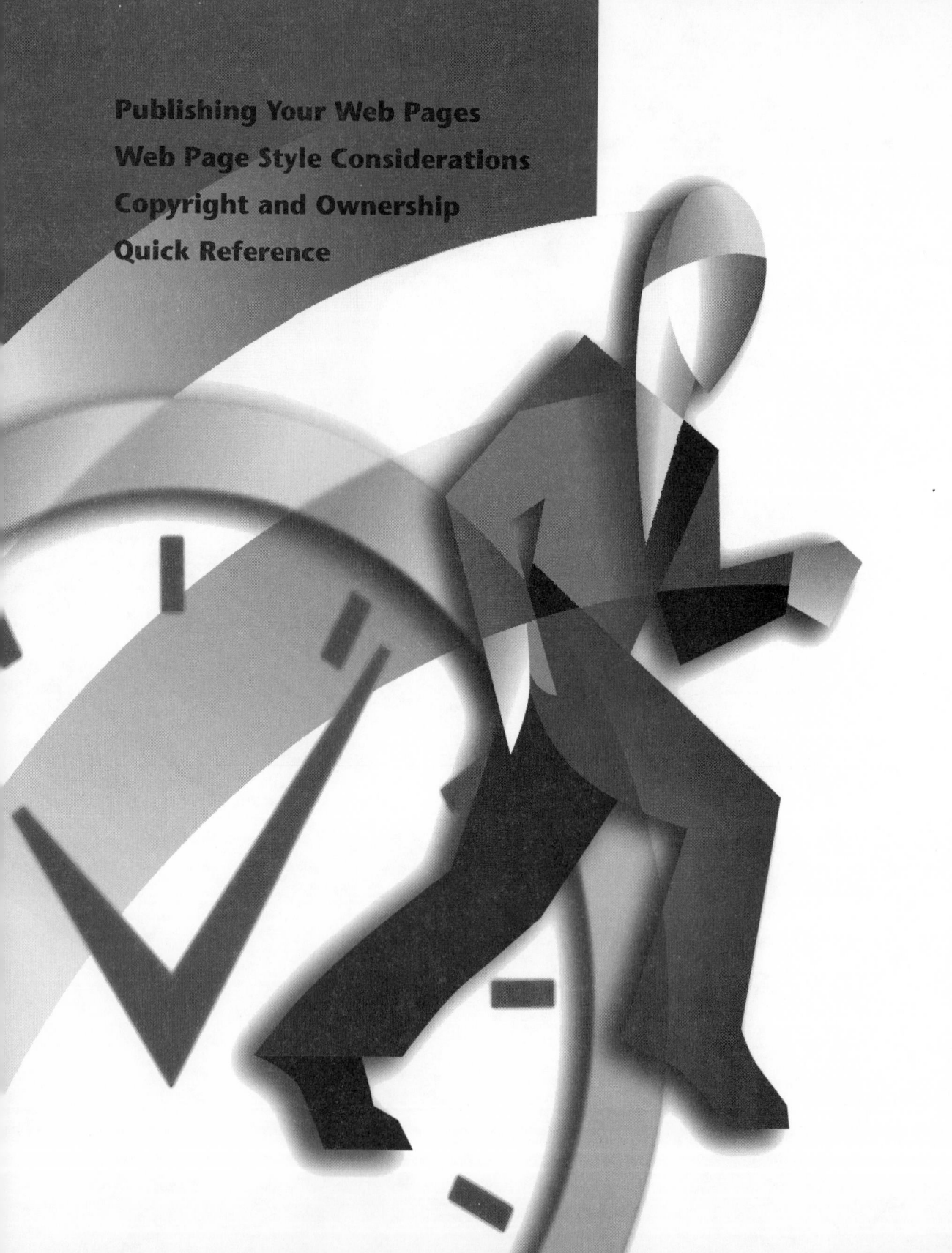

Publishing Your Web Pages

Web Page Style Considerations

Copyright and Ownership

Quick Reference

Chapter 8
Web Page Publishing and Design

Now that you have learned most of the basic mechanics of creating your Web pages, let's talk style. In this chapter, we'll cover some style, network, and site design issues that you should consider when creating your Web site. We'll also introduce you to the copyright law so that you can consider how to legally protect your creations. First, though, we're going to cover the general procedures you can use to publish your pages on the Web.

When you're done working through this chapter, you will know

- How to publish your Web pages on the Internet

- How to design your pages so that they are visually pleasing and reasonably quick to load

- How to include the proper copyright disclaimer so that you can legally protect your Web creations

PUBLISHING YOUR WEB PAGES

By now, you're probably dying to know how to actually get your Web page creations onto the Internet. Unfortunately, the specific steps to do are different for just about every type of Internet connection. So, we'll have to just talk in generalities here.

You probably have one of three types of connections to the Internet: You connect through one of the major online services, like America Online or CompuServe; you connect to either a regional or national provider of Internet services, like Netcom or your local phone company; or you get your connection from an employer whose systems are connected to the Internet. All of these providers can be referred to as *Internet Service Providers*, or *ISP*s. No matter which ISP you have, you must get your pages to their server. Then, in some cases, you must grant permissions to Web readers so that they may access your pages.

The major online services, such as America Online, often require you to use their special programs for creating and publishing Web pages. For example, America Online provides a program called AOLpress to its members. With programs like AOLpress, publishing your finished pages can be as easy as choosing File, Save As, and then specifying the URL where you want to save your files. If you're using a program like that, you probably don't need to read the next two sections. You might still want to read them, however, to improve your understanding of how the Web works.

GETTING IT THERE

The first step in publishing your Web pages (well, besides creating them) is to transfer those pages to your ISP's Web server. Your ISP might provide you with a nice graphical utility to do this or might force you to use a command-line utility, like *ftp* (a popular file transfer program that originated with the UNIX operating system). The goal is the same: to transfer the files that comprise your Web pages from your hard drive to the server that your ISP has connected to the Internet.

Teaching the intricacies of the ftp command or one of the many graphical versions of ftp is beyond the scope of this book. However, for any of these tools, the steps are similar. Generally, you must:

- Log onto your ISP
- Start the file transfer program
- Select the files to transfer
- Transfer the files

Some transfer programs are set up to transfer text files by default. If you try to transfer a non-text file, such as a graphic, the transfer program will treat the special codes that make up your file as if they were just plain text. This results in creating garbage out of your perfectly good file. Programs that operate in this manner offer a *binary* transfer mode to help in this situation. In binary mode, the codes that make up your file are transferred intact. In fact, both text and non-text files are transferred properly when in binary mode. So, if you are offered the choice, you might as well stick with binary mode when transferring any files.

To enable binary mode, you might need to enter a command or choose a menu option. For example, with the ftp program, you would type **binary** at the program's command prompt to change it to binary mode.

Here's how you would transfer all of the files from the C:\WEB folder on a personal computer to the ~\MYSTUFF folder on an ISP's server:

- Follow your normal procedures to connect to the Internet (dial your ISP).
- Open a command prompt (for example, by choosing *Start, Programs, Command Prompt* in Windows 95).
- Change to the C:\WEB folder by typing **cd \web** and pressing **Enter**.
- Start the ftp program by typing **ftp** and pressing *Enter.*
- Connect to your ISP's server by typing **open** and then the name of your ISP's server, and pressing *Enter.* You will need to provide your user name and password to be allowed access.
- Change to the ~\MYSTUFF folder by typing **cd ~\mystuff** and pressing *Enter.*
- Switch to binary mode by typing **binary** and pressing *Enter.*
- Transfer all of the files by typing **mput .** and pressing *Enter.*
- Confirm that all of the files have transferred by viewing a listing of the folder on the server by typing **ls** and pressing *Enter.*
- Quit the ftp program by typing **quit** and pressing *Enter.*

Of course, your exact steps will vary. Your ISP will be able to give you the exact details of how to upload files to its Web server.

SETTING PERMISSIONS

You only need to be concerned with this step if your ISP runs its Web servers on UNIX-based computers. How will you know if it uses UNIX? If they don't tell you, you will have to ask. If you are connecting to the Internet through a local or regional ISP, you will probably have to set security permissions.

UNIX is a multi-user operating system, meaning more than one person can use the same computer. In order to protect your data from others who might use the same computer, UNIX enforces security measures that make your data invisible to other users. That's not really what you want if you are trying to publish Web pages to the world. Other network operating systems popularly used as Web servers don't usually use the same security scheme. If your ISP uses one of those operating systems for its Internet servers you probably won't have to grant permissions to Web users.

Note: We've glossed over some gory network operating system details in those paragraphs above. But the essence of what we've included is true: On UNIX systems, you need to set file permissions, on other systems you (normally) don't have to worry about this step.

To make your Web files available to any user, you must use a UNIX command to change the permissions (UNIX calls it the *mode*) of a file. If your ISP provides you with a utility to transfer and publish your Web page files, that utility might automatically change the mode of your files for you. If not, you will have to use the UNIX *chmod* command, which is short for "change mode."

Let's say you want to publish a file called default.htm on a UNIX-based Web server. You would use the following command to change the mode of that file so that any user could read the file (but not change it):

```
chmod go+rx default.htm [enter]
```

Pretty intuitive don't you think? Just kidding! As klunky as is it, that command sets the mode of your file so that anyone can read it. If you want to set the mode for all of the files in a folder, change your current folder to that folder, then use this command:

```
chmod go+rx . [enter]
```

To set the mode on all of the files in your current folder and any folders below that folder, use:

```
chmod -R go+rx . [enter]
```

One last trick uses a different UNIX command, *umask*. The umask (short for un-mask) command has no effect on files already in your folder. However, it sets default permissions for any new files you put there. So, once you have set permissions for the files in your folder (using your friend, chmod), you can use umask to take care of any subsequent files you add. Use this command to set permissions as we described:

```
umask 022 [enter]
```

Hopefully, your ISP provides a more intuitive or graphical method for performing this necessary step.

WEB PAGE STYLE CONSIDERATIONS

When desktop publishing first burst on the scene in the 1980s, designers felt an irresistible urge to use every font loaded on their systems. Many Web pages show this same design philosophy. Those pages are loaded with big, richly colored graphics, complex backgrounds, and colored text. Unfortunately, such a design can appear cluttered and confusing.

Instead, let's consider a few ways that you can make your pages look more professional, easier to view, and quicker to view. In these next sections, you will learn how to:

- Choose and include graphical elements in a way that is visually pleasing to most viewers of your pages

- Design your pages to load quickly

- Design your pages so that they look good on different types of browsers that have different capabilities

- Design the pages of your site to use a consistent look and feel, and use similar page elements

GRAPHICAL DESIGN ISSUES

Probably the best way to create well-designed pages is to put yourself in the shoes of your readers (those who view your pages). Consider how your pages would look to those viewers and adjust your design accordingly.

For example, let's say you're designing a page for your company, whose corporate colors are gray and white (okay, so in this example, you're working for an unimaginative company). To follow corporate standards, you create a Web page with a light gray background and white text. Could readers actually read your text? Probably not. Your text and background colors shouldn't be too close or readability will suffer.

Consider these general guidelines:

- Choose colors that provide the greatest contrast between your text and your background. Remember that most people are used to reading black text on white paper. If your pages will include lots of text, you should try to emulate that paper experience. If you use a dark background, like black or dark blue, use a light color for the text, like white.

- If you're going to use background graphics, use simple graphics with faded or muted colors. You don't want your background graphics to distract readers from your foreground text or graphics.

Let's see some examples:

1. If your browser is not currently running, start it now.

2. From the HTMLWork folder, open the **BG1.HTM** file.

3. Observe the Web page. This page is poorly designed because the background graphic is complex and uses colors close to that of the text. The result is a page that is difficult to read.

4. Open the **default.htm** file. This is the file you have been creating throughout this book. You have carefully designed this file to be easy to read. You have used a white background with black text to provide the high contrast necessary for easy reading. Good job!

You can leave your browser open; you will need it in the next section.

NETWORK-RELATED DESIGN CONSIDERATIONS

You should consider how long it will take to download your pages when designing those pages. You don't want your readers to become bored waiting for your page to download. If they are the impatient type, they will probably move on and never see your pages.

While you cannot control the speed of the Internet, you can follow these guidelines to help control access speed:

- Avoid large or high resolution graphics as backgrounds. Instead, use small simpler graphics which can be repeated across the background to produce the effect you want.

- Instead of embedding large graphics in your pages, include smaller versions (sometimes called *thumbnails*) that are links to the full-sized versions.

- If you have a graphics program that will let you control the number of colors that your graphic uses, remove any colors not actually used in the graphic file. This will reduce the size of the graphic file and reduce the time it takes to load.

- Finally, create your Web site out of a collection of small pages rather than as one long page. Users will be able to download just the section they want without having to wait to download your entire site.

Let's see an example:

1. If you quit your browser after the last exercise, start it again.

2. From the HTMLWork folder, open the **BG2.HTM** file.

3. Observe the Web page. This page is poorly designed because the background graphic is so large. Consequently, the page takes a long time to load. Remember, your hard drive is hundreds of times faster than typical Internet connections. If your Web page loads slowly off of your hard drive, it will load painfully slowly when you publish it on the Internet.

4. Open the **default.htm** file. This is the file you have been creating throughout this book. The graphics you included are small and use minimal colors. You have carefully designed this file to be small and quick to load. Again, good job!

You can leave your browser open; you will need it in the next section.

BROWSER CONSIDERATIONS

To speed access, some users turn off the option that automatically loads images. Some users even use browsers, like Lynx, that cannot display graphics. If your pages rely on graphical elements, these users won't see your pages as you intended.

Another consideration you should be aware of is that the size and resolution of your screen are probably not the same as that of your user's computers. You might have your screen show 65,000 colors and a resolution of 800 by 600 pixels. Your readers might have their computers set up for 16 colors and only 640 by 480 pixels (the Windows 3.1 default settings). If your Web page just fits your browser window on your computer, you readers will have to scroll around to view your whole page.

Also, browsers automatically reformat the text of your pages to fit the window size. So, if you spend hours getting the text to line up just the way you want it, you will probably have wasted your time. Your readers are almost guaranteed to see your pages through different settings.

You can, of course, take the hard-line attitude of "who cares!" But in doing so, you will be cutting off many users from the beauty of your Web creations. Instead, follow these guidelines:

• Use graphics sparingly and only when appropriate. For example, use words for links rather than graphics which might not show up in a user's browser.

• Include alternate text when embedding graphics in your pages. Alternate text is text that appears in browsers that cannot display graphics (or when users have graphics turned off). Within the <IMG SRC> tag, add the option *ALT="your text goes here"* to include alternate text. For example, this line either loads a picture or some alternate text describing that picture:

```
<IMG SRC="mypict.gif" ALT="A picture of me!">
```

- Design for the Windows 3.1 default colors and resolution when creating your page layout. This means you're designing for the lowest common denominator. But, by doing so, you are assured that most everyone will see your pages as you designed them.

- If you want to absolutely control the line and paragraph layout of your text, put your text in a table. In doing this, you force your readers to scroll to see your text, but it will end up formatted as you intended.

Let's see an example of all this:

1. If you quit your browser after the last exercise, start it again.

2. Resize your browser's window so that it fills only one-quarter of the screen. Users with different monitor resolutions will see different portions of your Web page, just as you have simulated with this step.

3. Maximize your browser's window or resize to a size that you find appropriate.

4. Turn off the automatic loading of images. If you are using Navigator, choose **Options, Auto Load Images** to do this step.

5. Save your options. Again, if you are using Navigator, choose **Options, Save Options**.

6. Quit your browser, then re-start your browser. This ensures that images won't be loaded with any new pages you load.

7. From the HTMLWork folder, open the **bg3.htm** file.

8. Observe the Web page. Without its graphics, you will probably find this page difficult to navigate and interpret. The page's design relies on its graphics. You might wish to avoid such a design.

9. Turn on the automatic loading of images. If you are using Navigator, choose **Options, Auto Load Images** to do this step.

10. Save your options. Again, if you are using Navigator, choose **Options, Save Options**.

11. Reload the page to view it with its graphics. Now you can see how the page was meant to be seen. The links and their targets should be a little clearer.

You can leave your browser open; you will need it in the next section.

PAGE AND SITE DESIGN ISSUES

If you are going to be designing Web pages for your company or organization, you might want to consider creating a unified look and feel to those pages. A unified look makes the pages that make up your site recognizable, consistent, and in keeping with your corporate or organizational image.

Here are some elements that you can use consistently to create a site-wide look and feel:

- Use your organization's official colors for backgrounds and text to tie in your pages with your organization's image. You might need to deviate from your official colors to improve readability. (Computer screens provide much lower resolution than paper. So, even if your colors produce readable printed materials, they might not work for online materials.)

- Use your company or organization's logo on every page.

- Create standard navigation elements (buttons to the top of your site, for example) and use them on every page. These common elements will help users find their way around your site.

- Place standard footer information on each page, such as your organization's name, address, phone number, and e-mail address.

Let's look at a page that uses these consistent elements:

1. If you quit your browser after the last exercise, start it again.

2. Load the default.htm file that you have been creating throughout this book.

3. Observe the standard elements on this Web page. You placed this fictitious company's logo on every page of this site. You also included a standard navigation bar and a copyright statement on every page.

4. Click on the link to the **Tickets** page. Observe these same elements on this page.

5. Can you think of other site standards you might add to these pages? Can you think of other benefits to you or your page's users when you use standard page elements?

Hint: Other elements you could standardize are page layout, table styles, and graphical elements, such as bullets or link graphics. Benefits of standard elements include: Efficiency—you don't have to create a new layout for each page if you standardize; and ease of use—once your readers learn your layout, they will be able to easily navigate all of your Web site's pages.

You can leave your browser open; you will need it in the next section.

COPYRIGHT AND OWNERSHIP

In the United States, the copyright law automatically gives you protection for documents, including Web pages, that you create. While you do not have to place any special copyright information to gain this protection, a copyright statement notifies readers that your work is protected by law and should not be copied.

To copyright your work, add the word "Copyright," the copyright symbol (©), the year you first published the work, and your company's or organization's name to your document. As you learned in Chapter 5, you can create the copyright symbol by entering © or © into your HTML file where you want the symbol to appear. (Make sure to include the semi-colon, as shown above, after the codes when you enter them in your documents.)

If you will be creating Web pages for profit, you might wish to register your works with the United States Copyright Office (for a fee, of course). Doing so gives you some additional legal rights, such as the right to sue for copyright infringement. Depending on the type of work you are creating, a copyright lasts for 50, 75, or 100 years. And finally, The Berne Convention of 1988 standardized and formalized copyright protection internationally. Your work should enjoy the same legal protection outside of the United States as within the U.S.

We certainly are not providing you with complete or legally binding information about the copyright laws here. For that, you need to contact a lawyer who specializes in such law. You can find detailed information about copyright law on the Internet. This information will prepare you to speak intelligently with your lawyer, should you decide you need to consult an attorney.

The members of the misc.legal USENET News group have created a FAQ (frequently asked questions) document that will help answer many of your questions about copyright law. You can find this FAQ stored in six parts (each in a separate text file) at:

```
ftp://rtfm.mit.edu/pub/usenet/news.answers/law/copyright/faq
```

One last consideration we will mention is that you cannot control who views your Web pages once you publish them on the Internet. Your competitors can view your pages (and probably will) just as easily as your customers. You shouldn't put sensitive or proprietary information on your Web pages unless you really want the whole world to read about it.

You can check out the copyright FAQ now with these steps:

1. If you quit your browser after the last exercise, start it again.

2. In the location field, type **ftp://rtfm.mit.edu/pub/usenet/news.answers/law/copyright/faq** and press **Enter**. Once you have connected to this site, you will be presented with a list of documents with names like part1, part2, and so forth.

3. Click on **part1**. The first part of the FAQ document is loaded into your browser. This part contains useful summary information, such as a complete table of contents of the remaining parts.

4. When you're done reading, you can quit your browser.

QUICK REFERENCE

In this chapter, you learned about publishing your Web pages, how to create a quick-to-load and easy-to-use Web site, and how to copyright your pages.

This table summarizes the principles you learned in this chapter.

To Design This Aspect of Your Pages Well,	Do This
Visual appearance	Use dark text on light backgrounds or light text on dark backgrounds; use only simple or muted background graphics; place the whole page in a table so that you can control margins and text flow
Download speed	Include only necessary graphics; use thumbnail versions rather than full-sized graphics; don't use large background graphics
Image and consistency	Use navigation elements, colors, and page layout styles consistently across your entire site
Legal protection	Place a copyright notice with the word "Copyright" and the copyright symbol (©), the date of first publication, and your company or organization's name on every page

In the next chapter, you'll learn how to validate your HTML files so they will be the best you can make them.

Validating HTML Documents

Quick Reference

Chapter 9
Validating Your HTML Documents

You have learned how to create well-designed Web pages. Now, you need to make sure that those pages can be properly interpreted and displayed by as many browsers out there as possible. There are several tools available on the Web and as stand-alone utilities to help you with this task.

When you're done working through this chapter, you will know

- How to use a Web-based validation tool
- How to use a stand-alone validation tool

VALIDATING HTML DOCUMENTS

You have developed your Web documents and are ready to add them to your Web server to make them available to the world—almost. But before you make them available to everyone, you should try to validate their code. It is easy to forget to close a tag with an end tag or to use an incorrect tag. Most browsers will attempt to produce what you wanted, but sometimes you may get totally unexpected results.

Several popular validation checkers are available on the Web. They check the syntax, links, and document structure of your pages; they verify that tags were used in the appropriate section, that tags requiring closure were closed, and other aspects of your code. Most validators can check only those pages already placed on a Web server or snippets of code you type or paste into a textarea. Examples of these validators include Weblint; Kinder, Gentler Validator (KGV); and WebTechs Validation Service (formerly known as HALSoft). Some validators, such as HTML PowerAnalyzer from Talicom, can check local documents. Other HTML tools validate the pages as you create them.

As new browsers become available, you want the code you are writing now to work on them as well as it does on those browsers currently available. To ensure this, make sure that you are using only the HTML specifications, since the browsers are written to make sure that they are correctly interpreted. This process is most easily accomplished by running your code through a validation checker.

Even if your code is valid, it does *not* mean that you have a well-designed page. However, it is a step in the right direction. Using only the HTML specifications means that you will have the greatest possibility of getting your documents to run and look good on new browsers as they are introduced.

WHAT IS CHECKED

Different validation tools check different sets of potential problems. Some check only a specific thing such as the links or the spelling. Others check a full range of problems. Common items that validation tools check for include:

- Document structure
- Unknown tags or attributes
- The context of tags (were they used in the proper section?)

- That required tags were included (such as the TITLE in the HEAD section)

- Mismatched tags (such as opening with <H1> and closing with </H6>)

- Unclosed tags and extra tags

- Proper nesting of elements

- That Hn tags are used in the proper order (1 through 6)

- Upper and lower case usage

You can usually select which version of HTML you want the tool to check against, and whether to include Netscape or Microsoft extensions.

DOCTYPE

Validation checkers need to know which version of HTML code you are using in your document. Some of the validators allow you to specify this through the use of a form with checkboxes and radio buttons. The <!DOCTYPE ...> tag allows you to include in your document information on which version of HTML code you are using. This tag must be the first statement in your document. The version is specified by referring to the DTD or Document Type Definition. The DTD comprises the *SGML* (Standard General Markup Language) rules for a set of mark-up codes used by a class or set of documents, also known as a Rules File. SGML is a platform-independent standard used to create documents and archive information that enables you to output those documents to various media including printers, CD-ROM and the Web. HTML is a subset of SGML. Examples have been compiled at

```
http://www.w3.org/pub/WWW/MarkUp/html-test/catalog
```

and

```
http://ugweb.cs.ualberta.ca/~gerald/validate/lib/catalog.
```

Some examples from these locations include:

If you do not use a DOCTYPE tag and there is no place on the form to specify the version of HTML to check against, the validation service will just assume that you are using HTML 2.0. This can cause perfectly good code to be marked as an error. On the other hand, it can be good to know that code you have written might not be able to be interpreted by browsers that only support version 2.0, the most commonly supported version today.

Table 5.1   Examples of DOCTYPE Statements

Version	Statement
HTML 0, 1, 2	<!DOCTYPE HTML PUBLIC "-//IEFT//DTD HTML 2.0 //EN">
HTML with Netscape extensions	<!DOCTYPE HTML PUBLIC "-//Netscape Comm. Corp.//DTD HTML//EN">
HTML 3.2	<!DOCTYPE HTML PUBLIC "-//W3C//DTD HTML 3.2 //EN">

VALIDATING LOCAL DOCUMENTS

One way to validate documents is to check them even before you add them to the Web server. Not all validators are capable of doing this, but some are.

An example of a local tool for checking local documents is the HTML Power-Tools from Talicom. It can check a file or a group of files on a local drive. This set of tools includes a validator (HTML PowerAnalyzer), a tool to locate mismatched or unclosed tags (HTML Tag Pair Fixer), and a document converter (HTML To Text Converter).

If you would like to try HTML PowerAnalyzer, you can download it from Talicom's Web site, located at http://www.tali.com. Here is how you can get a copy:

1. Connect to the **http://www.tali.com** site. At the bottom of the *Talicom's HTML PowerTools* Web page, click on **Download Evaluation copies**.

2. In the appropriate row of the table, click on **Download From FTP Site #**. The upper row of the table is for a Windows 95 version of the application (HTML32.ZIP); the bottom row is for the Windows 3.x version (HTML16.ZIP).

3. When the Unknown File Type dialog box appears, click on **Save File**, then choose a directory to download to, such as **C:\NETSCAPE\VALIDATE**. After the file has been downloaded, unzip the file with PKUNZIP version 2.04g, WinZip, or another program capable of extracting .ZIP files.

4. From the directory where you unzipped the downloaded file, run **SETUP.EXE**. Follow the installation instructions on the screen, accepting all defaults.

If you want to use the registered version, examine the page at http://www.tali.com/purchase.html for ordering information.

If you have HTML PowerTools installed on your computer, you can try the following steps.

1. Start **HTML PowerAnalyzer**. If you are using the evaluation version of the program, acknowledge the licensing messages which are displayed.

2. Click on **Select Project**, then click on **New**.

3. In the Project Name text box, type **My project**. In the Project Code text box, type **proj1**. The project code can be up to five characters and is prepended to any report files that are related to the project.

4. In the Project Location box, browse for the **HTMLWork** directory. In the Files To Include text box, type **VALIDA1.HTM**, then click on **OK**. If you wanted to include more files, you could have left the .HTM in the Files To Include field, then after defining the project, you could have excluded any files you didn't want to check.

5. Verify that **My project (PROJ1)** is selected, then click on **Select**.

6. Click on the **Analyze HTML** icon, then click on **Proceed**. Now HTML Power-Analyzer does its stuff and checks your code.

7. Click on **Launch Report Viewer** to examine the errors that were found in this document. (If you have the Windows 3.1 version of HTML Power Analyzer, click on **View File Results** instead of Launch Report Viewer.)

8. Close the HTML PowerAnalyzer program by clicking on **OK**, then on **Close**, then on **Exit**.

Another validation option is to find a gateway which accepts local documents. Some of these gateways allow you to type or paste in code from a local file to be checked. One example is the gateway at

```
http://www.tiac.net/users/zach1/htmlcheck/htmlcheck.shtml#
checkcode.
```

Other gateways enable you to specify the path to a local file to be checked. An example is EWS Gateway at

```
http://www.cen.uiuc.edu/cgi-bin/weblint/upload.
```

Let's try using one (or both) of these gateways to check a local document.

1. In Navigator, access one of the gateways listed above (or another gateway you have found).

2. Depending on the site you are using, specify the path to the **HTMLWork\ VALIDA1.HTM** file in the File textbox, or paste the contents of **VALIDA1 .HTM** into the textarea. If you are pasting the contents into a textarea, you can open **VALIDA1.HTM** in WordPad, choose **Edit, Select All**, then choose **Edit, Copy** to place the contents of the file on the clipboard. Switch to Navigator and use **CTRL+V** to paste it into the textarea.

3. Click on the **Submit** button. Your code will be passed through the validation program and checked.

4. View the errors. Depending on the site used and any options checked, you may get a different number of errors than from another validation site.

VALIDATING HTML DOCUMENTS ON A WEB SERVER

Most validation checkers require that your code reside on a Web server. Some of these validation tools are Perl scripts, others are SGML-based. Weblint is a Perl script. Kinder, Gentler Validator and WebTechs Validation Service are both SGML-based validators.

These tools are available through many sites on the Web. Most of these sites provide a form which you use to enter information about the document you want to validate. Weblint is also available as a command-line program on platforms that support Perl.

What Is Perl?

Perl stands for the Practical Extraction and Reporting Language. It runs across multiple operating system platforms so it is ideal for use in writing scripts for the Web. It is good at scanning text files, extracting information from the file, and then creating a report from that information. This makes it a good choice to use as the programming language to develop a tool which will scan your HTML file, extract information, and create a report listing errors it finds in your document.

Weblint

Weblint is a Perl script written by Neil Bowers. It checks the syntax and style of HTML documents. It is named after the lint program, included with most C compilers, which examines C programs for suspicious or unnecessary code. (The C lint program checks for type mismatches between arguments used to call a function and those expected; variables declared but never used; unused functions; and uninitialized variables. It also points out potential portability problems—

things that run fine in your current environment, but may cause problems in other environments.)

Natively, Weblint runs as a command line program in UNIX. It has also been ported to Windows NT, Macintosh, and OS/2 environments. Many sites have built gateways to make it easier to use. These gateways are forms that enable you to enter an URL to be checked so that you do not have to install Weblint locally. Some of these gateways allow you to specify which items you want Weblint to check for (you choose from among those it can check for).

WebTechs Validation Service (or HALsoft)

This is a CGI script that uses an SGML parser to check the code. (*Parsing* is the analysis of a statement to break it down into pieces that can be interpreted by the program.) The code in your document is checked against a DTD which either you or the gateway specify. The CGI program parses the file and checks your code against the DTD. If the code conforms to the DTD, it is valid; if it doesn't, then an error report is generated. The errors can be rather cryptic since the premise is to show that something is correct rather than to identify a specific type of problem.

The HTML extensions that it supports include HTML 3.2, Mozilla, SoftQuad, and Microsoft Internet Explorer. The document you want to check can reside on a Web server, or you can type or paste in the contents of a local file to be checked. WebTechs runs on many versions of UNIX. You can also include the code for validation in your Web site. You can access the gateway at http://www.webtechs.com/html-val-svc/.

Kinder, Gentler Validator

Kinder, Gentler Validator, or KGV, is very similar to WebTechs. It produces an error list that many users find easier to understand than the Weblint error listing. The KGV list includes explanations of the errors, and the output has arrows that point directly to the code in question.

It is best to try to run your code through a variety of checkers. Each checker looks at and accesses your code in different ways, so each might come up with a different set of errors. By running your code through each of the validators discussed here, you can be quite sure that your document will not totally crash any browser.

The Kinder Gentler Validator gateway can be found at http://ugweb.cs .ualberta.ca/~gerald/validate/.

Let's try validating a document located on a Web server. You say you haven't got a server with a document on it to try? Try someone else's document! Just about any document you can access can be run through a validation service.

1. Access one of the gateways listed above or one you have found on your own.

2. Type the URL of the document you are checking in the appropriate text box. (If you haven't thought of one yet, how about trying **http://www .microsoft.com** or **http://www.netscape.com**.)

3. Examine any options available. Make any selections you want.

4. Click on the **Submit** button to send the document off to be checked.

5. Check the error log. Any surprises? Some sites that are accessed by literally thousands of users every day, when run through a validator, still have lots of errors or potential errors.

6. Try checking the same site through another gateway. Compare the results of the two validators. Were they the same or different?

QUICK REFERENCE

In this chapter you learned how to validate your documents to make sure they are in compliance with HTML standards. This ensures your documents can be read and displayed properly by most browsers.

Here's a quick reference for the techniques you learned in this chapter:

Desired Result	How to Do It
Specify which version of HTML to check against	Use the *DOCTYPE* tag at the top of the document to specify the version of HTML to check against
Validate a local document	Use an application such as Talicom's *HTML PowerTools* or a validation gateway on the Web which accepts local documents
Validate a document residing on a Web server	Use a gateway such as *Weblint, WebTechs Validation Service*, or *Kinder, Gentler Validator*

In the next chapter, you'll learn how to add links in your HTML files that connect to non-Web services on the Internet (like e-mail, FTP, USENET News, and more).

Links to Non-Web Services
Quick Reference

Chapter 10

Adding Links to Other Internet Services

Until now, we've been treating the Web as if it were the Internet. In this chapter, you will learn about other programs that run on the Internet. You will also learn how to create links on your Web pages that connect to those programs.

When you're done working through this chapter, you will know

- Which services, in addition to the World Wide Web, are available on the Internet

- How to create links within your Web pages that connect to those services

LINKS TO NON-WEB SERVICES

To many, maybe including you, the Internet and the World Wide Web are synonymous. Sure, the Web is the flashiest *service*, or program, available on the Internet, but it isn't the only one. Table 10.1 lists some of the other services that you can access over the Internet.

Table 10.1 **Internet Services**

Service	Purpose
Electronic Mail (e-mail)	Electronic mail is the online version of the typical postal service mail we have all used. You can send mail to and receive mail from anyone with a computer and an Internet connection. E-mail is actually the most popular use of the Internet.
FTP	The File Transfer Protocol, and the program you use to access it, ftp, enable you to transfer files between computers on the Internet.
Gopher	The Gopher system organizes files on the Internet. Then, rather than looking for files based on their names, you can search through menus of descriptions of files. When you select a file by its description, you automatically download that file. Much of the functionality of the Web was based on Gopher.
Telnet	Telnet enables your computer to emulate a terminal attached to another computer on the Internet. Using telnet, you can run programs as if you were actually sitting at that other computer.
USENET News	USENET (the User Network) is a world-wide discussion-based system. You can discuss an enormous range of topics with users around the globe via USENET. Discussion areas are categorized and called *newsgroups*.
Chat	Chat is like a real-time version of USENET—you communicate with other users by typing. The communication occurs as you type (with any time delay caused by the speed of your Internet connections). Discussion areas are categorized and called *rooms*.

Except for Chat, your browser most likely contains all of the functionality you need to connect to any of those systems. Chat usually requires a special access program.

Let's see a Web page that has links to some of these other services:

1. If your browser is not currently running, start it now.

2. From the \HTMLWork directory, open the **others.htm** file.

3. Observe the Web page. This page contains links to non-Web Internet services.

4. Move your mouse pointer over each of the links and view your status bar. The locations to which the links point show up in the status bar as you point to those links. Notice that the link addresses to the different services starting with prefixes other than http://.

5. Click on the link to **Greenwich Mean Time** (GMT). This links points to a "file" on a Gopher server. Actually, this file is a specially generated file (generated by that computer system) containing the continuously up-dated time in Greenwich, England. GMT is the official time of scientists, weather forecasters, and more. You can calculate your local time from GMT. For example, subtract five hours from GMT to calculate Eastern Standard Time.

   Note: This works with Netscape Navigator 2.0 and Internet Explorer 2.0. It does not work with Netscape Navigator 2.02 or 3.0, or Internet Explorer 2.0.

6. Click on **Back** to return to the others.htm page.

7. You can leave your browser open. You will need it in the next section.

ADDING LINKS TO INTERNET SERVICES

Up to now, you have been including links to Web pages and Web servers in your HTML documents. That practice is going to pay off here. Adding links to those other Internet services is just like adding links to Web services.

As you read Table 10.2, which lists the tags you can use to add these links, compare their format with the ones you use to add a link to a Web server. For example, you would use <A HREF="http://web_address">link text </A> to add a link to a Web address.

Did you notice that they all follow the same form and that the form matches the link format you use with Web addresses? Each starts with the *<A HREF="* part. This tells your browser to start creating a link. Then, each includes the name of the service (like *http://* or *ftp://*, though notice that *mailto:* doesn't

Table 10.2 **Link Format for Internet Services**

Opening Tag	Closing Tag	Why You Would Use This Tag
`<A HREF="ftp://`*`ftp_address`*`">`	`</A>`	To add a link to the primary directory of an ftp server

`<A HREF=`
`"ftp://ftp_address/path/`
`filename">`
	`</A>`	To add a link to a specific file, in the directory and on the server that you specify

`<A HREF=` `"gopher://gopher_address">`	`</A>`	To add a link to a Gopher server's address
`<A HREF=` `"mailto:`*`email_address`*`">`	`</A>`	To add an e-mail link that when clicked on will open your browser's e-mail window or your e-mail application (with the To address already filled in)

`<A HREF=`
`"news://news_server/`
`news_group">`
	`</A>`	To add a link to a particular newsgroup on the server you specify

include the double-slashes "//") followed by an address. Finally, each closing tag ends with ">. Then, you put whatever text you want to be highlighted as your link and finish with the </A> closing tag. That should be easy; let's do it!

1. Open **WordPad** or whatever editor you have been using to edit your HTML documents.

2. Open the **default.htm** file that you have been working with throughout this book.

3. Add the following lines right before the copyright statement section of your HTML file:

   ```
   <!-- A link to my own email address -->
   This file created by <A
   HREF= mailto:your_email_address >enter your name here</A>.
   ```

   If you don't have an e-mail address, you can use a fake address to see how this works. Use *fake@company.com*, for example.

4. Save your file and switch to your browser (if it's not running, start it now).

5. If the default.htm file is currently loaded, click on **Reload** so that you can view your recent changes. If it's not the currently loaded file, open **default.htm**.

6. Observe your new link; it looks like any other on this page. Put your mouse pointer over it and observe the status bar. Now you can see the difference; this link points to your e-mail address.

7. Click on your **mailto** link. The mail window of your browser should open.

8. If a mail window doesn't appear, your browser probably doesn't have built-in mail capabilities. You won't be able to finish this exercise, so skip ahead instead.

9. Enter a short message to yourself and then click on **Send** (or whatever you must do to actually send the message). After a while, that message should appear in your e-mail program's inbox. You don't have to wait for that to continue, though.

10. Close the mail window, if necessary. Congratulations! You successfully created a link to an Internet service other than the Web.

PRACTICE YOUR SKILLS

Let's try another one. This time, you'll create a link that points to one of the copyright FAQ documents that you learned about in Chapter 8. You'll make this link part of your copyright statement. That way, if someone reads your copyright statement and wants more information on what copyrights are, they can click on the link and read the FAQ.

1. Switch to your editor and, if necessary, open the **default.htm** file.

2. Change the copyright statement so that it includes the following link. Make the word "copyright" and the copyright symbol show up in the Web document highlighted as the link.

   ```
   <A HREF="ftp://rtfm.mit.edu/pub/usenet/news.answers/
   law/copyright/faq/part1">
   ```

3. Save your changes and view the document in your browser (don't forget to reload).

4. Click on your **ftp** link. Did it work? If not, compare it to this sample line, then correct your file and try again.

   ```
   <FONT SIZE=-1> <A
   ```

```
HREF="ftp://rtfm.mit.edu/pub/usenet/news.answers/law/
copyright/faq/part1">copyright &copy; </A> 1996 by
Jetaway Travel, Inc.</FONT>
```

5. If you will be continuing on with this book, you can leave your browser open. Otherwise, close it now.

QUICK REFERENCE

In this chapter, you learned about other services on the Internet. You now know how to create links within your Web pages to those other services.

Here's a quick reference for the techniques you learned in this chapter:

To Add a Link to Each of These Services ...	... Use This as the Opening Tag in Your HTML File:
FTP	<A HREF="ftp://*ftp_address*">
Gopher	<A HREF="gopher://*gopher_address*">
E-mail	<A HREF="mailto:*email_address*">
USENET News	<A HREF="news://*newsserver_address/ newsgroup_name*">

In the next chapter, you'll learn how to create forms that enable two-way communication between you and the users of your Web pages.

Chapter 11

Creating Forms with HTML

By now, you can create well-designed and feature-rich Web pages that publish information to visitors to your Web site. The next step in this book is for you to learn how to solicit input and involvement from those visitors, thereby making your pages interactive. Forms are the tool that enable you to create this interactivity.

When you're done working through this chapter, you will know

- How Web forms, and the mechanisms that support them, work
- How to create forms by entering HTML tags

INTRODUCTION TO FORMS

You probably have encountered forms in your journeys across the Web. Companies often use forms to gather information about users, like yourself, who download software. You might also have encountered surveys, subscription forms, and system log-on pages that use forms. Forms provide a means for Web page designers like you to open a two-way communication channel across the Web.

Consider the form as shown in Figure 11.1. You will notice that the form contains some locations for users to enter data. These are called *fields*. In two of the fields, users must type in the appropriate data; in one, they must choose from a drop-down list box; in the last set of fields, they must choose between one of two choices with a radio button. Finally, the form provides two buttons. When they click on the Submit button, users send the data to you. If they make a mistake, they can click on Reset to clear the data they have entered without sending any data to you.

FORM ELEMENTS

The figure above illustrated a few of the types of fields that you can use in your forms. Table 11.1 lists all of the fields (and the two buttons) that you can create in your forms.

Table 11.1 **Form Elements and Their Appearance**

Field Type	Description	Appearance in Netscape 2.0 for Windows 95
Text Box	Creates a single line text box for users to enter single lines of data.	`user data`
Text Area	Creates a scrollable text box for users to enter multiple lines of data.	

Table 11.1   **Form Elements and Their Appearance (Continued)**

Radio Button	Creates a radio button. This is useful when only one valid choice is available from a set of possible choices.	Checked ⊙ Unchecked ○
Check Box	Creates a check box. This is useful when more than one valid choice is available from a set of possible choices.	Checked ☑ Unchecked ☐
Select List	Creates a drop down list box from which users can select the data of their choice.	Choice 1 ▼
Password Box	Creates a single line text box. However, when users type in data, that data does not appear on their screens.	*********
Submit Button	Creates a Submit button. When users click on this button, the information they have entered into the form is sent to your server.	Submit
Reset Button	Creates a Reset button. When users click on this button, the data they have entered into the form is cleared. No data is sent to you.	Reset

Let's see a sample Web page that contains a form.

1. If your browser is not currently running, start it now.

2. From the \HTMLWork directory, open the **jwayform.htm** file.

3. Observe the Web page; it should match Figure 11.1 closely. This page contains a form. Can you identify the text box, select list, and radio button fields in this form? (Use the table above if you need help identifying these features.)

Figure 11.1
A sample Web page with a form

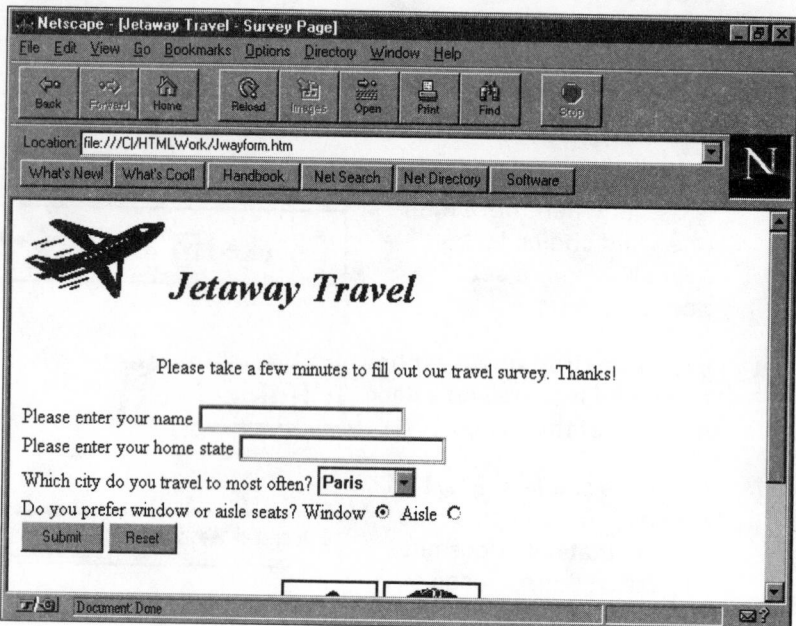

Let's examine the code that creates this from. This will help you see how a form is built using HTML tags.

1. Start by choosing **View, Document Source** to view the HTML tags that created this document (see Figure 11.2).

2. Briefly observe the code that created this page. Don't be overwhelmed. We'll go slowly. Start by noticing that this page contains <HTML> and <BODY> tags just like those you have been using throughout this book.

3. Now let's look at the part of the code that creates the form (see Figure 11.3). Scroll down, if necessary, to view the code containing the line that begins with <FORM ACTION=. This code begins the form. Now, look down in the code some more and you will find a closing version of that tag, a </FORM> tag. Forms, just like many other HTML elements, are built with an opening and closing tag. For now, let's skip the rest of the parameters in the opening form tag. We'll come back to those in a few moments.

4. If necessary, scroll back up to find the line that begins with "Please enter your name." Text that will prompt users to enter data is just normal text in your HTML file. However, notice the tag that follows: it begins with <INPUT TYPE= and contains a number of parameters. This is a form tag.

Figure 11.2
The source code for jwayform.htm

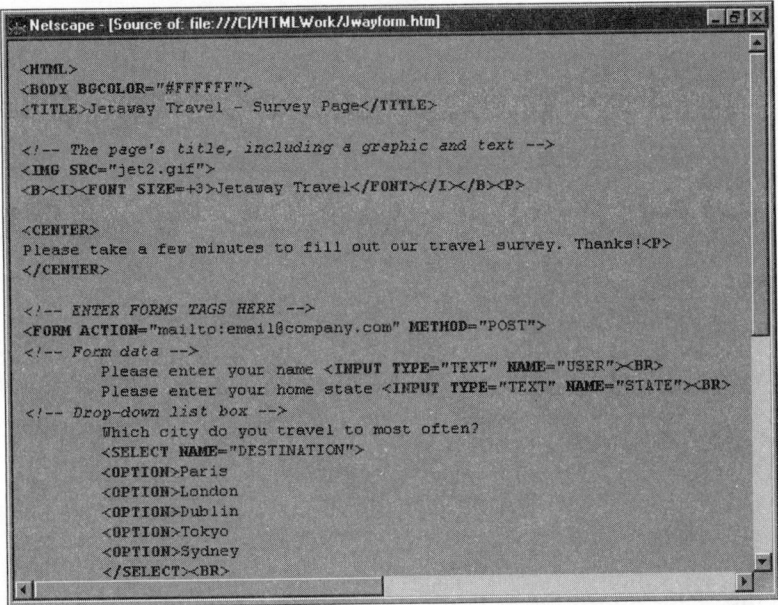

Figure 11.3
Viewing the Form code

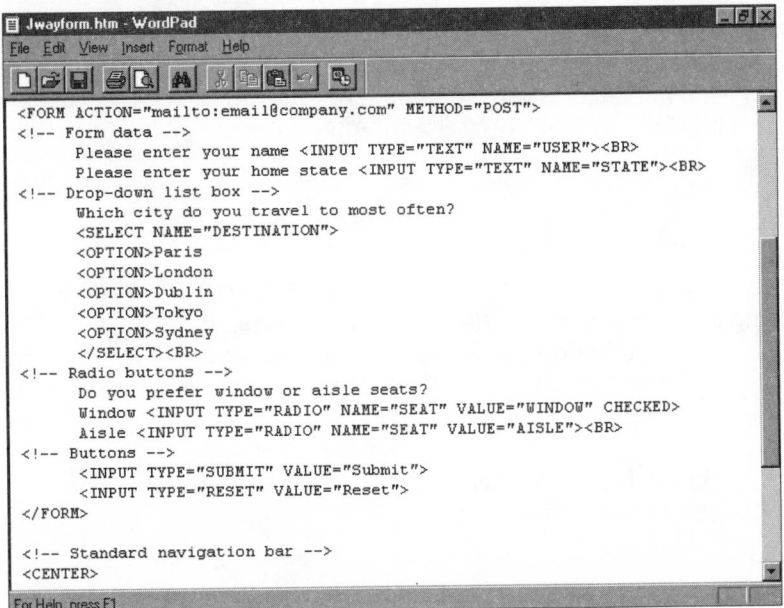

It and the others like it create text boxes, radio buttons, and more. In fact, observe the INPUT tag that contains the parameter TYPE="SUBMIT"— this is the tag that creates the submit button.

5. Close the source code window, but leave your browser running. Here's what the page looks like in real life:

> Please take a few minutes to fill out our travel survey. Thanks!
>
> Please enter your name [   ]
> Please enter your home state [   ]
> [Submit] [Reset]

Now that you have seen a form and the tags used to create it, let's create a form.

1. Open **WordPad** or your text editor.

2. Open the file **XSURVEY.HTM**. This is a partially completed HTML file. It contains all the tags that aren't involved with creating the form.

3. Add these lines after the line that contains "<!--ENTER FORM TAGS HERE -->" (make sure to substitute your e-mail address where indicated).

```
<FORM ACTION="mailto:your_email_address" METHOD="POST">
<!-- Form data -->
     Please enter your name <INPUT TYPE="TEXT"
NAME="USER"><BR>
<!-- Buttons -->
     <INPUT TYPE="SUBMIT" VALUE="Submit">
     <INPUT TYPE="RESET" VALUE="Reset">
</FORM>
```

4. Now, save the file with the name **SURVEY.HTM**.

5. Switch to your browser and load the **SURVEY.HTM** file. You should be looking at a form with one field and two buttons. If not, check your HTML code against the listing above, save, and reload the file in your browser.

6. Let's use this form. Enter your name in the field asking for your name.

7. Click on **Reset**. Poof! The data is gone. The reset button clears the form without sending the data anywhere.

PRACTICE YOUR SKILLS

For a little practice, add a field to your form. Then, you can enter some data and submit that data.

1. Switch to your editor. Add this line immediately following the line that creates the name text box.

   ```
   Please enter your home state <INPUT TYPE="TEXT"
   NAME="STATE"><BR>
   ```

2. Save your changes.

3. Switch to your browser and reload the page. You should see your new field on the form.

4. Enter your name and state into the appropriate fields.

5. Click on **Submit**. Poof! Your data is gone (again?). Actually, this time your data has been packaged up by your browser and sent off to the address that you specified in your HTML code. In this case, you specified that the data be sent to your e-mail address. Depending on the speed of your Internet services and the speed of the Internet in general, your data will arrive in your inbox in a few or maybe many minutes from now. You don't have to wait for it to arrive in order to continue.

A lot was happening in the HTML code that you used in your form. Let's take a closer look at that code.

1. View the source code for the document (choose **View, Document Source** in Netscape).

2. Observe the line that begins the form. It looks like this:

   ```
   <FORM ACTION="mailto:your_email_address" METHOD="POST">
   ```

   The first part is the tag name, FORM. This tag begins your form and has two parameters. The first, the ACTION parameter, tells your browser what to do with the data of the form when you click on the submit button. In this case, your browser is to e-mail the data to your e-mail address. The second, the METHOD parameter, controls how that data is sent to you. We'll cover METHOD later. So, we'll skip over it for now.

3. Observe the next important line in the HTML code (we're skipping over the comment line). It looks like this:

```
Please enter your name <INPUT TYPE="TEXT" NAME="USER"><BR>
```

The first part is just text that will show up in the browser window. The INPUT tag is responsible for creating the text box that follows the text. We know that this INPUT tag will create a text box because of the TYPE parameter. It says that the TYPE="TEXT" or "this input type should be a text box." Finally, the field is assigned a name (USER) so that when the data arrives, you can tell what the data pertains to. For example, if you received FIELD1="ROSE" from your form, would you know immediately whether this field pertained to the user's name or their favorite flower? Instead, by using a field name like NAME="FIRSTNAME" your data will be clearly formatted.

4. The next line just creates another text box. So, let's skip to the last two INPUT tags. These create the buttons on the form.

5. By specifying TYPE="SUBMIT" in your code, you inform the browser to place a Submit button on the form. While in our example, the button actually showed up on your screen with the word "Submit" on it, you can change the appearance of the button. That's what the VALUE parameter is for. Any text you enter for the VALUE is displayed on the button. What this means is that the parameter TYPE=SUBMIT designates what happens when a user clicks on the button rather than how that button is displayed. In the same manner, the next line of your code created the reset button.

6. Observe the next line, </FORM>. This is the form closing tag that ends the form.

7. Close the source code window.

Now that you've used a few of the form tags, let's discuss how they all work. What follows is a list of the forms tags and many of their parameters. In each of these, text in italics is just a placeholder. When you really use these tags, you'll have to replace that text with your real information.

```
<FORM ACTION="URL" METHOD="method"> </FORM>
```

This tag creates the form and sets parameters for the whole form. All of the tags that you enter to create your form must be between the opening and closing FORM tags. The opening tag requires two important parameters: ACTION and METHOD. In the ACTION field, you enter the URL (address) of the site to which users' data will be sent when they click on Submit. Generally, this address points to a special program, called your *CGI script* running on a Web server. (We'll introduce CGI scripts at the end of this chapter.) The METHOD parameter specifies how that data is packaged for the trip to your server. A section below covers this parameter in greater detail. But for now, you have two options, POST and GET, for this parameter. You will probably use POST exclusively.

```
<INPUT TYPE="type" NAME="name" VALUE="value" CHECKED
SIZE="#">
```

The INPUT tag is the form tag you will use most often. For with it, you can create many types of form fields. You specify which type of field to create by entering a code word in place of the *"type"*, for example: TYPE="radio". The value you enter for the NAME field will be included when the data of the form is sent to you. This will help you identify whether some data like "Rose" was from the part of your form asking a user for their name or their favorite flower. Some of the INPUT types accept an initial value. For example, in a text box, you could have an initial value, which appears in the form on a user's browser screen. Other INPUT types are checked or unchecked (such as radio buttons and check boxes). You can specify which field is checked by default with the optional CHECKED parameter. Finally, you can set the size in numbers of characters of two of the INPUT types, TEXT and PASSWORD. Table 11.2 describes the valid INPUT types that you can create.

Table 11.2   Valid Types for the INPUT Tag

Input Type	Description
TEXT	Creates a single-line text box. This type accepts the optional SIZE parameter.
CHECKBOX	Creates a checkbox. This type accepts the optional CHECKED parameter.
RADIO	Creates a radio button. This type accepts the optional CHECKED parameter.
PASSWORD	Creates a single-line text box that does not display back to the user the data they enter. This type accepts the optional SIZE parameter.
SUBMIT	Creates a Submit button. Any value you enter for the VALUE parameter is displayed on the button (by default, the word "Submit" is displayed).
RESET	Creates a Reset button. Any value you enter for the VALUE parameter is displayed on the button (by default, the word "Reset" is displayed).

```
<SELECT NAME="name"></SELECT>
```

Use this tag with the <OPTION> tag listed next to create a drop-down list box. Users choose from the options in your list. The open and close SELECT tags enclose the tags that create the elements of your drop-down list box.

```
<OPTION VALUE="value" SELECTED>option_text
```

Use this tag to create the elements of your drop-down list box. For each item that you wish to appear in your list box, enter an OPTION tag between the opening and closing SELECT tags. The text you enter after the OPTION tag (shown in the example line above as *option_text*) is the text that will be displayed to users of your form. That will be the data that will be sent to you when users click on Submit. However, you can override this action by specifying a VALUE. You might use this to transmit a code number rather than the full text of an option. Finally, you can specify that one option of the list be the default (be shown when the list hasn't been dropped down) with the optional SELECTED tag.

Note: This tag doesn't have a closing tag—it is automatically closed by the next OPTION tag or the </SELECT> closing tag.

```
<TEXTAREA NAME="name" ROWS="#" COLS="#"></TEXTAREA>
```

You can use this tag to create a scrollable, multiple-line text box into which users can enter text. You can specify the number of rows and columns that will appear on your form with the ROWS and COLS parameters, respectively. These parameters don't limit the amount of data that a user can enter. They simply limit how much area will be displayed on a user's screen.

Now that you know all about the form tags, you can add some additional fields to your form. In this next exercise you will add a drop-down list box to your form. Figure 11.4 shows how the HTML code will appear when you are finished with this exercise.

1. If necessary, open **WordPad** or your text editor and open the **SURVEY.HTM** file.

2. Add these lines between the line that creates the second text box (for the state) and the comment before the buttons. (Check Figure 11.4 if you're unsure of where to enter this HTML code.)

```
<!-- Drop-down list box -->
    Which city do you travel to most often?
    <SELECT NAME="DESTINATION">
    <OPTION>Paris
    <OPTION>London
    <OPTION>Dublin
    <OPTION>Tokyo
    <OPTION>Sydney
    </SELECT><BR>
```

Figure 11.4
The HTML code to create a form with a drop-down list box

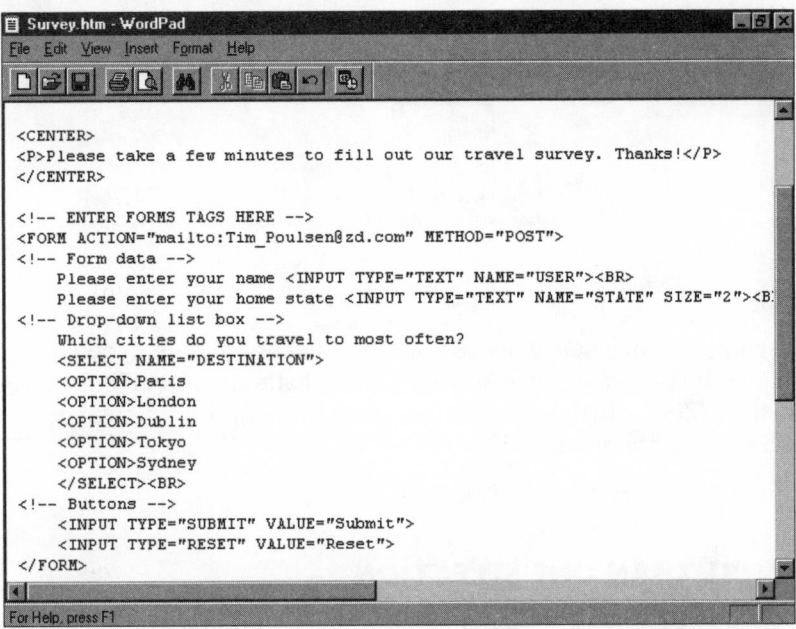

```
<CENTER>
<P>Please take a few minutes to fill out our travel survey. Thanks!</P>
</CENTER>

<!-- ENTER FORMS TAGS HERE -->
<FORM ACTION="mailto:Tim_Poulsen@zd.com" METHOD="POST">
<!-- Form data -->
    Please enter your name <INPUT TYPE="TEXT" NAME="USER"><BR>
    Please enter your home state <INPUT TYPE="TEXT" NAME="STATE" SIZE="2"><B
<!-- Drop-down list box -->
    Which cities do you travel to most often?
    <SELECT NAME="DESTINATION">
    <OPTION>Paris
    <OPTION>London
    <OPTION>Dublin
    <OPTION>Tokyo
    <OPTION>Sydney
    </SELECT><BR>
<!-- Buttons -->
    <INPUT TYPE="SUBMIT" VALUE="Submit">
    <INPUT TYPE="RESET" VALUE="Reset">
</FORM>
```

The <SELECT NAME="DESTINATION"> tag begins the drop-down list box. Each of the lines that start with <OPTION> become the entries in your list. Finally, the whole set of tags is closed with the </SELECT> tag.

3. Save the file.

4. Switch to your browser and re-load the **SURVEY.HTM** file. Your updated form should include the drop-down list box.

5. Enter your name and state.

6. Drop down the list box to observe the choices. The choices you entered in the code above should all appear in the drop-down list. Select one of the cities.

7. Click on **Submit**. This data will be e-mailed to you just like the earlier data.

> Please take a few minutes to fill out our travel survey. Thanks!
>
> Please enter your name [   ]
> Please enter your home state [   ]
> Which cities do you travel to most often? [Paris   ▼]
> [Submit] [Reset]
> **Paris**
> **London**
> **Dublin**
> **Tokyo**
> **Sydney**

LIST BOX SIZE

To make choices more easily accessible to the users of your Web site, you can display several choices at once by making the list box larger. To accomplish this, use the SIZE=*n* attribute, where *n* equals the number of selections you want to display in the list box. The syntax is:

```
<SELECT NAME="name" SIZE=n>
```

CHOOSING MORE THAN ONE SELECTION

By default, users can only make one selection from items in a list box. Use the MULTIPLE attribute with the <SELECT> tag to enable users to select more than one item at a time. The syntax is:

```
<SELECT MULTIPLE NAME="name">
```

To make multiple selections from items in a list box, you can click on the first item of your choice; then, while pressing the Ctrl key, click on another selection. Both items are then selected. To select all of the items in a list box, click on the first item; then, while pressing the Shift key, click on the last item in the box. All of the items between the first and last items are selected.

Let's modify the drop-down list you just created to use these two attributes.

1. In your text editor, change the <SELECT NAME="DESTINATION"> to <SELECT NAME="DESTINATION" **MULTIPLE SIZE=2**>. This allows users to select multiple cities. The list box will display two cities at a time.

2. Change the word city to **cities** in the line above the SELECT tag. Since you are allowing users to select multiple list box choices, this needs to change as well.

3. Save and view the file.

Please take a few minutes to fill out our travel survey. Thanks!

Please enter your name ⌷Sue Reber⌷
Please enter your home state ⌷New York⌷
                                          ⌷Paris   ⌷▲
Which cities do you travel to most often? ⌷London⌷▼
⌷ Submit ⌷ ⌷ Reset ⌷

---

4. Select **Paris**. While holding down the **Ctrl** key, select **London** and **Dublin**. If you wanted, you could select all of the cities using standard Windows selection techniques using **Shift** or **Ctrl** while clicking the mouse.

5. Click on Reset to clear the data from the form. If the fields do not clear, just reopen the file for a fresh start.

DEFAULT SELECTIONS

To specify an item in a list box as the default selection, use the SELECTED attribute with the <OPTION> tag. When you use this attribute, the corresponding item is already highlighted when you load the Web page. The syntax is:

```
<OPTION SELECTED VALUE="value">description
```

Let's make one of the cities the default in our list.

1. In your text editor, change <OPTION>London to <OPTION **SELECTED VALUE="London"**>London. If you wanted, the value could have been a code such as LON or City2.

2. Save and view the file.

3. Examine the cities list box. Is London already selected? If so, good! If not, try reopening survey.htm. If it still isn't, check your code against that in step 1 and make sure you reloaded the page.

In the next exercise, you will add two radio buttons. As you probably know from working with other programs, you can only select one radio button at a time. If you click on one radio button of a set, the others are deselected. Radio buttons are useful when you want users to choose from a set of mutually exclusive choices. (In other words, when you want people to make a choice be-tween the options.)

1. If necessary, open **WordPad** or your text editor and open the **SUR-VEY.HTM** file.

2. Add these lines after the line containing </SELECT>
.

```
<!-- Radio buttons -->
    Do you prefer window or aisle seats?
    Window <INPUT TYPE="RADIO" NAME="SEAT" VALUE="WINDOW"
CHECKED>
    Aisle <INPUT TYPE="RADIO" NAME="SEAT"
VALUE="AISLE"><BR>
```

Here, the INPUT tags create the radio buttons. The NAME parameters de-fine the data that will be sent to you. They also define which radio but-tons on your form comprise the same set. (You can have more than one set of radio buttons on a form. Clicking on a button in one set doesn't af-fect the buttons in other sets.) The VALUE parameter is the data that will be sent to you when users check that radio button. Finally, when users first load your form, the window radio button will be checked because of the CHECKED parameter.

3. Save the file.

4. Switch to your browser and re-load the **SURVEY.HTM** file. Your updated form, with a pair of radio buttons, should be displayed. If both buttons come up checked, reopen the file to fix this bug.

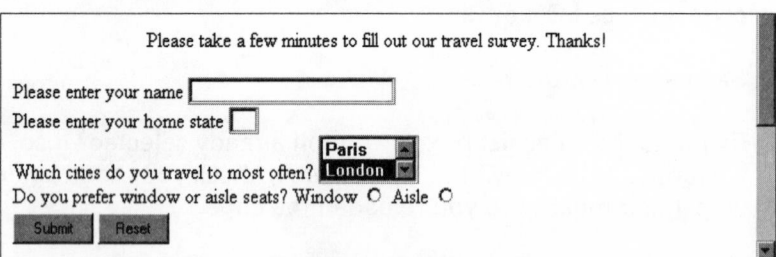

5. Enter your name and state. Choose a city from the drop-down list box.

6. The window radio button is already selected (your code specified that). Click on the **aisle** radio button: It becomes selected and the window radio button is deselected. Choose your actual preference for seating.

7. Click on **Submit**. This data will be e-mailed to you just like the earlier data.

CGI, POST, AND GET

Well, we have been putting this off, but let's cover the METHOD part of the opening FORM tag. Also, we'll discuss the Common Gateway Interface (CGI). Both are very important if you plan to use forms for more than a few casual applications.

Up to now, we have been using METHOD="POST" without explaining much of what's going on. Actually, when you or a user clicks on a submit button, your browser can compile the form data in one of two ways before sending. The method an HTML programmer like you chooses is based on what's going to be done with the data when it reaches its destination. You have two choices, POST and GET, which are described in Table 11.3.

Table 11.3   Form Methods

Method	Definition and Purpose
POST	When you use this method, a browser compiles form data in such a way that it can be simply recorded on your server such as in a log file. This method is commonly used for sign-in lists, surveys, on-line order entry, and so forth.
GET	When you use this method, the browser compiles the data in such a way that your server can read the data, interpret it, and return information to the user based on their choices. For example, if you had a form that let users access records from a database based on entries they provided in a form, you would use the GET method when defining your form.

You will probably use the POST method far more often that the GET method.

Once the data gets to your server, you will probably want to do something with it. In our examples, the data was mailed to you so you have limited options. Probably all you could do with it is to cut and paste that data into a log file and use some other application to analyze or manipulate the data. Powerful forms applications operate on the data more directly. In those situations, Web programmers write CGI programs to process the data they receive from their forms.

CGI isn't a programming language. It is actually a programming standard that defines how programs communicate with each other and with a Web server. A CGI-compliant program is generally called a *script*. When data from a form is sent to your script, your Web server receives the data, starts a copy of your CGI script, and gives it the data just received. What your script does with that data is up to you (or the programmer you hire to write the CGI script for you).

You can use just about any programming language to create a CGI script, such as C or C++. The most popular language used to create CGI scripts is the PERL programming language popular on UNIX computers.

CGI scripts must be installed on your Web server according to your Web server's documentation. You will need administrator-level access to the server to perform this step. If you are not the server administrator, for example, if your Web access is through a service provider, you will need to contact the server's administrator to get your script installed.

CGI scripting can be quite complex and you have many choices of which programming language to use to create your scripts. CGI scripting is well-beyond the scope of this book. There are many CGI references available, however.

PRACTICE YOUR SKILLS

Let's create a link from the Jetaway Travel home page to your survey page so that users can find and complete your survey.

1. In your text editor open the **DEFAULT.HTM** file.

2. Add these lines immediately before the lines that create your unordered list.

```
<!-- Link to survey -->
    <CENTER>
    <P>Please fill out our <A
HREF="survey.htm">survey</A>.<P>
    </CENTER>
```

3. Save and view the file. Your new link to the survey page should now be part of the Jetaway Travel home page as shown in Figure 11.5.

4. Click on **survey** to go to the survey page. Here's your page with the form.

5. Click on the **home graphic** to return to the home page.

Figure 11.5
The Jetaway Travel home page with link to Survey form

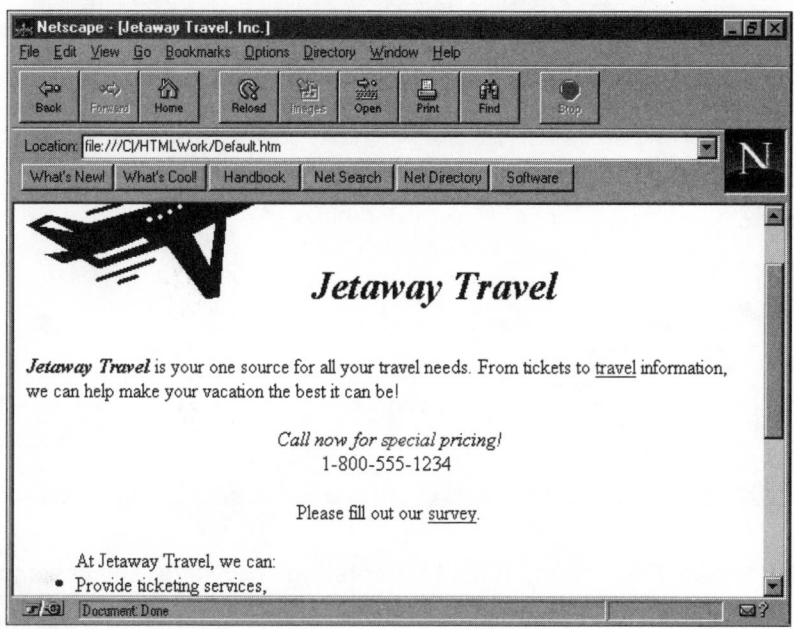

SETTING INPUT TYPE ATTRIBUTES

Input type attributes are available to further customize input fields. You can control the display size of an input field as well as the maximum number of characters users can enter into a field.

DISPLAY SIZE

The default display size of a text or password input field is 20 characters (although this is not the maximum number of characters you can enter into an input field). To change this setting, use the SIZE="*n*" attribute, where *n* stands for the size of the field in number of characters displayed.

Let's try specifying the display size of a field.

1. In your text editor open **Survey.htm** and find the input field for entering your state:

```
<HTML>
<TITLE>Jetaway Travel - Survey Page</TITLE>

<BODY BGCOLOR="#FFFFFF">

<!-- The page's title, including a graphic and text -->
<P><IMG SRC="jet2.gif"><FONT SIZE=+3><B><I>Jetaway Travel</I></B></FONT></P>

<CENTER>
<P>Please take a few minutes to fill out our travel survey. Thanks!</P>
</CENTER>

<!-- ENTER FORMS TAGS HERE -->
<FORM ACTION="mailto:Tim_Poulsen@zd.com" METHOD="POST">
<!-- Form data -->
    Please enter your name <INPUT TYPE="TEXT" NAME="USER"><BR>
    Please enter your home state <INPUT TYPE="TEXT" NAME="STATE"><BR>
<!-- Drop-down list box -->
    Which cities do you travel to most often?
    <SELECT NAME="DESTINATION" MULTIPLE SIZE=2>
    <OPTION>Paris
    <OPTION SELECTED VALUE="London">London
    <OPTION>Dublin
```

2. Add SIZE="2" to the input field for entering your state. The line should now read <INPUT TYPE="TEXT" NAME="STATE" **SIZE="2"**>.

3. Save and view the file.

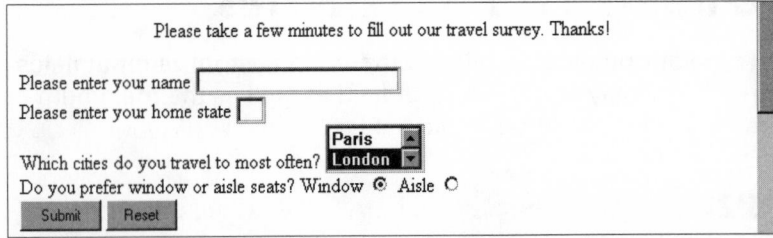

4. In the State field, type **Minn**. Were you able to type all four letters? You should have been able to; the field scrolls to allow you to enter as many characters as you want.

5. Click on the **Reset** button to clear the information from the field.

MAXIMUM NUMBER OF CHARACTERS

The default setting for the number of characters you can enter into a text or password field is unlimited. To change this setting, use the MAXLENGTH="*n*" attribute, where *n* equals the maximum number of characters you can enter into a field. This setting is helpful to avoid having individuals enter too much information into a field where only a small amount of information is required. Once a form is submitted to the author of the page, the information is usually entered into a database or processed in some other way. Receiving too much information where only a little information is expected can cause problems with a database, result in the loss of information, or cause the information to be processed incorrectly.

Let's try setting the state field to only allow two characters.

1. In your text editor, add **MAXLENGTH="2"** to the state input field. The entire line should now read <INPUT TYPE="TEXT" NAME="STATE" SIZE="2" MAXLENGTH="2">.

2. Save and view the file.

3. In the state field, type **Minn**. What happened? After you have entered two characters, the field no longer scrolls and you cannot enter the rest of the information. A beep might sound to alert you to the end of the field.

4. Click on the **Reset** button to clear the information from the field.

ALIGNING INPUT FIELDS

To add visual appeal to your form, you might want to align the input fields. HTML provides two methods of doing this.

The first method to align input fields is to use the <PRE> and </PRE> tags. Text between those tags is displayed exactly as it is typed in your text editor. You can use tabs to align the <INPUT TYPE=...> tags on the screen in the text editor. When you view the document in Navigator, the resulting fields are aligned. Text inside of the <PRE> and </PRE> tags is displayed in a fixed-width font.

The second method to align input fields is to use the <TABLE> and </TABLE> tags. With this method, you create a table that contains table rows and table cells but not table borders. Each prompt for information and each input field is contained in its own table cell and is therefore aligned. Because the table does not have borders, the text and fields are displayed as being aligned, but it is not obvious that the information is in a table.

Text within the <TABLE> and </TABLE> tags will be displayed in the default font. The displayed result of this method of aligning input fields is more visually appealing than that achieved by using the <PRE> and </PRE> tags.

Let's examine a document which uses a table to align fields.

1. In Navigator, open **JWFORM.HTM**.

2. Examine the personal information section of the form, as shown in Figure 11.6. All of the fields are aligned.

Figure 11.6
Aligning fields in the Jetaway Travel Customer Application Form

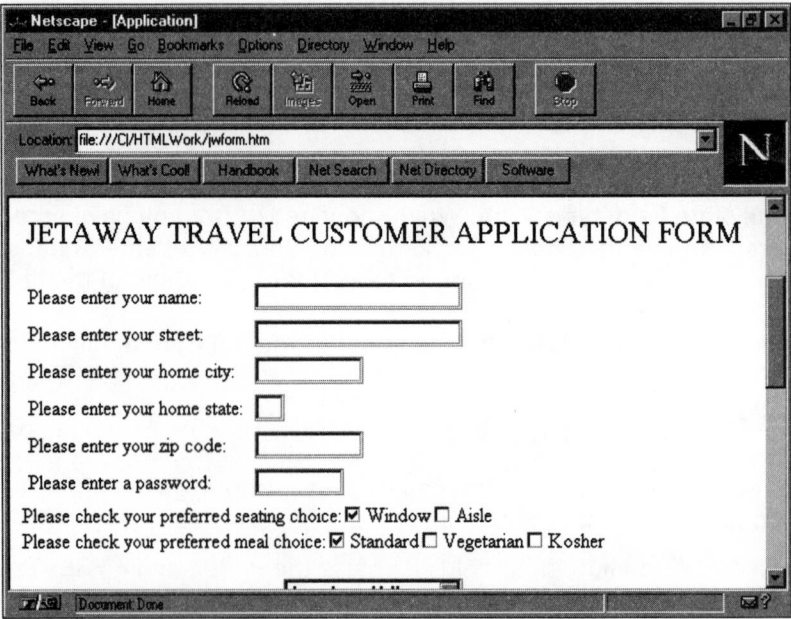

3. View the document source to see how the table tags were used to achieve this alignment of text and input fields, as shown in Figure 11.7. The textual information is in the left column of the table, and the input field is in the right column of the table.

4. Close the document source window.

Figure 11.7
The Document Source for Jwform.htm

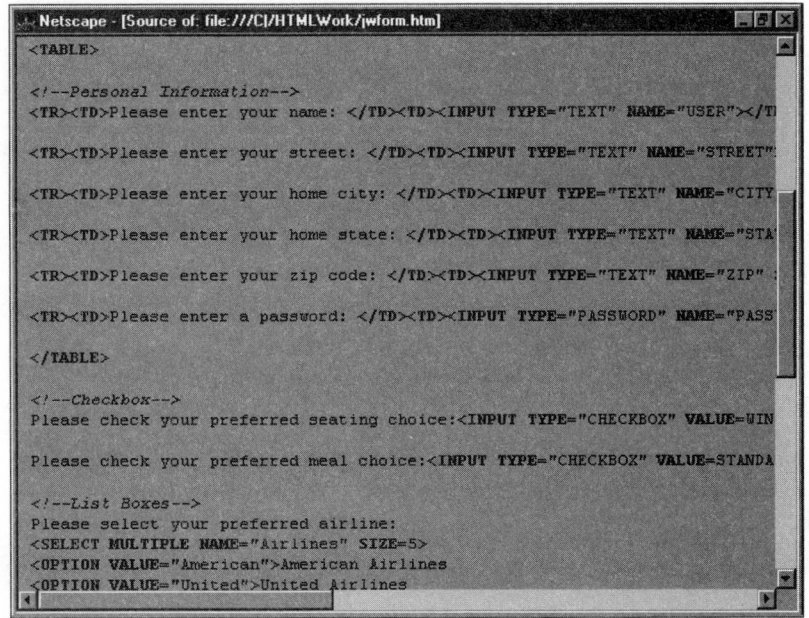

```
Netscape - [Source of: file:///C|/HTMLWork/jwform.htm]
<TABLE>

<!--Personal Information-->
<TR><TD>Please enter your name: </TD><TD><INPUT TYPE="TEXT" NAME="USER"></TD

<TR><TD>Please enter your street: </TD><TD><INPUT TYPE="TEXT" NAME="STREET"

<TR><TD>Please enter your home city: </TD><TD><INPUT TYPE="TEXT" NAME="CITY"

<TR><TD>Please enter your home state: </TD><TD><INPUT TYPE="TEXT" NAME="STA

<TR><TD>Please enter your zip code: </TD><TD><INPUT TYPE="TEXT" NAME="ZIP"

<TR><TD>Please enter a password: </TD><TD><INPUT TYPE="PASSWORD" NAME="PASS

</TABLE>

<!--Checkbox-->
Please check your preferred seating choice:<INPUT TYPE="CHECKBOX" VALUE=WIN

Please check your preferred meal choice:<INPUT TYPE="CHECKBOX" VALUE=STANDA

<!--List Boxes-->
Please select your preferred airline:
<SELECT MULTIPLE NAME="Airlines" SIZE=5>
<OPTION VALUE="American">American Airlines
<OPTION VALUE="United">United Airlines
```

CREATING A TEXTAREA

Text is comprised of characters displayed on a screen. In a Web page, text is created by the author of the page and is displayed for others to view. You might, however, also want to encourage feedback or ask for lengthier information from the individuals who visit your site. To receive this feedback or information, you need to provide an area for lengthier input.

Use the <TEXTAREA> and </TEXTAREA> tags for this purpose. The syntax is:

```
<TEXTAREA ROWS=n COLS=n NAME="name"></TEXTAREA>
```

The ROWS=n attribute defines the number of rows that will be displayed. The COLS=n attribute defines the number of columns that will be displayed. One column equals one character. The number of lines of text that you can enter into the textarea is infinite. The COLS and ROWS attributes control only the displayed size of the textarea, not the number of lines available for input.

Let's add a textarea to your document.

1. Switch to your **text editor** (**Survey.htm** should be open).

2. Immediately above the line that begins with <!--Buttons-->, enter:

   ```
   <!--Textarea-->
   <P>Please tell us what you think about Jetaway Travel:</P>
   <TEXTAREA ROWS=5 COLS=20 NAME="OPINION"></TEXTAREA></P>.
   ```

   This prompts users to give feedback about the company. The space on the page will be 5 rows high and 20 characters wide.

3. Save and view the file.

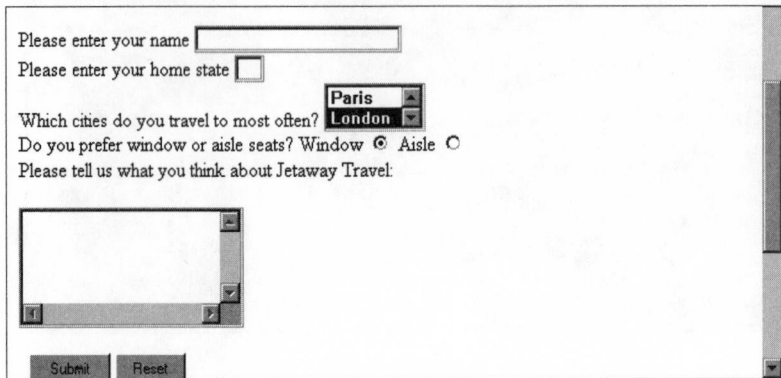

4. Enter text that extends beyond the right margin into the textarea. Notice that the textarea keeps scrolling to the right. To get to a new line, you must press the **Enter** key.

5. Delete the text in the textarea by clicking on the **Reset** button.

PRACTICE YOUR SKILLS

1. Use WordPad to add the following line below the line that begins with "Please tell us what..."

   ```
   Left box: What have we done well? Right box: How can we
   improve? <BR>
   ```

2. Add another textarea with the same number of rows and columns. Start a new line to type the tags for easier readability. Name the second textarea: **IMPROVE**. Change the name of the first textarea from OPINION to **WELLDONE**. Delete the closing paragraph tag from the existing line that begins with <TEXTAREA.... and add a closing paragraph tag at the end of the new textarea line.

3. Save and view the file.

4. Try out the updated form.

WRAPPING INPUT

To make it easier to read the information entered into a textarea, use the WRAP attribute. You can choose between WRAP=VIRTUAL and WRAP=PHYSICAL. WRAP=VIRTUAL wraps text at the end of each displayed line in the textarea. However, when the information is submitted, it is still sent as one line of text. WRAP=PHYSICAL also wraps text just as WRAP=VIRTUAL does. However, when the text is submitted, line break codes are included. These codes indicate the end of each displayed line in the textarea.

When you add WRAP=*value* to the TEXTAREA tag, the bottom scroll bars are no longer necessary and do not display.

Let's try setting the wrapping attribute to enhance the ease of readability when entering text into a textarea by wrapping text within the displayed area.

1. Switch to your **text editor**.

2. In the first textarea tag, after NAME="WELLDONE" and before >,enter:

   ```
   WRAP=VIRTUAL.
   ```

   The whole line should now say:

   ```
   <TEXTAREA ROWS=5 COLS=20 NAME="WELLDONE""
   WRAP=VIRTUAL></TEXTAREA>.
   ```

3. Save and view the file. The bottom scroll bar has disappeared from the first textarea.

4. Enter text into the textarea. Text is wrapped to the next line at the end of each line in the textarea, but is still submitted as typed.

PRACTICE YOUR SKILLS

1. Use your text editor to set the second textarea to **WRAP=PHYSICAL**.

2. Save the file, view it, and enter text into the textarea. On the screen the input looks the same as with WRAP=VIRTUAL. It is, however, submitted with line break codes at the end of each wrapped line.

3. Delete the text by clicking on the **Reset** button.

QUICK REFERENCE

In this lesson, you learned how to create a form on your Web page. You added fields, text boxes, drop-down list boxes, radio buttons, buttons, and textareas to your document. You examined ways to align the text and input fields. You also learned about the mechanisms that you can use to process the data that you receive from your forms. Here's a brief summary of the tags you used in this chapter to create forms on your Web pages. (Remember, the text in italics is just a placeholder. You need to enter your real data in place of that text.)

To Create This Form Element ...	... Use This Tag or Set of Tags
The form itself	<FORM ACTION="*URL*" METHOD="POST"> *remainder of your form tags* </FORM>
Text box	<INPUT TYPE="TEXT" NAME="*name*">
Drop-down list box	<SELECTNAME="*name*"> *option tags* </SELECT>
Elements in a drop-down list box	<OPTION *SELECTED*>*text*
Radio button	<INPUT TYPE="RADIO" NAME="*name*" *CHECKED*>
Submit button	<INPUT TYPE="SUBMIT" NAME="*name*">
Reset button	<INPUT TYPE="RESET" NAME="*name*">
Textarea	<TEXTAREA ROWS=n COLS=n NAME="name" WRAP=VIRTUAL or PHYSICAL></TEXTAREA>

Automatically Updating Pages

Counting the Hits

Interactive Documents

Java Applets in HTML Documents

Quick Reference

Chapter 12

Creating Dynamic and Interactive Documents

You have probably seen and used some of the spiffy new
Web pages that contain programs that let you perform calculations of
various sorts, or scroll messages across the screen. Some pages also
"magically" update the page being displayed—anything from displaying a totally different page to updating how many visitors the site has
received. In this lesson, you will learn how you can create those kinds
of pages.

When you're done working through this chapter, you will know

- How to include JavaScript code in your document
- How to include a Java applet in your document
- How to dynamically update pages when they are displayed

AUTOMATICALLY UPDATING PAGES

Several of the most recent browsers enable you to dynamically update Web pages by using two techniques: client pull and server push. Common uses for these techniques include:

- Creating the equivalent of a slide show by displaying a series of documents at a specified interval
- Taking the user directly to a second site (a nice feature for sites that have been moved)
- Updating data at specific intervals (for example, updating stock quotes at five-minute intervals)
- Displaying your page in the character set of any language (for example, making your page available in English and Japanese by using the META attribute Charset= and setting the appropriate MIME character set)

SERVER PUSH

Server push is a method of dynamically updating browser screen content with data sent from the server to your browser. The HTTP connection is left open and the server sends more data for your browser to display. This connection remains open until the user stops the data stream (with the Stop button), until all of the data is transferred, until a specified time limit is reached, or until some other mechanism is triggered.

You implement server push via a CGI (Common Gateway Interface) program on a Web server. The program keeps the connection open and "pushes" a continuous stream of data to the browser.

CLIENT PULL

Client pull is another method of dynamically updating browser screen content with data sent from the server to the browser, along with information as to when to update the data. The connection is closed after data is sent and a new connection is opened for any new data that needs to be sent.

You implement client pull by using the <META> tag in your document. However, this feature is only available to browsers that support META. The META tag can only be placed inside of the HEAD elements. No CGI script is required. The browser does the work specified by the action defined in the META tag.

You can find a good explanation and comparison of client-pull and server-push updates at

http://www.netscape.com/assist/net_sites/pushpull.html.

THE META ELEMENT

The <META> tag must appear within the HEAD element. This tag has three attributes:

- *HTTP-EQUIV* specifies the attribute associated with the META element. The value *REFRESH* is a Netscape-specific extension that allows you to update a Web page.

- *CONTENT* specifies how long (in seconds) before the REFRESH occurs and *URL* specifies the Web page that will be displayed when the page is updated.

- *NAME* specifies a name for the information if an HTTP-EQUIV attribute is not specified.

Let's try creating a dynamic document using client pull that will automatically load a different page after a few seconds.

1. In your text editor, open **CLPULL.HTM**.

2. After the </TITLE> line, enter

   <META HTTP-EQUIV="REFRESH" CONTENT="5; URL=update.htm">.

   The REFRESH value tells Netscape Navigator to load a new page. The CONTENT attribute has two values enclosed in quotes and separated by a semi-colon. The value 5 specifies how many seconds to wait before doing the REFRESH. The URL specifies which page to display after the five seconds are up.

3. Save and view your file. After five seconds the UPDATE.HTM page should be displayed. If it isn't, double check that you have spelled everything correctly in the META element and that you placed the punctuation in the correct places.

COUNTING THE HITS

Many sites display the number of *hits*, or times the site was accessed. Usually, you implement this feature through a CGI script or a C program which creates a GIF file containing the number. Several popular sites on the Web are hosts for such counter programs. Some require that CGI scripts be run on your server. A popular site for those of you who cannot run CGI scripts on your server is WebCounter at http://www.digits.com. This is a remote site which can be used for counting hits. WebCounter is available for a small fee. Access the site, then click on the WebCounter graphic for full details on using Web-Counter.

If you want, you can try accessing the WebCounter site and registering. Add the appropriate code as detailed at their site to your document. The next time you load the document, you will see how many times your document has been accessed.

INTERACTIVE DOCUMENTS

Up to this point you have been creating nice, useful, but static pages. You can also design interactive pages by using CGI scripts or complex server code.

Two examples of interactive pages include:

- A page with a message that scrolls in the status bar
- A page with a program that enables users to enter and calculate data

JAVA

You can also create interactive pages by using Java. Java is an object-oriented, platform-independent programming language. Two basic levels of code can be written in Java. They are described in Table 12.1.

Table 12.1   Two Levels of Java Code

Type	Description
Applications	Programs that are compiled into machine-independent byte code and that can run standalone. An example is the HotJava browser.
Applets	Programs that are compiled into machine-independent byte code and that require a Java-enabled browser to run the applet. The name of the applet must be embedded into the HTML document or the applet will not run.

JAVASCRIPT

JavaScript was developed by Netscape and Sun, and is based on Netscape's LiveScript scripting language.

JavaScript is un-compiled code embedded in an HTML document that is interpreted by the browser when the document is loaded.

Not all browsers support JavaScript. You can hide the JavaScript lines from those browsers so that the browser does not attempt to interpret these lines as HTML code. One way to hide the code is to place the SCRIPT elements and the JavaScript code inside the HEAD elements. The other way is to place the JavaScript inside comment tags.

ADDING JAVASCRIPT TO A DOCUMENT

You must use the SCRIPT tags to add JavaScript code to a document. The opening SCRIPT tag specifies the language used, for example

```
<SCRIPT LANGUAGE="JAVASCRIPT">.
```

If you want the script to be loaded and interpreted before any of the rest of the HTML code is loaded, place the SCRIPT tags and the JavaScript code inside of the HEAD elements.

We are not teaching you JavaScript creation; the focus is on incorporating existing JavaScript into an HTML document.

Let's examine a couple of documents that include JavaScript and see how to incorporate it into those documents.

1. In your text editor, open **CONVERT.HTM**. This file contains the JavaScript code, but not the SCRIPT tags necessary for the HTML document to run the script. CONVERT.HTM is pictured in Figure 12.1.

2. Notice where the JavaScript code is placed. The code is *inside* the HEAD tags. Anything placed inside the HEAD tags is not displayed on the browser screen. By placing the JavaScript here, browsers that do not support JavaScript are not confused by these lines.

3. On a new line following the TITLE tags, enter **<SCRIPT LANGUAGE= "JavaScript">**. This specifies that the code coming up is JavaScript code.

4. On a new line just before the closing HEAD tag, enter **</SCRIPT>**. This specifies that the end of the JavaScript code has been reached.

5. Save and view the file. It should look like Figure 12.2.

Figure 12.1
Viewing JavaScript code

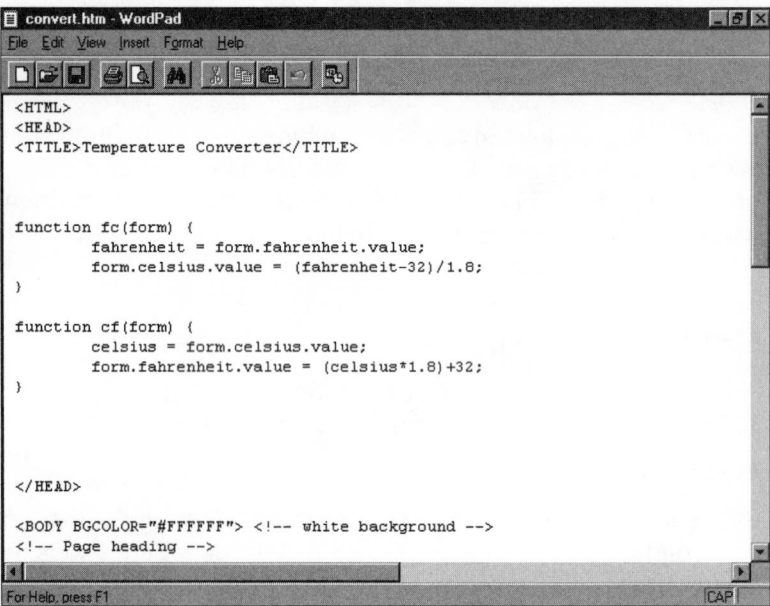

Figure 12.2
The Temperature Converter page

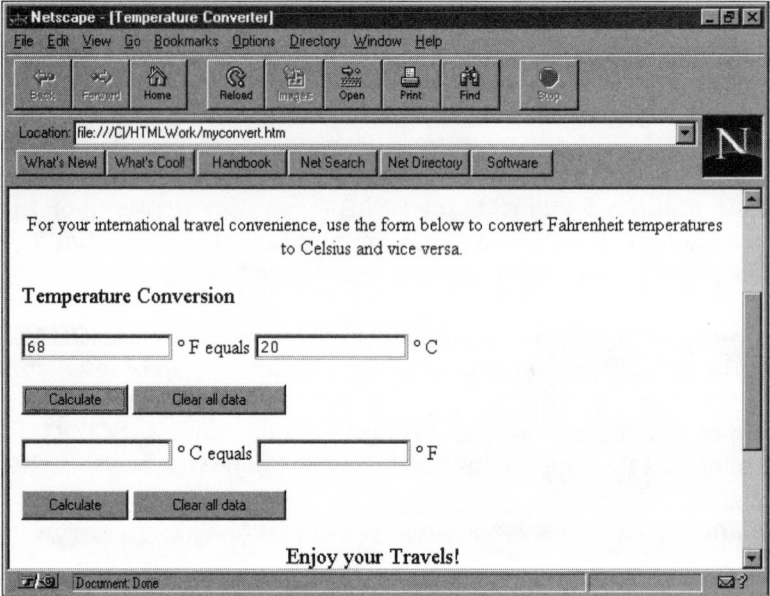

6. Try it out! If necessary, scroll down until both sets of conversion fields are visible. A form was defined that enables you to enter data, which the Java-Script will calculate. In the first Fahrenheit text box, type **68**, then click on **Calculate**. Click on **Clear All Data** to prepare to perform another calculation.

Now, let's try adding some JavaScript to the **DEFAULT.HTM** file you have been building throughout the book. This code will add a scrolling message in the status bar of your document when it is opened.

1. In your text editor, open **SCROLL.TXT**. This is the JavaScript code which will produce the scrolling text in the status bar.

2. Choose **Edit, Select All**, then choose **Edit, Copy**.

3. Open **DEFAULT.HTM**. In the Head section, paste the contents of the clipboard.

4. On a line before the code you pasted in, type **<SCRIPT LANGUAGE= "JAVASCRIPT">** and press **Enter** (see Figure 12.3).

Figure 12.3
Entering JavaScript code

```
<HTML>
<HEAD>
<TITLE>Jetaway Travel, Inc.</TITLE>
<SCRIPT LANGUAGE="JavaScript">
var window_size = 0;

//These two lines are the message that is scrolled in the status
//window

var Status1="Planning a family vacation soon?";
var Status2="Call us at 1-800-555-1212 for information on Family Discount Sp

function StartMarquee(initial_size) {
     window_size = initial_size;
     ScrolledMessage(window_size);
}

function ScrolledMessage(scrollto) {
     var StatusLine;
     var msg = " ";
     var i = 0;
     var speed = 5;
```

5. On the following line, type **<!--Hide the code** and press **Enter** (see Figure 12.4).

Figure 12.4
Hiding JavaScript code

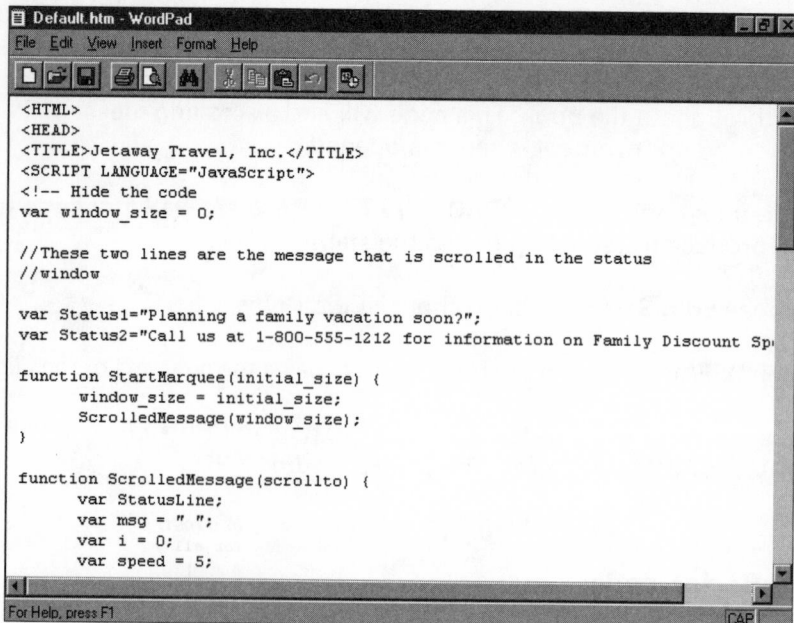

```
                                                                        _|8|X|
Default.htm - WordPad
File  Edit  View  Insert  Format  Help

[toolbar]

<HTML>
<HEAD>
<TITLE>Jetaway Travel, Inc.</TITLE>
<SCRIPT LANGUAGE="JavaScript">
<!-- Hide the code
var window_size = 0;

//These two lines are the message that is scrolled in the status
//window

var Status1="Planning a family vacation soon?";
var Status2="Call us at 1-800-555-1212 for information on Family Discount Sp

function StartMarquee(initial_size) {
     window_size = initial_size;
     ScrolledMessage(window_size);
}

function ScrolledMessage(scrollto) {
     var StatusLine;
     var msg = " ";
     var i = 0;
     var speed = 5;

For Help, press F1                                                       CAP
```

6. On the line following the code you pasted in, type **// end of hidden code-->** and press **Enter**.

7. On the following line, type **</SCRIPT>** and press **Enter** to specify the end of the JavaScript code (see Figure 12.5).

8. Inside the body tag, add the attribute onload="StartMarqee(200)". The new body tag should be similar to <body background="bluerock.gif" text=white onload="Start Marquee(200)".

9. Save and view the file. Notice the text that scrolls across the status bar at the bottom of the browser window.

JAVA APPLETS IN HTML DOCUMENTS

You can run Java applets from within your HTML documents provided you have a browser that supports Java applets. The Windows 3.1 version of Netscape does not support running Java applets.

No special server is needed to run the applets; you can simply use your Web browser.

Figure 12.5
Finishing the JavaScript code

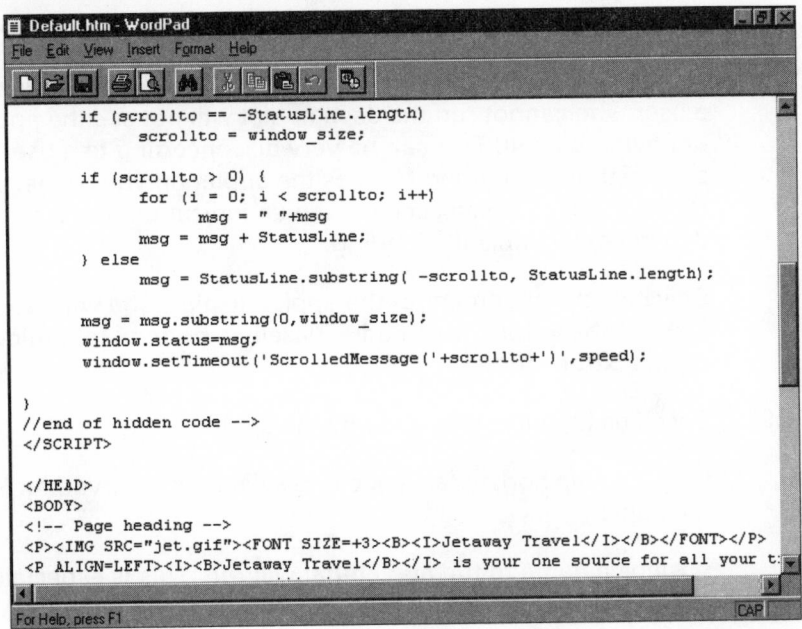

```
        if (scrollto == -StatusLine.length)
            scrollto = window_size;

        if (scrollto > 0) {
            for (i = 0; i < scrollto; i++)
                msg = " "+msg
            msg = msg + StatusLine;
        } else
            msg = StatusLine.substring( -scrollto, StatusLine.length);

        msg = msg.substring(0,window_size);
        window.status=msg;
        window.setTimeout('ScrolledMessage('+scrollto+')',speed);

}
//end of hidden code -->
</SCRIPT>

</HEAD>
<BODY>
<!-- Page heading -->
<P><IMG SRC="jet.gif"><FONT SIZE=+3><B><I>Jetaway Travel</I></B></FONT></P>
<P ALIGN=LEFT><I><B>Jetaway Travel</B></I> is your one source for all your t
```

THE APPLET TAG

The APPLET tag is used to specify which Java applet you want to run. The required attributes are described in Table 12.2.

Table 12.2 **Required Attributes for the APPLET Tag**

Attribute	Description
CODE	Specifies the filename of the Java applet
HEIGHT	The size, in pixels, of the initial height of the display area for the applet
WIDTH	The size, in pixels, of the initial width of the display area for the applet

The optional APPLET attributes are described in Table 12.3

Table 12.3 **Optional Attributes for the APPLET Tag**

Attribute	Description
ALT	Text defined with this attribute is displayed by browsers that cannot run the Java applet. If you do not include this attribute, a user who cannot run the Java applet will not see the applet or anything at all. This can be very disconcerting to a user since if there is nothing besides the applet on your page, all they will see is a blank screen and an indication that the document has finished loading.
ALIGN	Specifies the alignment of the applet display. The values include absbottom, absmiddle, baseline, bottom, left, middle, right, texttop, and top.
CODEBASE	Specifies the base URL used by the applet.
HSPACE	Specifies the horizontal space in pixels to be reserved for the applet.
NAME	Assigns a name to the applet that will run. This is especially useful when there are multiple applets included on your Web page that need to communicate with each other.
VSPACE	Specifies the vertical space in pixels to be reserved for the applet.

THE PARAM TAG

You can use the PARAM tag to specify parameters that will be passed to the Java applet. The attributes are NAME and VALUE. An example of this tag is:

```
<PARAM NAME="varname" VALUE="0">
```

ADDING AN APPLET TO A DOCUMENT

The APPLET tags are used to identify which applet the browser will run. You need to specify the name of the applet and the height and width of the space in which it will run. Before the closing APPLET tag, you can add additional HTML code that browsers which cannot run the applet will run instead.

Let's create a document that includes a Java applet and find out whether your browser is capable of running Java applets.

1. Switch to your text editor and open **JAVAPPLT.HTM**.

2. After the <!--Add applet here--> comment line, type

```
<APPLET CODE="Jet.class" HEIGHT=228 WIDTH=360>
<H1>If you see this message, your browser could not load
the Java applet</H1><BR>
</APPLET>
```

3. Save and view the file (see Figure 12.6). Did your browser run the applet or display the message?

Figure 12.6
The JavaApplet

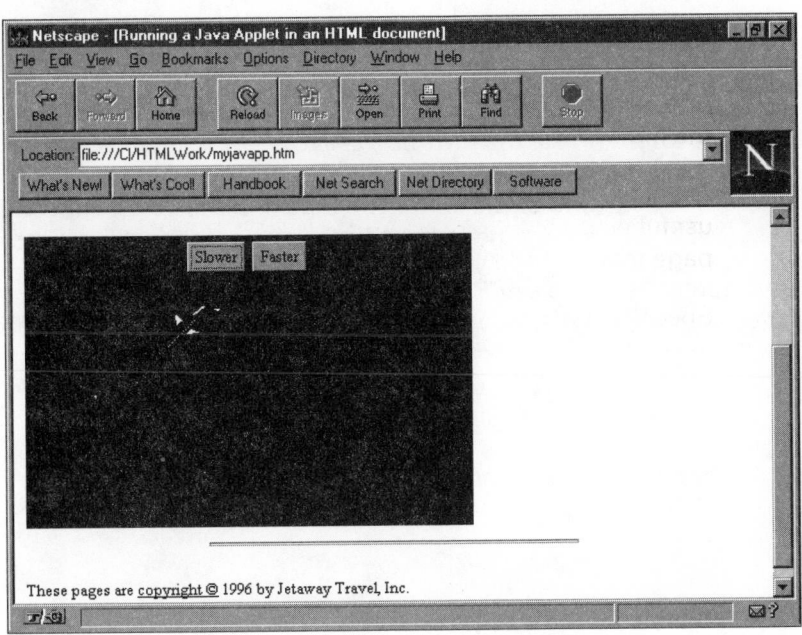

QUICK REFERENCE

In this lesson, you learned how to create a page that is dynamically updated each time it is run. You also learned how to incorporate JavaScript and Java applets into your HTML documents.

Here's a brief summary of the tags you used in this chapter to create dynamic and interactive Web pages.

To Do This ...	You Need To
Automatically display a different HTML document in 5 seconds	Use *<META HTTP-EQUIV="REFRESH" CONTENT="5; URL=filename.htm">*
Count the number of hits your Web page receives	Install a program that counts the number of times the page is accessed on your server or register with a service that provides such a program.
Add JavaScript to your Web page	Place the *<SCRIPT LANGUAGE="JAVASCRIPT">* at the beginning of the JavaScript code and *</SCRIPT>* at the end of the code. The tags and the JavaScript code should be in the HEAD section of the document.
Add a Java applet to your Web page	Use *<APPLET CODE="filename.class" HEIGHT=nnn WIDTH=nnn></APPLET>*. Remember to either use the *ALT* attribute or place other HTML code between the APPLET tags for those users who cannot run the Java applet.

In the next chapter, you'll learn how to add frames to your Web pages.

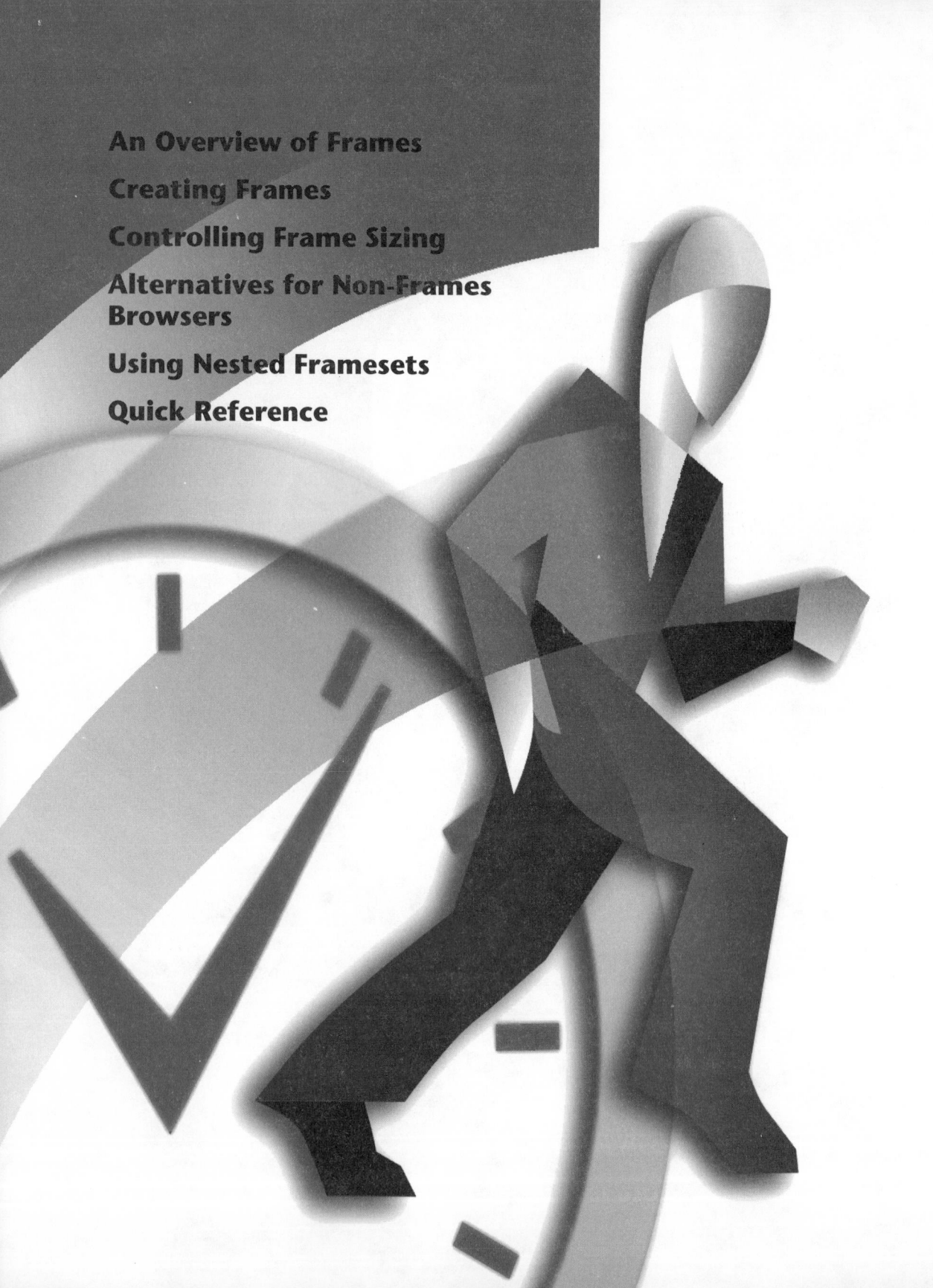

Chapter 13
Adding Frames to Your Web Pages

Frames! They seem to be everywhere you turn on the Web today. You might not even know you are using a page containing frames unless you try to navigate forward and back using the standard browser buttons and end up in a totally different place than you expected! They are recognizable by the separate windows that divide the screen. Not every browser supports frames, so you will need to be careful about where and how you use them. We will provide you with some guidelines and alternatives for those users who cannot use frames.

When you're done working through this chapter, you will know

- What a frame document and Web page containing frames looks like
- How to create and control the appearance of frame documents
- What a page containing nested framesets looks like

AN OVERVIEW OF FRAMES

By using frames, you can create two or more independent windows that divide your screen. This makes your display more visually appealing and enables you to better organize data. You can also use frames to display more than one page at a time, and the individuals visiting your Web site can access and use your pages with greater ease. You can see the difference frames can make by looking at Figure 13.1 below.

Figure 13.1
A comparison of information with and without frames

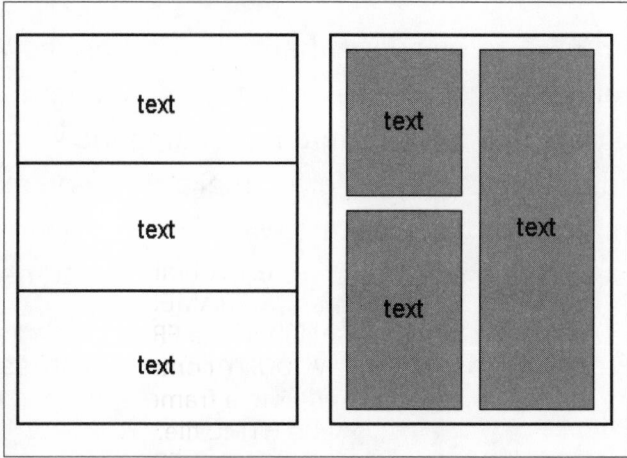

In Figure 13.1, the picture on the left illustrates how regular text would look on the page. The picture on the right illustrates how, by using frames, you can better organize the text and make it more visually appealing. Figure 13.2 below shows what a page looks like with two frames.

Figure 13.2
A frames page with two frames

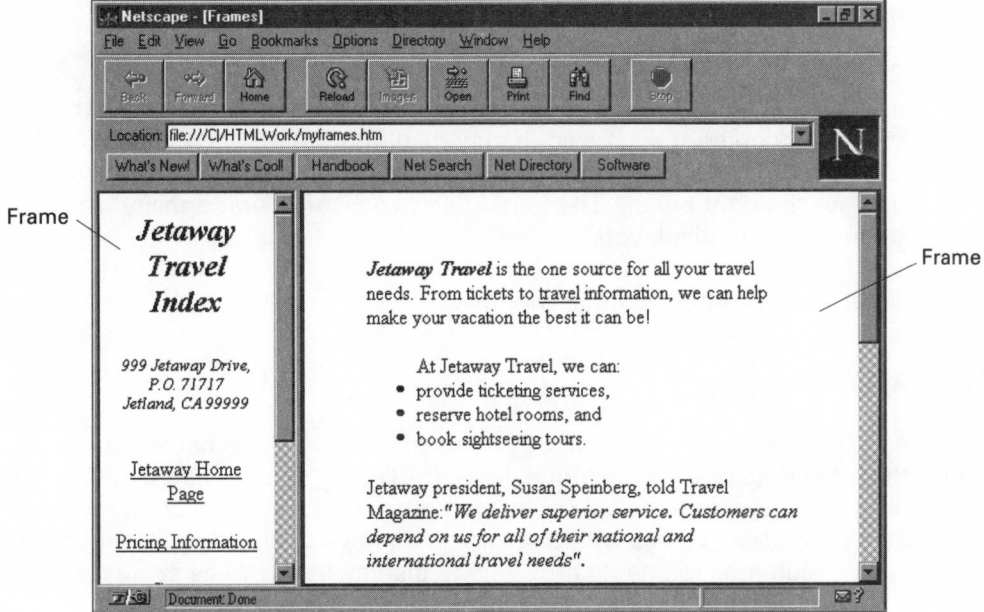

You can scroll individual windows if the amount of data in the page does not fit in the window. By default, scroll bars are automatically applied when necessary. You can scroll and change each window or frame independently of any others.

Frame definitions are contained inside a FRAMESET container. To create a FRAMESET container, use the <FRAMESET> and </FRAMESET> tags. You cannot use a BODY container in a document that contains a FRAMESET container because the FRAMESET container replaces the BODY container in a frames document. You do not enter any actual content into a frames document; instead, each frame uses as its content a separate HTML file. If a browser encounters a BODY section in a document that also uses a FRAMESET container, it ignores the frame information. Only the <FRAME> tag or nested <FRAMESET> containers are allowed inside of the <FRAMESET> and </FRAMESET> container tags.

You have to define a minimum of two windows or frames for browsers to be able to display frames. Some browsers, however, cannot display frames. For those browsers, you need to provide either a warning message or an alternate page that displays when the frames page is loaded.

Let's examine a document that contains frames.

1. In your browser, open **2FRAMES.HTM**. Notice how the screen is divided into two panels. The left panel is an index of documents that you can choose from and which will be displayed in the right panel. (**Note:** If your browser doesn't support frames you won't be able to either.)

2. Choose **View, Document Source** to view the HTML source code. (If you are using a browser other than Netscape Navigator, the command to view the document source code may be different.) The first FRAMESET tag defines how the page is split (25 percent for the left panel and 70 percent for the right panel). The remaining two FRAME tags specify which documents are displayed.

3. Close the Document Source window.

CREATING FRAMES

To create a frame, use the <FRAMESET> and </FRAMESET> container tags to provide the outer structure for the frame, and the COLS= *"values"* and ROWS=*"values"* attributes to define the size of the columns and rows for each frame. Separate each of the values with a comma. You have to specify a minimum of two rows or columns to enable browsers to display frames. The syntax is:

```
<FRAMESET COLS="values" ROWS="values"></FRAMESET>
```

It is safe to specify either only rows or only columns; the attribute you omit automatically receives a value of 100 percent. You can express values in one of three ways:

Value	Example
Absolute Pixels	<FRAMESET ROWS="50,100,200">
Percentages	<FRAMESET COLS="25%, 50%, 75%">
Relative Scale	<FRAMESET COLS="*, 4*, 2*">

Absolute pixels specify an absolute number of pixels for each column or row. Percentages specify a certain percentage of the page's width or height for each column or row. Relative scales specify a proportional amount of the available space. In the relative scale example above, column one would receive one-seventh of the page, column two four-sevenths, and column three two-sevenths.

You can also use all three specifications together. An example of this is:

```
<FRAMESET ROWS="75,30%,*,2*">
```

In this example, the first row would receive a height of 75 pixels; the second row would receive 30 percent of the entire page's height; the third row would receive one-third of the remaining space's height; and the fourth row would receive the remaining two-thirds.

The next element you need to define is the <FRAME> element. One <FRAME> tag is required for each row or column you defined with the <FRAMESET> tag. The syntax for the <FRAME> tag is as follows:

```
<FRAMESET COLS="values">
<FRAME SRC="url">
<FRAME SRC="url">
</FRAMESET>
```

The <FRAME> tag is not a container tag and therefore does not require an end tag. The SRC attribute defines the URL of the HTML page which will provide the content of the corresponding frame. The source HTML page has to be complete, meaning that it has to contain the <HTML>, <HEAD>, and <BODY> container tags with text and other tags contained in the body section.

In the generic example above, the two <FRAME> tags illustrate both the need for at least two defined rows or columns within the <FRAMESET> element, and the need for matching <FRAME> definitions. If you define only one <FRAME> tag, the other frame will display empty.

Let's try creating your own frames document. This will be an index document for your favorite travel agency, Jetaway Travel.

1. In your text editor, open **FRAMES.HTM**. This document contains just the beginnings of an HTML document.

2. On a new line just after the </HEAD> line, add the following:

```
<!--Frames-->
<FRAMESET COLS="50%, 50%">
<FRAME SRC="index.htm">
</FRAMESET>
```

3. Save and view the file. Notice that only one frame appears because only one source URL was specified (index.htm).

4. In your text editor, add a **frame** with a source URL of **fjet.htm**.

5. Save the FRAMES.HTM file in your text editor.

6. In your browser window, reopen **FRAMES.HTM**. Throughout this lesson, you will need to reopen rather than reload the documents in your browser when you make changes to the file. Both frames now contain information.

SETTING FRAME NAMES

You can use the NAME attribute to assign a name to a frame. In most cases, you would assign a name in order to link to the frame from other frames that are displayed at the same time. The syntax is:

```
<FRAME SRC="url" NAME="name">
```

Names must begin with an alphanumeric character. For the NAME attribute to be useful, you have to define a link to the name in another HTML document. One practical scenario you can create is to have one frame's source document act as an index with links to all the other pages that you want individuals to visit. In the index document, you specify a BASE TARGET as the name of the frame in which you want to displaylinked documents. Clicking on a link in the index document displays the linked document in the other frame.

Let's set a frame name and then link to that name.

1. In the index frame, select **Pricing Information**. The frame is filled with the pricing information page, and the index is no longer accessible.

2. Reopen **FRAMES.HTM** to reload **INDEX.HTM** in the left frame.

3. In your text editor, change the line <FRAME SRC="fjet.htm"> to <FRAME SRC="fjet.htm" **NAME="default">**.

4. Save the file.

5. Open **INDEX.HTM**.

6. On a new line directly below the <TITLE> line, type **<BASE TARGET= "default">**.

7. Save the file.

8. In your browser window, open **FRAMES.HTM**. (Remember to reopen and not reload the file or it won't work correctly.)

9. Click on the **Pricing Information** link in the index frame. The pricing information page now appears in the right frame, leaving the index visible.

10. Try out some of the other links in the index frame.

NAVIGATING FRAMES

Not only do frames organize the display of your Web pages, but you can also use them to navigate through the pages with greater ease than you can by using your browser's Back and Forward functions. If you click on a frame to make it active and then click once with your right mouse button, you will see a menu that enables you to navigate the frame.

- If you have only viewed one document in the frame in addition to the default document, you can choose to go backward in the frame.

- If you have viewed more than one document and have gone backward at least once, you can also go forward in the frame.

- If you have viewed only the first document in a frame, the menu does not have any valid selections.

The menu allows you to navigate the frames without having to reload the entire starting page and repeat your steps from there. If you are using Netscape Navigator 3.0, "Internet Shortcut" will be a valid selection, and will always be available on the menu.

Let's try navigating frames so you can become familiar with the navigation menu.

1. Click anywhere in the **right frame** to make it the active frame.

2. Click once with the **right** mouse button to display a pop-up menu.

3. Choose **Back In Frame**. You will move backward through the previously viewed frames.

4. Click once again with the **right** mouse button to display the pop-up menu.

5. Choose **Forward In Frame**. You will move forward to the next frame.

CONTROLLING FRAME SIZING

You initially control the size of frames by defining columns and rows in the <FRAMESET> tag. However, you (or anyone visiting your Web site) can resize the frames to any desired size. This can be practical, depending on what your needs are. However, it can also hinder the proper display of your pages as you intended them to be displayed. The NORESIZE attribute enables you to specify that your frames cannot be resized. The syntax is:

```
<FRAME SRC="url" NORESIZE>
```

In a display with multiple adjoining frames, you do not need to add the NORESIZE attribute to all adjoining frames. The fact that one frame cannot be resized automatically means that the others cannot be resized either.

Let's see what a user can do to the size of frames.

1. Move the cursor over the left edge of the right frame. The mouse pointer will turn into a double-headed arrow.

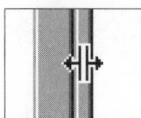

2. Press and hold the **left** mouse button. Drag the arrow to the left (a black line appears) until the left frame occupies approximately one third of the page. Release the mouse button. This will resize the left frame. It also re-sizes the right frame which automatically fills the remaining two thirds of the page. Notice how the text in the frames adjusts to the new frame size.

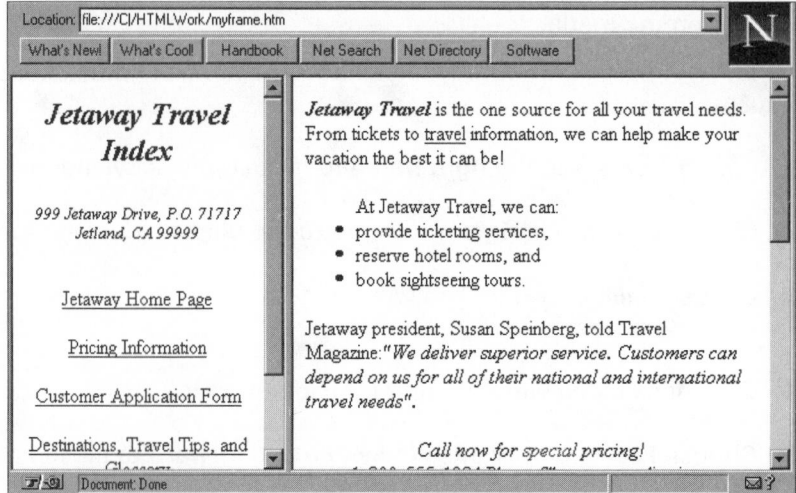

3. What do you think happens to the size of the frames when you reopen the page? Try it and find out. Yup, they're right back to splitting the page 50-50.

Now let's see what happens when you disable the resizing function of frames.

1. In your text editor, open **FRAMES.HTM**.

2. Change the first percentage of the FRAMESET COLS= parameter to **25%** and change the second to **70%**. This will permanently change the layout of the frames on the page. You may have noticed that our numbers never add up to 100 percent. That is because the other 5 percent of the page is occupied by the scrollbars. Some browsers display frames more success-fully when this is the case.

3. Change the <FRAME SRC="index.htm"> line to <FRAME SRC= "index.htm" **NORESIZE**>.

4. Save the file.

5. In your browser window, reopen **FRAMES.HTM**.

6. Move the mouse pointer over the left edge of the right frame. The double-headed arrow no longer appears and the frame cannot be resized. Since there are only the two frames, you could have achieved the same result by placing the **NORESIZE** attribute in the other FRAME tag.

CONTROLLING SCROLL BARS

Frames automatically place scroll bars in a window if the content of a page does not fit into the frame's display area. You might find that, at times, scroll bars can take away from the visual appeal of your page. You can control the placing of scroll bars with the SCROLLING attribute. The attribute has three values:

Table 13.1 **Scrolling Attribute Values**

Value	Description
AUTO	This setting is the default if the SCROLLING attribute is not used.
YES	This setting causes scroll bars to be placed both on the right and bottom of the frame.
NO	This setting prevents scroll bars from being placed in the frame.

The syntax is:

```
<FRAME SRC="url" SCROLLING="value">
```

Let's try controlling whether a frame has scroll bars or not.

1. In your text editor, add **SCROLLING="NO"** between "index.htm" and NORESIZE. The entire line should now read

```
<FRAME SRC="index.htm" SCROLLING="NO" NORESIZE>.
```

Figure 13.3 shows what the page will look like after adding SCROLLING="NO".

2. Save the file.

3. In Navigator, open **FRAMES.HTM**. Notice that the left frame, or index frame, does not have any scroll bars.

4. In your text editor, change SCROLLING="NO" to SCROLLING="**YES**".

Figure 13.3
A frame with the SCROLLING attribute set to No

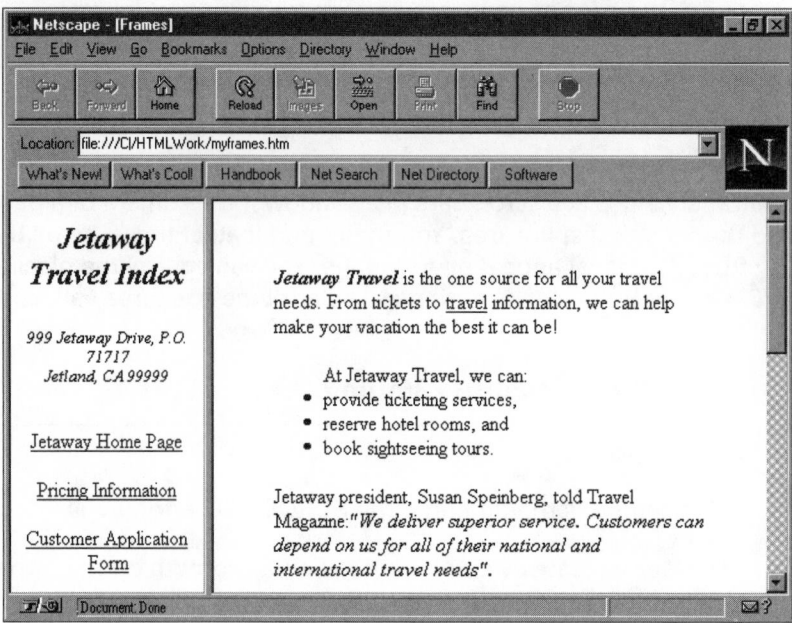

5. Save the file.

6. Switch to your browser window and open **FRAMES.HTM**. Notice that the left frame now has scroll bars on the side and the bottom.

7. Switch to your text editor and delete **SCROLLING="YES"**. This will return to the default of automatic scrolling (see Figure 13.4).

8. Save the file.

Figure 13.4
A frame with the SCROLLING attribute set to Yes

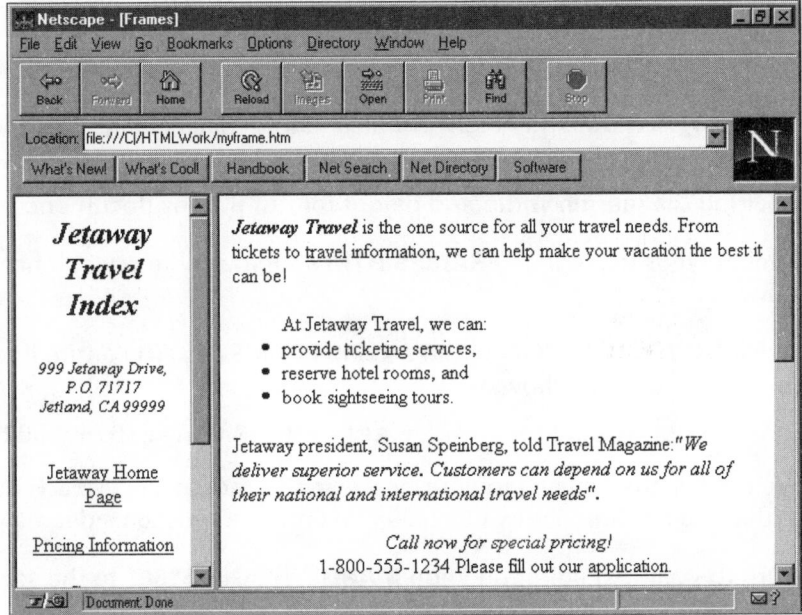

PRACTICE YOUR SKILLS

1. In your text editor, change the right frame to have scrollbars on the right and bottom of the frame.

2. Save the file and verify your changes in your browser.

3. In your text editor, change the right frame to set scrollbars to appear automatically where appropriate.

4. Save the file and verify your changes in your browser.

CONTROLLING FRAME MARGIN WIDTH AND HEIGHT

You can use the MARGINWIDTH="*n*" and MARGINHEIGHT="*n*" attributes to control the margin settings of a frame. The value is expressed in pixels. The syntax is:

```
<FRAME SRC="url" MARGINWIDTH="n" MARGINHEIGHT="n">
```

Controlling margin width and height enables you to make a page more visually appealing.

Let's try setting the margin width and height for our frames document.

1. Switch to your text editor. **FRAMES.HTM** should still be open. If not, open it now.

2. Add **MARGINWIDTH="50"** to the second FRAME tag. The entire line should now read as follows:

```
<FRAME SRC="fjet.htm" NAME="default" MARGINWIDTH="50">.
```

3. Save the file, then switch to your browser and reopen **FRAMES.HTM**. Notice that the left frame now has a 50 pixel margin on each side.

4. Return to your text editor and add **MARGINHEIGHT="50"** to the second FRAME tag. The entire line should now read as follows:

```
<FRAME SRC="fjet.htm" NAME="default" MARGINWIDTH="50"
MARGINHEIGHT="50">.
```

5. Save the file, then switch to your browser and reopen **FRAMES.HTM**. Notice that the top margin now extends 50 pixels down from the top of the right frame (see Figure 13.5). If you scroll down, you will notice the bottom of the document in the right frame has a 50 pixel bottom margin.

ALTERNATIVES FOR NON-FRAMES BROWSERS

Some browsers are not capable of displaying frames. You can provide either a warning message or a completely separate page for individuals using a non-frames browser. Otherwise, a non-frames browser will display a blank page. The <NOFRAMES> container tag is used to handle this situation. The syntax is:

```
<NOFRAMES>text</NOFRAMES>
```

Place this container tag after the </FRAMESET> tag. The text contained inside the <NOFRAMES> and </NOFRAMES> tags is regular text marked up with HTML tags, which provides users with an alternate page if their browser does not support frames. Non-frames browsers display the information contained inside the <NOFRAMES> and </NOFRAMES> tags and disregard the <FRAMESET> and <FRAME> definitions.

Figure 13.5
A frames document with margin width and height spacing

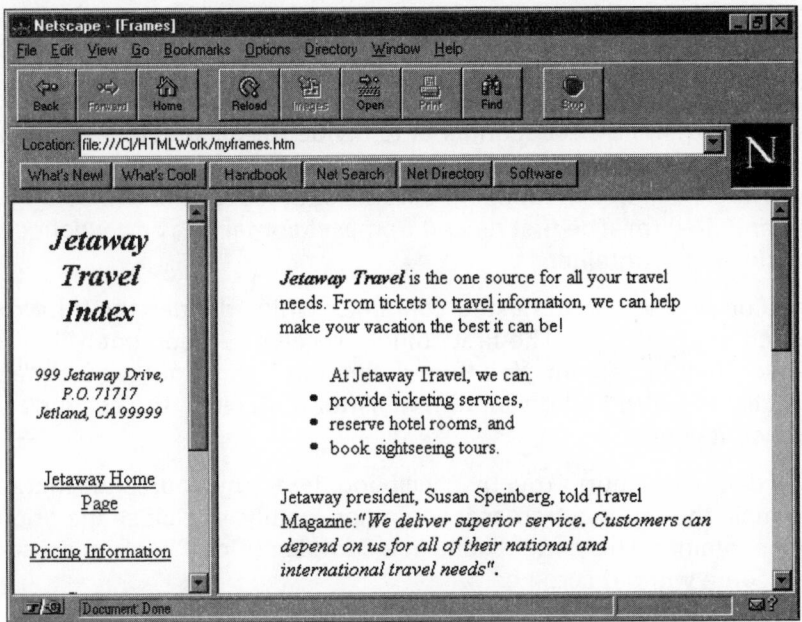

USING NESTED FRAMESETS

You can nest frameset containers to create complex grids of frames. When nesting framesets, you place one or more framesets inside another. This process enables you to organize data more efficiently and to enhance the visual appeal of your page. Below is an example of nested frameset containers:

```
<FRAMESET ROWS="25%, 30%, 30%, 14%">
<FRAME SRC="header.htm" SCROLLING="NO">
<FRAMESET COLS="25%,70%">
<FRAME SRC="index.htm" MARGINWIDTH="10" MARGINHEIGHT="10">
<FRAME SRC="fjet.htm" NAME="default" NORESIZE
MARGINWIDTH="25" MARGINHEIGHT="17">
</FRAMESET>
<FRAMESET>
<FRAMESET COLS="70%,25%">
<FRAME SRC="celsius.htm">
<FRAME SRC="discount.htm" SCROLLING="NO">
</FRAMESET>
<FRAME SRC="footer.htm" SCROLLING="NO">
</FRAMESET>
```

In this example, with the opening of the first frameset container, you define four rows. The first row takes up 25 percent of the page, the second 30 percent, the third 30 percent, and the fourth 14 percent. Notice that the percentages do not add up to exactly 100. It is often advantageous to leave one to five percent of the page unassigned so that the browser can fill it in gracefully.

Next, you define the frame source for the first row, header.htm. Then you define the first nested frameset container to divide the second row into two columns. The first column receives 25 percent of the row's width, the other 70 percent. The next step is to define the frame sources for the two columns, index.htm and fjet.htm. The first nested frameset container is now defined, and you can close the container.

Next, you open the second nested container, which divides the third row into two columns as well. The first column receives 70 percent of the row's width, the other 25 percent. You then define the frame sources for the two columns, celsius.htm and discount.htm. After that, close the second nested frameset container.

Now you define the fourth row by specifying the frame source for that row, footer.htm, in the original frameset container. Finally, you close the original frameset container. This code results in a complex grid of six frames, some with and some without scroll bars.

Keep in mind that even though you can create just about any kind of grid you can imagine, sometimes too much complexity can actually take away from the visual appeal and organization of your page. In addition, the more complex the page, the longer it takes to load. Always consider the ultimate goal of making your pages user-friendly. You want people to come back to visit again and again.

Let's examine a document which contains nested framesets.

1. In your browser, open **NFRAMES.HTM**. Notice that the nested framesets created a grid on the page.

2. View the **Document Source**. Notice the order in which the frameset tags are opened and closed.

3. Close the document source window.

4. Compare your screen to Figure 13.6. Does the design of the page look practical to you? Some of you might say yes, a lot of information can be displayed at once; others might say no, there is too much information and it is difficult to read the text in the scrolling frames.

Figure 13.6
A frames document containing nested framesets

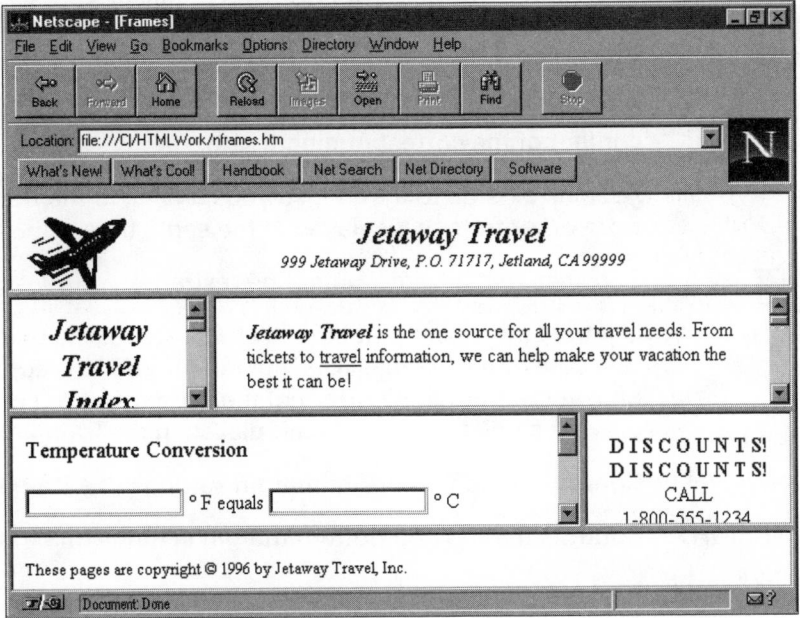

QUICK REFERENCE

In this chapter you learned that frames produce windows that divide your screen into independent, possibly scrollable, sections. The benefits of using these frames can include organization of data and display of data on the screen, enhanced ease of use, improved accessibility of data, and the ability to display more than one page at a time. You also learned that some factors to consider when using frames include

- You have to define a minimum of two windows or frames in order for browsers to display frames.

- Some browsers cannot display frames, so you need to provide a warning or alternative page for those users.

- All content of frames must be contained in documents separate from the frames document.

Only FRAME and FRAMESET tags are allowed in a frames document. However, other code can be included between the NOFRAME tag for nonframe browsers. FRAMESET container tags provide the outer structure for the frame.

The COLS and ROWS attributes of the FRAMESET tag specify the size of columns and rows for each frame.

Here's a quick reference of the FRAME attributes used in this lesson.

Attribute	Use
SRC	Defines the URL of the HTML page which will provide the content of the corresponding frame.
NAME	Assigns a name to a frame so you can link to the frame from other frames displayed at the same time.
NORESIZE	Specifies that a frame cannot be resized.
SCROLLING	Controls the placement of scroll bars. Values include *AUTO* (the default if SCROLLING is not used), *YES* to place scroll bars at the right and bottom of the frame, and *NO* to prevent scroll bars from being placed in the frame.
MARGINWIDTH	Controls the left and right margin settings of a frame.
MARGINHEIGHT	Controls the top and bottom margin settings of a frame.

Other tags used in this lesson include

Tag	Use
NOFRAMES	Used for non-frames browsers
BASE TARGET	Used in the index document to specify the default frame in which linked documents will be displayed.

Congratulations, you made it all the way through the book. You're now ready to design and create your own compelling Web pages.

SKILL BUILDER 4

Here's a chance for you to practice the skills you have learned throughout this book. We'll give you this practice by giving you a real world task to perform.

If you're like many browser users, when you start your browser it connects to your browser manufacturer's home page. If this is true, then you have to wait for that page to download each time you start your browser. How about making your own home page (one that will reside on your hard drive, though, not on the Internet)? You can do that now: You're an HTML programmer!

1. Start by writing a list of a few of your favorite Web sites on a piece of paper. For now, you can keep the list short, maybe five or six sites. You can add more to your page later.

2. Start **WordPad** or your editor.

3. Create the heading section of your HTML document using the **<HTML>**, **<HEAD>**, and optionally, the **<META>** tags. Fill in the appropriate information, if you use the <META> tag.

4. In your heading section, use the **<TITLE>** tag to give your Web page a title. You could use a title like "My Home Page," or "My Favorite Links."

5. Start the body of the document with a **<BODY>** tag that sets the background color to white and the text color to black.

6. Add a centered, bold line that says "**My Home Page**." Make the text two sizes larger than normal text.

7. For the body of your page, create a two-column table with no border. You might want to turn on the border until you get your HTML code debugged, though.

8. In the first column, create your links to the favorite sites you recorded earlier. Use the **<A HREF>** tag. Make sure that the link text (that which shows up in your browser) is clear as to where the link will take you.

9. In the second column, write a brief description of each of those sites. For example, you might want to note what you found useful at each site for later reference.

10. Save your file as **MYHOME.HTM**. (Actually, you can use any name you like. This name will do just fine because it makes clear what the file contains.)

11. Start your browser and load your new file.

12. If your file does not load correctly, fix your HTML code. Test each of the links to make sure you entered the HTML code correctly. Turn off the table border if you had turned it on. Make any corrections necessary, then reload your document to test again.

13. When your document works correctly, make this file your home page. The easiest method is to load the file as you have done. Now, select the all of the text in the Location field at the top of your browser window. Press **Ctrl+C** to copy that information. If you're using Netscape, choose **Option, General Preferences**. If necessary, click on the **Appearance** tab. In the Startup section of the dialog box, click on **Start with Home Page Location**. Select any text already in the text field below that radio button and press **Ctrl+V** to paste in the URL of your file. Click on **OK**.

14. Try it out now; click on **Home**. Your new home page should load. If it does not, repeat the procedures in step 13 or enter the path manually.

15. Now that you have a simple home page, jazz it up. Add a background graphic, if you like (you could download a background graphic from Netscape's site; see Chapter 7). Add some other graphics if you would like. You could even make those graphics links to your favorite sites. Because this file is being loaded from your hard disk, it will load quickly. You do not need to be as concerned with design, because only you will use this page.

16. When you're done, close WordPad and your browser.

17. Finally, keep this page updated as you find new great sites. (Don't forget to remove old sites that you no longer find cool!)

Creating Your Work Folder

The process of creating your work folder varies depending on the operating system you are using. In this appendix, we'll describe the process of creating your work folder (or directory) in Windows 3.1, Windows 95, and the Macintosh platforms.

CREATING YOUR WORK FOLDER IN WINDOWS 95

Follow these steps to create your work folder and copy the data files from the data disk in the back of the book:

1. Turn on your computer. After a brief internal self-check, Windows 95 will load and might prompt you for a password.

2. If prompted, type your password and press **Enter**. Momentarily, the Windows 95 desktop will be displayed.

3. From the Windows 95 desktop, click on the **Start** button to open the Start menu. Point to **Programs** to open the Programs menu, and select **Windows Explorer**. You can use the Windows Explorer to manage the folders and files on your computer.

4. In the Tree pane, click on the **plus** sign (**+**) to the left of the My Computer branch, if necessary, to expand it so that you can view both the floppy-disk drive and the hard drive. This branch may also contain folders such as the Program Files and Windows folders.

5. Click on the **hard-disk** icon (C:). From the menu bar, choose **File, New Folder** to create a new folder. You will copy the contents of the data disk to this folder. The new folder is displayed in the Contents pane and is highlighted so that you can rename it now.

6. Type **HTMLWork** and press **Enter** to assign the name to the new folder.

7. Remove the data disk from its envelope at the back of this book. Insert the data disk (label up) into the appropriately sized disk drive. Determine whether this is drive A or drive B.

8. The easiest way to copy the files from the floppy disk to your HTMLWork folder is by dragging them. Display the contents of the **3 1/2 Floppy (A:)** or **(B:)** branch. (Click on the branch in the Tree pane.) Then, choose **Edit, Select All** from the menu to select all the files in the Contents pane.

9. Drag the selected files to the HTMLWork folder in the Tree pane. (The folder name should be highlighted before you release the mouse button.) As the files are copied, a message box graphically displays the files flying from one folder to another.

10. Click on the Explorer window's **Close** button to close the Windows Explorer.

CREATING YOUR WORK DIRECTORY IN WINDOWS 3.1

To create your work directory and copy the files from the data disk, follow these steps:

1. Turn on your computer. If you are in Windows, go to step 2. If you are in DOS, skip to step 4.

2. Within Windows, locate the *Program Manager* and if necessary open it into a window.

3. Double-click on the Program Manager's **Control-Menu** button and click on **OK** to exit from Windows to DOS.

4. The DOS prompt appears:

   c:\>

   (Your DOS prompt may differ somewhat from this.)

5. Type **md HTMLWork** to create an HTMLWork directory at the root of your hard drive.

6. Type **cd HTMLWork** to make HTMLWork the active directory.

7. Remove the data disk from its envelope at the back of this book. Insert the data disk (label up) into the appropriately sized disk drive. Determine whether this is drive A or drive B.

8. If the data disk is in drive A, type **copy a:*.*** to copy the data files from the disk to your HTMLWork directory.

   If the data disk is in drive B, type **copy b:*.***

9. Type **dir** to verify that the files were copied to **HTMLWork**.

10. Start Windows.

Appendix B
HTML and Web References

In this appendix, we will introduce you to some background information about HTML and the Web, plus we will give you some pointers to locations on the Web that you can visit for HTML development assistance. Finally, we will briefly introduce a few of the types of Web page creation programs currently available.

HTML VERSIONS

HTML is a work-in-progress. While it was originally developed by scientists (particle physicists, to be exact) for scientists, HTML now supports all kinds of users from all over the globe. The early versions supported only textual information; new versions support a bewildering array of multimedia data. This is all possible because HTML itself is constantly evolving.

Shortly after developing HTML, Tim Berners-Lee of the European Particle Physics Laboratory (CERN) worked with the Internet community to create the World Wide Web Consortium, called the W3 for short. W3 now controls how HTML evolves. Well, at least on paper that's how it works.

Netscape Communications, Microsoft Corp., Sun Microsystems, and others are constantly adding new features to HTML. To use these features (surprise!) you have to use that vendor's browser. Normally, vendors then give their new additions to the W3 in the hope that W3 will add their extensions to the next standard version of HTML. Sometimes that happens, sometimes it doesn't.

Since its founding, the W3 has issued three standard versions of HTML: HTML 1.0, HTML 2.0, and HTML 3.2 (agreeing on what would be in HTML 3.0 got so contentious that they skipped it and went right on to 3.2!). The table below lists some (but not all) of the tags that have been included in each of these standards.

Table 5.1   The Three Standard Versions of HTML

HTML 1.0	HTML 2.0	HTML 3.2
The basic heading tags: <HTML>, <HEAD>, and <TITLE>	All of the HTML 1.0 tags	All of the HTML 1.0 and 2.0 tags
The basic content tags: <BODY>, <A HREF>, <A NAME>, <HR>, <P>, , <IMG SRC>, <UL>, <OL>, and the six levels of headings, <H1> through <H6>	<FORM> and related forms tags	Paragraph alignment with the <P ALIGN> tag
The basic character formatting tags: <STRONG>, <EM>, <B>, <I>, <PRE>, and <BLOCKQUOTE>	Alignment of text around images with the <IMG ALIGN> tag	Superscript and subscript characters with the <SUP> and <SUB> tags, respectively

Table 5.1   The Three Standard Versions of HTML (Continued)

HTML 1.0	HTML 2.0	HTML 3.2
The character (escape sequence) codes	Support for image maps with the <IMG SRC HREF="*url*" ISMAP> tag	Height and width attributes for images with the <IMG WIDTH= HEIGHT=> tag
		Support for tables with the <TABLE> and related tags

Netscape Communications has been more aggressive than Microsoft in adding features to HTML. (Can you believe it, a company more aggressive than Microsoft?!) Most of Netscape's extensions have been incorporated into the standard versions of HTML.

For example, Netscape added tables, the ability to specify page and text colors, set font sizes, and create a page with frames—multiple "pages" within one Web page. Of these, only the frames feature has not been added to the HTML standard.

Microsoft, for its part, has added the ability to specify the type of font to use, background colors for tables, and support for some Microsoft programming tools (such as ActiveX). Most of these have been, or are in the process of being added to the HTML standard.

For definitive information on the latest standards, plus information on coming developments, you can visit the home of HTML on the Web, the W3 Consortium's site. Their main address is http://www.w3.org. But, you will find the specifications and descriptions of the HTML standards at http://www.w3.org/pub/WWW/MarkUp. (Careful, this address is case-sensitive.)

John December of December Communications, Inc., maintains a comparison of the HTML versions at http://www.december.com/html. You can also use Yahoo! or another search site to find tons of HTML information on the Web.

ONLINE REFERENCES FOR HTML DEVELOPMENT

Having trouble figuring out how to add a particular HTML feature to your Web pages? Why not go right to the source, the Web itself, for help? Here are a few of the many sites that provide how-to information and style suggestions:

```
http://www.logicalops.com/html-help
```

Logical Operations maintains tutorial and sample HTML files as well as pointers to a selection of the other HTML-assistance sites on the Web.

```
http://www.netscape.com/assist/net-sites
```

Netscape Communications maintains many pages with much information on creating Web pages.

```
http://www.dsiegel.com/tips/index.html
```

David Siegel's page of Web style guidelines.

```
http://www.boutell.com/faq
```

A FAQ (frequently asked questions) document of HTML and Web information.

```
http://www.december.com/html
```

The Web Quick Reference, maintained by John December of December Communications, Inc.

```
http://www.hwg.org/
```

The Web site of the HTML Writers Guild.

```
http://www.yahoo.com/Computers_and_Internet/Software/Data_
Formats/HTML/Guides_and_Tutorials/
```

The catalog page from Yahoo! that lists the many sites providing HTML assistance.

HTML DEVELOPMENT TOOLS

While this book focused on writing your HTML code by hand, you could use an HTML development tool instead. Many companies offer programs with which you can generate your Web pages, sometimes without even considering the HTML that goes on behind the scenes.

HTML development tools can be roughly categorized into three types: add-ons to existing programs, HTML editors, and site development and management tools. Each of these categories is covered below with an example. (These sections are not complete, nor are they meant to be reviews or endorsements of any products.)

ADD-ON PROGRAMS

Add-on programs are modules that you add to your existing programs, say your word processor, enabling you to save your documents as HTML files in addition to your programs' default file formats. The advantage of this approach is that you can continue working in the familiar environment of your current applications yet still be able to generate Web documents.

Microsoft, for example, has released the Internet Assistant for each of its basic Office applications. With the Internet Assistant loaded, you could work in Word, for example. When you have finished creating your document, you simply choose File, Save As, and choose HTML as the file type. Voila! Your Web page is complete.

Many productivity applications now include the ability to save documents as HTML files right out of the box. For example, the newest version of Word Perfect includes the ability to save your files as HTML files. You don't need to download or install any extra software. However, since the ability to save files as HTML started as an add-on to the vendor's basic products, we have categorized these tools together.

The two downsides of this approach are: Add-ons typically do not support the latest HTML features, and you typically have to tweak the HTML code to get a really professional looking Web page. Even so, you will probably find using these tools to be significantly easier than coding a bunch of pages by hand.

HTML EDITORS

HTML editors are like word processors for creating Web pages. Some of these editors offer full WYSIWYG (what you see is what you get) environments. Others simply automate entering most of the HTML tags by letting you choose from dialog boxes or menus.

Some HTML editors are extensible; that is, you can easily add in support for new HTML features as they become available. The simpler editors don't offer this feature, which means you might not be able to take advantage of new HTML features until the vendor updates the editor.

Netscape's Navigator Gold, Adobe's PageMill, and Quadsoft's HoTMetaL Pro are three examples of the many HTML editors currently available.

SITE DEVELOPMENT AND MANAGEMENT TOOLS

Site development and management tools are the most comprehensive Web development tools. Site development and management tools enable you to create Web pages, verify and correct links across your site, control who edits your Web pages, and much more. Adobe's SiteMill and Microsoft's FrontPage are examples of this type of program.

Site development and management tools can offer you great benefits. For example, let's say you wanted to change a link that was included in every document on your Web site (for example, a standard copyright disclaimer). Coding by hand, you would have to manually edit each and every page (and hope you didn't make any mistakes). With a site development tool, you could use a menu or dialog box to specify the change. Then, the tool would do the work for you, editing all of your documents.

Unfortunately, to take advantage of this power, you must have a powerful computer and be prepared to work exclusively within the site development tool's environment. If you don't do so, the tools can sometimes become confused, creating havoc with your Web site. This attention to detail can be a small price to pay, however, to reap the benefits these tools offer.

Index